PREACHING *Like* CALVIN

THE CALVIN 500 SERIES

PREACHING *Like* CALVIN

SERMONS FROM THE 500TH ANNIVERSARY CELEBRATION

EDITED BY

DAVID W. HALL

P&R PUBLISHING
P.O. BOX 817 • PHILLIPSBURG • NEW JERSEY 08865-0817

Italics within Scripture quotations indicate emphasis added.

Printed in the United States of America

Library of Congress Cataloging-in-Publication Data

Preaching like Calvin : sermons from the 500th anniversary celebration / edited by David W. Hall.
p. cm. -- (The Calvin 500 series)
Contains sermons delivered at the Commemorating Calvin Conference, July 9-11, 2009, Geneva, Switzerland.
Includes bibliographical references and index.
ISBN 978-1-59638-097-4 (pbk.)
1. Reformed Church--Sermons. 2. Bible--Sermons. 3. Sermons, English--21st century. I. Hall, David W., 1955- II. Commemorating Calvin Conference (2009 : Geneva, Switzerland)
BX9475.P74 2010
252'.0421--dc22

2010008350

I affectionately dedicate this volume to the fifteen preachers herein—today's all-star team of Calvin expositors. I count each of you as a dear friend, and I wish to thank you all, along with your wives and children, for graciously creating another venerable company of pastors in Geneva—in this case, rearranging your schedules to join the Calvinistic Woodstock, as one of our participants called it! More importantly, each of you is a faithful trumpet—regularly heralding God's Word from pulpits in ways that change lives, as the Spirit works with the Word.

Above all, I thankfully dedicate this work to those who are not all-stars—to that worldwide company of Calvinistic expositors, who faithfully pray, study, apply, and proclaim God's Word in thousands of pulpits each week. More listeners will hear your words weekly than those of the all-stars, and although you may not be known to many outside your circles, you are known to God and to your flocks.

May all who faithfully proclaim the Word of God follow the trail of John Calvin to see churches and cultures changed by the steady, weekly, true exposition of the breathed-out mind of God. I pray that we will leave behind eloquence, superior wisdom, charm, fad, and gimmickry to "proclaim the testimony about God . . . [and] to know nothing . . . except Jesus Christ and him crucified" (1 Cor. 2:1–2).

Contents

Editor's Note

Each of the sixteen chapters in *Preaching Like Calvin* is the text of a sermon delivered in celebration of John Calvin's 500th birthday. All but one of these sermons were delivered in July 2009 at St. Pierre's Cathedral in Geneva, Switzerland, where from 1536 to his death in 1564 John Calvin preached over two thousand sermons.

Preaching Like Calvin faithfully preserves the original sixteen sermon texts, including their original "shape" and, in some cases, brief preaching notes and preaching outlines. Our goal has been for the written versions of the sermons to mirror the oral form in which they were delivered, thus ensuring, as much as possible, that the written word is a facsimile of the spoken word. To achieve this goal, we have retained the authors' original wording and paragraph breaks, limiting editorial work to matters of spelling and punctuation.

It is my sincere hope that these sermons will encourage and motivate us afresh to embrace and proclaim the gospel with godly boldness and for his glory alone.

Once again, I and all the contributors are deeply indebted to the editorial excellence of John J. Hughes and the proofreading expertise of Karen Magnuson, and we all wish to express our thanks to them.

Soli Deo gloria.

David W. Hall
Executive Director, Calvin500

Foreword

On July 10, 1509, in the town of Noyon in Picardy, some sixty miles from Paris, Gerard and Jeanne Calvin rejoiced in God's gift of a son to them. They named him John. It is this John Calvin whose birth we are commemorating five hundred years later, with such descriptions as "one of the great and transformative forces of modern history" (Dr. Phillip E. Hughes). Professor Gerald Bray tells us that "today, more people read Calvin's writings than those of any Christian outside of the New Testament." A recent assessment of his magnum opus, *The Institutes of the Christian Religion*, describes it as "the finest summary of Christian theology ever to have been written."

Such high praise leaves us less than surprised that it was felt appropriate to arrange a commemoration of John Calvin in July 2009 in the church where he taught and preached in Geneva, Switzerland. Calvin500 was a celebration of Calvin's life and work in the form of a series of sermons reflecting the preaching of Calvin himself. For this occasion, Dr. David Hall put us all in his debt by bringing together some of the outstanding preachers of the Reformed church today. Personally, I have reveled in the expositions of Scripture that were given at this commemoration, and now are in more permanent form in the book you hold in your hands. I have no doubt that John Calvin would have delighted in them, too.

What, then, were the great characteristics of this man that made him in so many ways a unique figure in the history of Christianity? Let me suggest three.

John Calvin Was a Man of Gigantic Intellect

There are many reasons for making such a statement. The quality and quantity of his literary output alone would give ample testimony to his remarkable gifts of intellect. Some fifty-nine volumes of the *Corpus Reformatorum* come from Calvin's fertile mind. He wrote full and scholarly commentaries on every book of the New Testament (with the exception of Revelation) and a large part of the Old Testament, several books of sermons, and, of course, the magisterial *Institutes of the Christian Religion*, which eventually extended to half a million words, and which Calvin himself saw as the centerpiece of his life's work.

Another feature of Calvin's mind was his extraordinary consistency. J. I. Packer makes this significant comment in this connection: "Any statement of view in any of Calvin's writings, early or late, may be taken as integral to his thought throughout. Those scholars who study particular themes in Calvin cross-sectionally have no need to raise questions of changing opinions from one work to another. No such changes took place. Calvin's theology, first to last, was a great tapestry of Biblical strands of thought, masterfully woven, and all of a piece."[1]

Calvin also had a prodigious memory. His friend Theodore Beza tells us that in his dictation of profound and complex material, he might be interrupted for several hours, but would then return to dictate precisely where he had left off. According to Beza, he had no need of "memos"; whatever he required to know, he never forgot.

1. J. I. Packer, *Honoring the People of God: The Collected Shorter Writings of J. I. Packer* (Carlisle, UK: Paternoster, 1999), 144.

John Calvin Was a Man of Extraordinary Industry

Beza says, "He took little sleep." He preached ten sermons every two weeks, produced and revised *The Institutes of the Christian Religion,* wrote full commentaries on most of the books of the Bible, lectured on theology three days every week, attended meetings of the Consistory, instructed the clergy, participated in civil government, and received innumerable visitors who sought his counsel. Perhaps most remarkable of all was that he did all this while suffering from serious ill health, including asthma, gastritis, violent headaches, and probably pulmonary tuberculosis.

John Calvin Was a Man of Remarkable Godliness

Benjamin Warfield wrote of Calvin, "No man ever had profounder sense of God than he." Recounting his conversion, Calvin says, "Having thus received some taste and knowledge of true godliness, I was immediately influenced with an intense desire to make progress." There can be no doubt that the great aim of his life and the motivation for everything he did and said was contained in his motto, which Abraham Kuyper reminds us was not just *Deo gloria* but *soli Deo gloria*. J. I. Packer concludes that he was "Bible centered in his method, God centered in his outlook, Christ centered in his message. He was controlled throughout by a vision of God on the throne and a passion that God should be glorified."

Our response to his life could rise no higher than to embrace his motto *soli Deo gloria*.

The Rev. Eric J. Alexander
Former Pastor, St. George's-Tron Parish Church
Glasgow, Scotland

Abbreviations

CO	John Calvin, *Ioannis Calvini opera quae supersunt omnia*, ed. Guilielmus Baum, Eduardus Cunitz, and Eduardus Reuss, 59 vols; *Corpus Reformatorum* series, vols. 29–87 (Brunswick: C. A. Schwetschke and Son, 1863–1900)
CTJ	*Calvin Theological Journal*
ESV	English Standard Version
HTR	*Harvard Theological Review*
Institutes	John Calvin, *Institutes of the Christian Religion*, various editions
KJV	King James Version
NASB	New American Standard Version
NICNT	New International Commentary on the New Testament
NIV	New International Version
Vg.	Vulgate
WCF	Westminster Confession of Faith
WTJ	*Westminster Theological Journal*

1

Reformation, Calvinism, and Lessons Learned—Nehemiah 8:1–4a and 9:1–3, 16–21

David W. Hall

Ann and I have been privileged to watch the unfolding, the maturing, and the cultivation of Calvin500. As we met last Sunday (July 5, 2009) for worship, we were in the church—that dates to the 12th century—in Calvin's Geneva, and for the week we heard several dozen presentations by Calvin scholars and enjoyed fifteen of the finest expositions of Scripture in St. Pierre Cathedral over a five-day conference. I wish to thank the church for the privilege of allowing me to be involved and for your support. It was a high point for us to hear the echoes of psalms bouncing off the same walls, using some of the same tunes, prayers, concepts, and creeds as our forefathers did. We were blessed by being surrounded by a great cloud of witnesses, who, at times, seemed very close.

Bob Godfrey spoke of Calvin's "cherished text," finding that Calvin often referred to John 17:3: "For this is eternal life: to know the only true God," which later became the motto of Harvard College. A humble Archbishop of Uganda mounted the stairs to the pulpit, only after making a sincere protest because he was awed by following Calvin, and brought us a bold message. Phil Ryken preached on the always-open door for the gospel.

Geoff Thomas, a Reformed Baptist, summed up the simplicity of predestination in a few questions between a pastor and a member:

> Pastor: How are you saved? Parishoner: By God's grace.
> Pastor: Did God save you or did you save yourself? Parishoner: God did.
> Pastor: Did he do so on purpose or by accident?

Sinclair Ferguson called us to relate all things to Christ alone. And Ted Donnelly, from Northern Ireland, challenged us to live out Romans 8:35–39, even while not in luxury hotels as on a tour, but as with five young martyrs who were killed at Lyon at the hands of Roman Catholic persecutors in the 1550s, while Calvin tried to console them. They, like we, sang psalms to one another and summoned each other to heroic courage.

We heard many great quotes and illustrations at the conference, which is the major preaching conference for this commemorative cycle. Outstanding studies were presented, and much fellowship was renewed. Importantly, these messages provide a current apology for the vitality of Calvinism, and they are exemplars to modern audiences of what living Calvinism looks like and sounds like today.

One of the painful lessons, however, is to observe how Calvin's church—once bustling, burgeoning, and exporting the faith—is now often marginalized in its own city and in the world. Surrounded by obvious signs of modernity, hedonism, and unbelief, most of us questioned: what happened to the faith that once changed the world? How could it shrink, vanish, or succumb to the spirit of the age? Of course, we also ask—and to some degree, each of these sermons asked—how can we avoid that same fate? Also we ask: is it right to look back?

A Renewal or Reformation from Time to Time Is Necessary

In Nehemiah's time, there was a return to faith—a vital revival and reformation. The three primary features of it were: return to the Word, repentance from and recognition of sin, and refocus of priorities.

Calvin found and highlighted the same features. As I share my comments with you today, I want to begin and end with the book of Nehemiah—bookending some of my other thoughts.

I would hope that a celebration of a past event would stimulate folks to return faithfully to their faith and live it out. They may have to change some things, as in Nehemiah's time, and they may have to rebuild. But that is better than spinning farther and farther away from the truth.

That is, after all, the reason to have a commemoration: to call folks back to the strong and living aspects of a tradition. No tradition should be perpetuated if it is not thoroughly biblical and helpful. We should not, in these events, focus on the outward or glorify previous human beings. We should take their faith, their thought, their moral examples and benefit from those. Notwithstanding, we ought not to worship any ancestor, even a hero like Calvin. We should seek to learn from him and his disciples to the degree that they imitate Christ.

In this Old Testament example, we see: a strong decline, a rebuilding that follows that decline, and light that follows darkness.

The Heart of Calvinism Can Bring These: Three Points of Calvinism

If we expect Calvinism to endure and bring other reformations like the one in Nehemiah's time, we should make sure we know what we are talking about. For simplicity's sake, and rather than using the customary five points, I shall summarize Calvinism under three points that should be taught in the home, the church, and the school. The other sermons herein form a collage of how Calvinism may be rightly understood.

The Glory and Sovereignty of God

From the *Institutes'* beginning preface, John Calvin portrayed the human condition as "naked of all virtue," enslaved, blind, and weak. The purpose of this depiction was to preclude all occasion for self-glorying and give all glory to God. Human beings, thought Calvin, should be stripped of "vainglory" to "learn to glory in the Lord."

Five centuries after Calvin's birth, John Piper suggests that a fitting symbolic banner over Calvin's work could be: *Zeal to Illustrate the Glory of God*. Whether in life or on his deathbed, Calvin professed to propound only "what I esteemed to be *for the glory of God*." At the 500th anniversary of Calvin's birth, Calvinism's essence is tied to "passion for the absolute reality and majesty of God."

Also, at Calvin's 400th anniversary Princeton giant Benjamin Warfield summarized: "No man ever had a profounder sense of God than [Calvin]." Whether it is "this relentless orientation on the glory of God" (Piper), or the "all-embracing slogan of the Reformed faith: the work of grace in the sinner as a *mirror for the glory of God*" (Vos), or Calvin's own words, the glory of God distills the meaning of Calvin's message.

Warfield summarized: "The Calvinist is the man who has seen God, and who, having seen God in his glory, is filled on the one hand, with a sense of his own unworthiness to stand in God's sight as a creature, and much more as a sinner, and on the other hand, with adoring wonder that nevertheless this God is a God who receives sinners."

Calvin described this world as *theatrum Gloriae*. For him, every aspect of life from work to worship and from art[1] to technology bore the potential to glorify God. Creation is depicted as a platform for God's glory[2] or a "dazzling theater,"[3] displaying God's glorious works. Such comments support Lloyd-Jones' later claim that for Calvin "the great central and all-important truth was the sovereignty of God and God's glory."

British evangelical James I. Packer concurs that Calvin's Christianity rested on a vision of God enthroned and reigning majestically: "How often Calvin used the words 'majesty' and 'glory'! How often he dilates on the greatness of God! The passion corresponded to the vision. It was the passion expressed in that great phrase which has become the slogan of Calvinism—*soli Deo gloria*!"

If the glory and sovereignty of God is the first note of Calvinism, the second enduring hallmark of Calvinism is the fall of man.

The Fall of Man

Calvinism, if it is to resemble Nehemiah's reform, will manifest a stubborn realism and retain limited expectations. We expect neither the world nor ourselves to be perfect; we are not utopian. And the better Calvinists quickly learn that this applies to our own inner lives as well; for every morning, the first visage we see in the mirror is one of depravity. This is not something that we will outgrow nor end with an educational remedy. If we jettison the doctrine of sin, along with its necessary remediation only by Christ, we will not serve to reform or aid those around us.

1. *Institutes*, 1.11.12.
2. Ibid., 1.14.20.
3. Ibid., 1.5.8; 2.6.1.

Calvin's doctrine was a bracing tonic for the accumulated arrogance of the day, complete with its opulence and outer success. The Renaissance hubris would fall, however, like the subprime mortgage market in 2008. Calvin's faith in God, not man, filled that gap. The fallenness of human nature continues to exemplify Calvinism in all ages.

The third signature of Calvinism is calling to the world.

Calling to the World

All vocations can give glory to God. All walks of life can be noble, helpful, and God-oriented. The clergy have no corner on the marketplace, and many who are not ministers are and have been used for great things.

Vocation and daily work are good. Calvinism calls us out of the cloister, far from the hiddenness of the monastic life, and into the world with the shining, powerful message of God.

These make Calvinism different from every other religious scheme. And this is the faith that is spreading.

The Spread of Calvinism and Why It Doesn't Die

This week I wondered: do you think John Calvin might be surprised five centuries after his birth to find three men of African descent in his pulpit or to find more Calvinists in the Southern Baptist Convention than in the Presbyterian Church in America? It was sheer joy to note the participation by the many brothers and sisters below.

- Several of the "guardians" (deaconal assistants) at St. Pierre Cathedral were Turkish-Kurds, having come to the faith.
- Koreans and Chinese populated Geneva and may be the leading visitors to this area.

- The largest seating capacity for a sanctuary of any Reformed church (seating five thousand) is in the heart of downtown Jakarta, Indonesia, pastored by a Chinese Calvinist, Dr. Stephen Tong.
- Chinese Calvinism is growing, and may prove to be one of the most exciting stories of our century.
- Africans blessed us, with the sermon by a most humble Archbishop (of Uganda) Henry Orombi, with his assistant, Onesimus Asiimwe. On another occasion, the Rev. Dr. Setri Nyomi (of Ghana), the president of the World Alliance of Reformed Churches, welcomed us as brothers and sisters.
- Our church supports a strong Calvinist, the Rev. Jean Paul in Haiti with Reformation Hope International. He knows the hope for Haiti is the Reformed faith.
- We met Dr. Peter Vimalasekaran, originally from Northern Ireland, but who is leading a German Gypsy ministry in Fribourg.
- Sebastian Heck, from our presbytery and a former intern at Grace Presbyterian in Douglasville, Georgia, is replanting a Reformed denomination in Heidelberg, Germany.

Conferences on Calvin this year were held in unlikely places such as Rome, Italy; St. Petersburg, Russia; Prague; South Africa; Toronto; and Boston. Others met in Holland, France, New Zealand, Australia, and South Carolina and California.

Dr. Michael Milton of Reformed Theological Seminary (Charlotte, NC) calls this "Global Calvinism" because it is catholic/biblical Calvinism. And that Calvinism is spreading.

How Living Calvinism Is Expanding Today

Who would have imagined the following news stories in the first half of this year?

- The third most potent idea in a CNN/Time poll in April 2009 was "New Calvinism."
- More books have been published on Calvin this year than in any other previous year. For example, Calvin500.com has released a CD that contains 97 volumes of Calvin materials.
- University campuses, especially in the East, are cropping up with independent young scholars who dare to question tradition, and in so doing find that Calvinism is one of the few ideological platforms that is both stable and capable of transforming dated structures.
- The *New York Times, Washington Post,* and *USA Today,* over this July anniversary week, each featured a piece on the significance of Calvinism, even if begrudgingly.
- National Public Radio did a story on "Calvinmania" sweeping Europe, while CBN carried a feature of Calvin's anniversary.
- One thousand gathered in Boston over the July 4 weekend to recall the virtues and energy of the Reformation.
- Vibrant, local churches celebrated in their own ways; and many tours visited historic sites of the Reformation.

So our faith is not dying out; or is it?

A Cautionary Tale: How the Mighty Are Fallen

One church told me that it, a Reformed Baptist congregation in Lausanne, is the only church in Switzerland to hold to the "doctrines of grace." While some might dispute that, it at least reflects the severe dwindle that has characterized Calvinism for the past two centuries.

Many of you have heard the oft-repeated slogan that "the church is always but one generation away from extinction." All it takes for the church to die is for one generation to drop the baton.

Few people attend St. Pierre parish, maybe one hundred fifty to two hundred per Sunday, with a very high median age.

In much of Geneva today, Calvin is an embarrassment. He was called by one tour guide in Chaminix: "Osama Bin Calvin." That is how Calvin is respected in his own land.

The church can become secular in a hurry! This is the sad tale of Europe. Will ours end similarly?

What happened to a movement that was so vital, so revolutionary, so influential? God's Word, the supernatural, evangelism, and discipleship were abandoned. Arts, culture, intellect, and leisure were substituted.

So back to Nehemiah and reformation. Nehemiah 1–7 provides the setting; then in chapters 8–9 we see four things:

1. Recovery of the Word—8:3–4 (note pulpit level in v. 5, which shows the proper emphasis)—and authority of the Word—8:8 (not human opinion).
2. Return to Holy Times/ Seasons—8:9. These people, once reformed, began to set aside the Sabbath for worship. The Feast of Booths (8:13) was celebrated as it had not been for a thousand years, since Joshua's time!
3. Realistic appraisal of moral sin—9:2–3. They confessed their sin for a quarter of the day, and that after standing for the reading of God's Word for a quarter of the day.
4. Admiration of how God worked in the past—9:6–15 and 17ff.

Why is memorializing important? Many of you have fond memories of earlier services, and often thinking back will trigger a certain feeling—sometimes even actions. Let me pose two self-reflective questions about memorializing how God works in the past.

First, does God instruct us to look backwards and remember the past? Or is this little more than backwards navel-gazing to aggrandize ourselves or our tradition?

Some might think this activity to be wrong in itself—a case of wrong focus. Of course, it probably is wrong to look back to the past if one seeks to enshrine it as automatically better than any other day or to think that one's own tradition or family is superior to all others. To focus on the past with an aim to find that no descendants measure up is perhaps closer to idolatry than to a godly remembering.

The belief that all is new also speaks against remembering the past. For if the new is always and automatically better, then there's little need in looking back to the past.

But both of those are abuses; does God ever say to look back and remember? We think so. Memorials are prominently featured in the early chapters of the book of Genesis:

- The rainbow at the end of the flood is a reminder that God would never send a flood like this again. Noah's altar signified that the seasons would continue.
- Several times, Abram builds an altar to mark an event (13:4, 18). Once he even planted a tree to memorialize a treaty (21:33). Abraham purchased a cave at Machpelah to bury his wife Sarah; he would later be put to rest there.
- Isaac dug a well to mark God's promise and a treaty.
- When Jacob had a dream of how God would use him, he built a pillar of stones to mark where he'd had such a deep experience with God (28:18).

So it seems that all the patriarchs built memorials of some events, and they were good.

Passover also provided a call for and the prompt for remembering. The forerunner to the Lord's Supper was designed to be a part of an annual celebration. Each year, God wanted his people to remember a specific miracle: the deliverance from Egypt and the culmination of the ten plagues. God not only ordered that this be recalled every year, but also planted a prompt in the service. In order to ensure that each family recalled this, God planned for the inquisitive younger family members to ask, "What do these stones mean?" (Josh. 4:6),[4] and the parents would explain the miracle of the exodus, hopefully pointing to God's providence and salvation by the blood. The Lord had his people remember this particular event for years.

In Joshua, remember what may be learned from 4:6–7. As Israel crossed the Jordan River, each tribe had a representative carry a stone "to serve as a sign among you. In the future, when your children ask you, 'What do these stones mean?' tell them that the flow of the Jordan was cut off before the ark of the covenant . . . These stones are to be a memorial to the people of Israel forever." Later in that chapter, God wanted those in the future to inquire and learn of God's acts (4:21).

God wanted his people to remember great lives, miracles in nature, the exodus, the crossing of the Jordan, and other significant acts. The reason is two-fold: (1) we are ever so forgetful, and most of us treat each new day as divorced from yesterday—we tend to think we're the first ones ever to face something new; and (2) God knew that the retelling of these things would help keep us on track. Some things, indeed, do deserve a retelling, while many should not be repeated at all.

But the point is this: the Lord does not expect his truths to be carried on without some retelling. If we assume that everyone automatically knows everything, we need not rehearse events. But human beings are not that way, and to fail to memorialize—to move into neutral—may lead not only to forgetfulness but to decay. The reality is that we all have to repeat some things.

Next ask a second question: why is this activity important, and how does it help us?

We get out of the "total present tense" and take a long-term view. It is good to know that the whole world does not revolve around us and just us. Not only is there a very large world out there, but there is also a very long span of time that God has

4. All quotations of Scripture in this chapter are from the NIV.

been working. If one lives only in the "now," he'll likely not plan, likely not make judgments except for the short run. If we get too present-tense-focused, we may also get very selfish.

The Lord commends a long-term view for us, and one of the things that helps is if we look back at the past to learn how previous saints dealt with certain issues. We can find that we have friends from the past. We may discover good counselors, and church history can keep us from many a mistake. In fact, most heresies are old ideas brought back by someone who thinks he's created a new idea. Some knowledge of the past helps us.

We also compare ourselves to God's standards; that is good.

If you return to Nehemiah 9, note also three warning signs in 9:16: presumptiveness, rebel/obstinate, and disobey.

Could this be an anatomy and could it not be that the first (presumptiveness) begins a declension that follows in similar trajectory? This might be a warning catalogue. Do you begin a spiritual decline with overconfidence? Presumptiveness? Thinking that God will only bless you and never be displeased with you?

Then do you move to being set in your sin, happy to rebel?

Finally, do you move into being obstinate as a rule toward the things God is calling you to?

Also, Nehemiah 9:26–29 shows how extremely patient God is, and yet we rebel and turn our backs toward him.

This is why periodic renewals are important and needed!

And if such gatherings are used to call us back to God and his ways, then they are positive.

History may, in fact, show that a long cycle of decline has bottomed, and Calvinism is on the way back! A couple of young British authors now have a book on the *New York Times* best-seller list that is entitled *God Is Back*! Could that be some of the future of Calvinism? If, as we think, it is a genuinely superior system of doctrine, then once irrational factors are muted, it should regain ground. We may be witnessing that cyclical revival, following two centuries of loathing by hostile critics.

Notwithstanding, since none of us are endowed with predictive prophetic gifts, maybe we can begin with a review of highlights in the area of success and failure. These might protect us and keep us on track as we face the future.

What Worked and What Didn't Over the Half Millennium: Five Huge Success Stories

Receiving immigrants and persuading them. Calvin's Geneva doubled in population during his lifetime, and he welcomed Italian, Polish, French, and English exiles. He was probably not strategic enough to consider how they would return to their homelands, radiating the truths learned in Geneva. More likely, he was simply doing his Christian duty, but he did not insist on ethnic homogeneity. Calvin discipled all *ethnoi,* knowing that being in *imago Dei,* each could be an ambassador.

Spreading Calvinism through educational centers. Calvin's Academy, which was modeled on those in Lausanne and Strasbourg, taught thousands and trained the next generation of leaders. Over time, wherever Calvinist ministers planted churches (Nyon, Neuchatel, Lyon, etc.), academies popped up. Calvin sensed early on that "ideas had consequences," and he sought to cultivate those.

Implanting Calvinists in strategic leadership sectors. Many of the refugees to Geneva were from the nobility. Accordingly, Calvinism spawned more disciples in the ruling class in various countries than most other branches of the Reformation. Leaders like Admiral Coligny, and readers like the King of Poland, were impressed with Calvin's reforms. Seeking strategic leaders is one of the successes that early Calvinists experienced.

Fueling Calvinism by infusing economies. Calvinism virtually transformed the commerce and business of the day. Modern, market-based economies finally were liberated and found their buttresses in the Calvinistic work ethic, in the tendency to invest, and through the business leaders of Reformed churches. Calvinism likely would not have spread without this favorable economic climate, and it used it optimally.

Codifying truth via catechisms, classic works, and regular preaching. Calvinists were quite successful in crystallizing the faith. They formed catechisms and adopted creeds wherever they went. As such, their extent quickly became multigenerational, all very logo-centric, and preaching became the news of the day—good or otherwise.

Such were some of the Calvinist methods that succeeded and that will probably guide us for the future.

However, there were and are glaring errors as well.

Notorious Calvinist Failures

Pettiness, censoriousness. From the earliest disagreement with Luther (due to the stridency of Dr. Luther as much as anything), Calvinists have, regrettably, been notorious for splitting hairs and communion with each other. Often there is more concern about a leader's status and recognition, and it is not uncommon to have a judgmental demeanor that hardly attracts converts. Focusing mainly on one's agenda has been a large Calvinist failure.

Racial discrimination. In certain geographical areas, some of God's children were viewed as second- or third-class citizens by aristocratic Calvinists. Calvin himself, of course, did not succumb to this, but some disciples actually crafted ingenious and self-serving rationales to discriminate against races. Future Calvinism, if it is to succeed, must not repeat this mistake.

Class-orientation, as if only upper classes could benefit from Calvinism. Similarly, because many of the original Calvinists were wealthy or from the nobility or aristocracy, it was an easy confusion to think that to be a prerequisite or fruit of Calvinism. In fact, to the degree that Calvinists are mono-classists, they will lose people to the socialism of the day.

Affair with Unitarianism and Socinianism. Calvinism, perhaps because of its emphasis on the mind, became quick prey to new rationalistic movements. Socinius and his children, the Unitarians, quickly recovered much territory that Calvin's disciples won, and it never returned to the Calvinist column. While we wish to harness the intellect, both compromise with the world and arrogance from educational successes can lead future Calvinism astray.

Attempting to rule by force (e.g., as the Servetus case points up). Calvinists must recall that "though the wrong seems oft so strong, God is the ruler yet," and that we cannot force human consciences to agree with or submit to our faith. Often the zeal that accompanies Reformation movements becomes quite regrettable down the road. Mature statesmen and wise counselors must call those back from the brink if they move into conquering by political or external might.

So as we face the future, seeing both Nehemiah's and Calvin's reforms, we should be careful to apply biblical truth and not imitate the culture of our day.

One very difficult thing to resist is the altering of the ancient faith in the attempt to make it relevant. It is hard to make the case that Calvinists have been very good at this. All too often the church or its leaders are seduced by the sirens of contemporaneity. How tempting to be conformed to the patterns of this world. Perhaps this 500th celebration will remind us to use delicate care in translating the faith, for something precious can be lost in the translation. However, it must be translated.

The faith that echoes the name of Calvin might be tested by these five hallmarks:

1. It downplays the grandeur of unredeemed man. Sin, in other words, must always be preached.
2. It champions the power of God (not institution or self) to change our world. Calvinism does not depend on technique but on spiritual power.
3. It opposes wrong schemes of earthly power (hierarchicalism); it espouses dispersed power.
4. It calls us to take our living faith into the marketplace of ideas.
5. It is Trinitarian, calling us to carry the cross and to trust the Spirit.

One earlier historian (Ford Lewis Battles) in 1976 summarized well how Calvinism could continue, first by denying that he was advocating an "antiquarian enterprise," then by posing and answering this question:

> Can the form of Christianity commonly known as Calvinism survive in the modern world? It cannot survive unless, first, it is known; secondly, believed; thirdly, practiced. Calvin, the theologian, was captive to his own time and place, but also transcends the sixteenth century. The more I study that great interpreter of Jesus Christ, the more contemporary I discover him to be, and the more dated I find so called 'contemporary theology' to be.[5]

Based on this, future success will probably not deviate from past successes. Wisdom—and if we learn anything from these commemorations—suggests that we emphasize the following as we move forward:

1. Hold to God's truth from age to age. Be confident enough in it that the tendency to compromise diminishes in com-

5. Jim O'Brien, "Ford Lewis Battles: 1915–1979, Calvin Scholar and Church Historian Extraordinary," *CTJ* 15, 2 (November 1980): 187.

parison to the greatness of God. The awareness that the church, our lives, and Scripture itself is enduring inspires perseverance, even when times are tough.
2. Always target the education of the next generations.
3. Seek to translate into the vernacular, without neutering the content (printing, Internet, media, etc.).

As Chesterton put it, while lamenting both passivity and the infatuation with idea-novelty: "If you leave a white post alone it will soon be a black post. If you particularly want it to be white you must be always painting it again; that is, you must be always having a revolution. Briefly, if you want the old white post you must have a new white post."[6] He was likely correct to warn that if past virtues were not championed, they would inevitably deteriorate due to adverse conditions. He understood that if things are simply left alone, those are abandoned to a torrent of change. Chesterton seemed to grasp something of why God wants memorials.

4. Century in and out, strong local churches will keep the flame burning. Calvin knew there were no substitutes for the local church.
5. Mission and colonizing are regular parts of our lives.

So our memorial is hardly out of place or counterproductive. It is but a launchpad.

In the case of this volume, these sermons came from a memorializing event. Calvin500 convened in Calvin's Geneva in order to have sermons preached from Calvin's pulpit. The symbolism of intent and continuity could hardly be missed. And these sermons were offered as attempts to repaint a homiletical fencepost.

In these, we hear the echoes of Calvin's voice through a host of talented preachers—many of these will be the finest of their

6. G. K. Chesterton, *Orthodoxy* (London: Lane, 1909), 210–11.

generation. Each, I think, upholds the wisdom of Ford Battles' advice on the conditions necessary for Calvinism to have a future: "first, it is known; secondly, believed; and thirdly, practiced." That sage advice sums up the goals of this present work. These also provide a fine example of thriving Calvinism.

Why will Calvinism last? Not because of John Calvin but because of how close he drew to the enduring truths God gave us.

Perhaps we can phrase the challenge this way: are we building Christ's church for the next five hundred years so that people in 2509 will look back on us as we have been noting the contributions of those born in 1509? What kind of Christians we are and our children will be, from this point on, will be of considerably more consequence than the thoughts or births of those five hundred years earlier.

There is a story of an Austrian nobleman, who, raised from the ranks of the common people, was taunted once by a group of haughty princes because of his lack of pedigree. "Gentlemen," however, he replied, "you are correct; you are descendants; I am an ancestor." Wouldn't you rather be the ancestor of a new Reformation like Nehemiah's and Calvin's than the descendant of an old one? Most of us would prefer to lend our hands toward the building of five hundred glorious years of future history than merely be the products of five hundred years of great history past.

Is It Calvin's Faith or God's Word That Lasts?

Finally, each should make sure that we know Christ the Redeemer and that we need his mediatorial work on our behalf. Most of us could use strong and more regular reminders that we are needy sinners and that God in his Word provides the way.

Let us not have overconfidence, presumptiveness, lethargy, or indifferentism. Calvin said: "Faith cannot be long mulled to sleep without being at last quenched."[7] What is needed from this commemoration, as it was in Nehemiah's time, is to declare a "truceless war" against anything that attacks the worship, truth, or honor of God. Will you join together for that?

I ask each of you, in every way possible, to lend your hand to that great calling. As debtors to God's mercy, let us renew ourselves to God's Word, holy times and seasons, repentance from sin, rebuilding the future, and learning from God's past.

Delivered July 12, 2009, at Midway Presbyterian Church, Powder Springs, Georgia.

7. W. Robert Godfrey, *John Calvin: Pilgrim and Pastor* (Wheaton, IL: Crossway, 2009), Kindle edition, Location 2461–74.

2

In Christ Alone—Philippians 3:8–12

Sinclair B. Ferguson

Calvin's Prayer before the Sermon:

Let us call upon our good God and Father, beseeching him, since all fullness of wisdom and light is found in him, mercifully to enlighten us by his Holy Spirit in the true understanding of his word, and to give us grace to receive it in true fear and humility. May we be taught by his word to place our trust only in him and to serve and honor him as we ought, so that we may glorify his name in all our living and edify our neighbor by our good example, rendering to God the love and obedience which faithful servants owe their masters, and children, their parents, since it has pleased him graciously to receive us among the number of his servants and children.

Finally, my brothers, rejoice in the Lord. To write the same things to you is no trouble to me and is safe for you.

> Look out for the dogs, look out for the evildoers, look out for those who mutilate the flesh. For we are the real circumcision, who worship by the Spirit of God and glory in Christ Jesus and put no confidence in the flesh—though I myself have reason for confidence in the flesh also. If anyone else thinks he has reason for confidence in the flesh, I have more: circumcised on the eighth day, of the people of Israel, of the tribe of Benjamin, a Hebrew of Hebrews; as to the law, a Pharisee; as to zeal, a persecutor of the church; as to righteousness, under the law blameless. But whatever gain I had, I counted as loss for the sake of Christ. Indeed, I count everything as loss because of the surpassing worth of knowing Christ Jesus my Lord. For his sake I have suffered the loss of all things and count them as rubbish, in order that I may gain Christ and be found in him, not having a righteousness of my own that comes from the law, but that which comes through faith in Christ, the righteousness from God that depends on faith—that I may know him and the power of his resurrection, and may share his sufferings, becoming like him in his death, that by any means possible I may attain the resurrection from the dead.
>
> Not that I have already obtained this or am already perfect, but I press on to make it my own, because Christ Jesus has made me his own. Brothers, I do not consider that I have made it my own. But one thing I do: forgetting what lies behind and straining forward to what lies ahead, I press on toward the goal for the prize of the upward call of God in Christ Jesus. Let those of us who are mature think this way, and if in anything you think otherwise, God will reveal that also to you. (Phil. 3:1–15)

On the 2nd of May 1564, John Calvin sent a brief letter to his longtime friend William Farel. He expected these to be the words of his final farewell to the old comrade who had first threatened him with God's judgment if he would not serve Christ in the city of Geneva. "I draw my breath with difficulty, and every moment I am in expectation of breathing my last." And then he added: "It is enough that I live and die for Christ, who is to all his followers a gain both in life and death. Again I bid you and your brethren farewell."[1]

Three weeks later—enough time for Farel to pay one last visit—Calvin took his final breath in this world. According to his wishes, his body was laid in an unmarked grave, there to await the resurrection.

It would have seemed strange beyond words to this emaciated, disease-ridden, fifty-four-year-old man that five hundred years later his words would be cited at the beginning of a conference celebrating his life and ministry.

I am not sure he would have altogether approved. But perhaps he would look kindly on the fact that the opening sermon would be drawn from Paul's Letter to the Philippians and echo his conviction that Christ is a gain to believers in both life and death.

Calvin was, of course, alluding to Paul's words in Philippians 1:21 and pointing us to the heartbeat of the gospel, of the Christian life, and of all his own teaching—Christ is everything, and everything we need God has supplied for us in Christ alone.

But later, in this great Christ-centered and Christ-saturated passage in Philippians 3, he returns to the same theme and expounds it in greater detail. It is a celebration of the gospel, an exaltation of Jesus Christ, and it expresses a profound consecration to him.

It would not be surprising, if you had the audacity to ask Calvin to give you a "life text"—a bold request indeed!—if he suggested these words. They certainly constituted Paul's "life text."

What is the apostle's burden here? He was concerned that his beloved Philippians should not be diverted from the Lord Jesus Christ. He seeks to prevent them from being led astray by

1. Jules Bonnet, ed., *The Letters of John Calvin*, trans. M. R. Gilchrist (Philadelphia: Presbyterian Board of Publication, 1858), 4:1559–64, 364.

"the circumcision party" by recounting his own experience. First, he tells us what he was by nature. Second, he describes what he found in Christ. Third, he explains what he became by grace.

What He Was by Nature

No one would doubt, surely, that Saul of Tarsus was a "type A" personality—highly motivated, deeply driven, and ambitious to the core of his being. Moreover, if any man ever had reason to boast in his accomplishments in this world, in what he calls "the flesh," *especially religious accomplishments*, that man was Saul of Tarsus.

He had entered into a remarkable inheritance: "circumcised on the eighth day, of the people of Israel, of the tribe of Benjamin, a Hebrew of Hebrews" (3:5). No mere eighth-generation South Carolinian, seventh-generation Floridian, sixth-generation Texan! His roots went back to the patriarchs of distant antiquity. Not for nothing did he bear the name of the first king of Israel.

He was not only a Jew, he was a Jew first class—a five-star Jew!

Added to this was what gave him self-confidence. "As to the law," he was a Pharisee. By personal choice, he had elected the narrow way. He had been educated in Jerusalem at the feet of the great Gamaliel "according to the strict manner of the law of our fathers" (Acts 22:3). Not only so, but his life was marked by an ongoing adherence to his commitment to holiness—"as to righteousness under the law" he had seen himself as "blameless." He could have said to a Decalogue-commanding counselor what the rich young ruler had said in response to Jesus: "All these I have kept from my youth" (Luke 18:21). There was little if any sin-consciousness here.

But there was more.

Added further to this was his performance. He mentions it in an ominous expression of his commitment to the Pharisaic way: "as to zeal, a persecutor of the church" (3:6). Such zeal seems strange and perverse to us. But his own eyes were blind to the twisted heart that drove him on with such violence to hound down and extirpate the followers of him who came to save sinners.

But then he had met Christ on the road to Damascus, and everything changed.

Or did it?

In recent years, in part stimulated by the late Krister Stendahl's famous essay "The Apostle Paul and the Introspective Conscience of the West,"[2] many Pauline students and scholars have come to hold that Saul's experience was not really a Damascus Road *conversion* so much as a Damascus Road *calling*. He did not experience a classical "Western" conversion from legalism to grace, from sin to Christ. Rather, the Damascus Road encounter was a call to one who lived in grace to recognize Jesus as the Messiah. Thus, Stendahl argued, there is no Augustinian, Luther-like, or Bunyanesque conviction of sin, despair of self, or desperate sense of the need for a Savior to be found here.

I am not so sure. Why?

For several reasons.

For one, it was never the logical implication of Pharisaism to annihilate the followers of Jesus.

Nicodemus had made that clear during our Lord's ministry (John 7:50); Gamaliel himself, no matter how his words are assessed, also made it clear in the days of the apostles (Acts 5:34).

2. Krister Stendahl, "The Apostle Paul and the Introspective Conscience of the West," originally a paper presented to the Annual Meeting of the American Psychological Association in 1961 and later published in *HTR* 56 (1963): 199–215. It has been republished in *Paul Among Jews and Gentiles and Other Essays* (Philadelphia: Fortress Press, 1976), 78–96.

These men were Pharisees—indeed more than average Pharisees, leading Pharisees—men to whom other Pharisees listened attentively. No destructive zeal here!

Why then the enraged obsession that Paul vividly describes?

> For you have heard of my former life in Judaism, how I persecuted the church of God violently and tried to destroy it. And I was advancing in Judaism beyond many of my own age among my people, so extremely zealous was I for the traditions of my fathers. (Gal. 1:13–14)

The New Testament seems to me to provide an entire series of clues to the fact that there was more to the Damascus Road than recognizing that Jesus was the Messiah. In truth, to use Calvin's description of his own spiritual awakening, God subdued Saul of Tarsus "by an unexpected conversion."[3] Unexpected, indeed, but conversion it was.

The clues are as follows:

This man who happily assumed that he was blameless, without any troubling consciousness of sin or guilt, lived in Jerusalem. There, as a Jew of Cilicia, in all probability he attended the synagogue of the Cilicians to which Acts 6:9–10 refers.

As a young man Paul had a driving ambition to outstrip all of his contemporaries. He had made remarkable advance. But then he found himself caught with others in controversy with one particular man.

The man's name was Stephen. He was a Christian. He had an extraordinary knowledge and understanding of his Hebrew Bible, and from it he reasoned and taught about Jesus Christ, the messianic Savior. No one could counter his arguments.

3. John Calvin, *Commentary on the Book of Psalms*, trans. James Anderson (Edinburgh: Calvin Translation Society, 1845), 1:xl. In "The Author's Preface," Anderson translated Calvin's words *subita conversione* as "by a sudden conversion," but the sense of *subita* here (as Calvin recognized elsewhere) may be "unexpected" rather than "sudden." Ibid.

> And Stephen, full of grace and power, was doing great wonders and signs among the people. Then some of those who belonged to the synagogue of the Freedmen (as it was called), and of the Cyrenians, and of the Alexandrians, and of those from Cilicia and Asia, rose up and disputed with Stephen. But they could not withstand the wisdom and the Spirit with which he was speaking. (Acts 6:8–10)

For one young man, advancing beyond his contemporaries, but unable to overcome Stephen in biblical discussion, this evoked a strange new experience that proved to be a crisis.

Paul, I believe, describes that experience in a deeply personal paragraph in Romans 7:

> If it had not been for the law, I would not have known sin. I would not have known what it is to covet if the law had not said, "You shall not covet." But sin, seizing an opportunity through the commandment, produced in me all kinds of covetousness. Apart from the law, sin lies dead. I was once alive apart from the law, but when the commandment came, sin came alive and I died. The very commandment that promised life proved to be death to me. For sin, seizing an opportunity through the commandment, deceived me and through it killed me. (Rom. 7:7–11)

Why does he focus on the final commandment? Not because he had kept the others perfectly but because his first searing consciousness of the power of sin seems to have emerged in connection with coveting.

Saul had no special need to covet before—jealously to wish to possess what another had. If anyone had reason for confidence in the flesh, he had. Nobody could put greater confidence in the flesh—nobody stood above Saul of Tarsus when it came to matters of the faith. He had burning zeal and an ability that placed him head high above his peers.

What then was the locus of the covetousness of Saul of Tarsus? If he surpassed all others in accomplishment, of what or of whom was he jealous? What brought the first consciousness of the dark side within? What drove him eventually to frenzy?

The answer seems clear enough from the way Luke links two names in the Acts of the Apostles: Saul and Stephen. Nobody could better Stephen in the heated discussions of the meaning of Scripture. And from the hints Luke gives, this was accompanied by an outstanding degree of godliness of character. Stephen had a fine reputation, was marked by unusual wisdom, and was full of the Spirit of the Lord Jesus Christ. Is it accidental that Stephen is mentioned first in a list that is clearly not in alphabetical order and is singled out for special description as "a man full of faith and of the Holy Spirit" (Acts 6:3, 5)?

Only two options were before the burningly ambitious Saul as he heard Stephen and then watched the grace in which he died. The first, to seek, find, trust, and surrender to the Master whom Stephen proclaimed. The second was to get rid of him and everyone like him. And so Saul set out to destroy the church of Jesus Christ, "breathing threats and murder against the disciples of the Lord" (Acts 9:1), fighting all the way to silence the voice of conscience that bore witness to the sinfulness, rebellion, and alienation of his life.

Yes, indeed, the shadow of guilt lay across Saul's heart. No wonder he was in a frenzy of activity to destroy the church and to silence Stephen forever. Despite his best efforts, he was not able to silence the voice of Stephen's blood as it cried, "You sinful man, you can never silence the conscience that condemns you."

And so it proved to be. This man—proud, self-sufficient, covetous, and angry, who would destroy the Savior's people rather than yield to him—was brought to his knees before the Savior he persecuted. He was "subdued" (as Calvin himself might say) "by an unexpected conversion." Yes—unexpected to those who knew him, unexpected even to Christians who might have been praying for him, and, yes, unexpected to Saul himself.

But it was not unexpected to the Lord Jesus.

What, then, was the impact of this "unexpected conversion"?

What He Found in Christ

The conversion of Saul of Tarsus is described from the historical perspective in Acts 9:1–22 and in his personal testimonies in Acts 22:1–21 and Acts 26:4–23. Here in Philippians 3, Paul tells the same story but now from a theological perspective.

Clearly Paul remained an ambitious man. Ambition in itself is not wrong. But his ambitions were thrown into reverse gear. Or, perhaps better, ambitions that had been in reverse gear, ministering to the flesh, idolizing religion, were now thrown into forward gear. They were redeemed, cleansed, and recentered on the Lord Jesus Christ.

Philippians 3:7–15 are verses saturated with references to the Lord Jesus.

Sometimes when we expect to see someone we have not met for some time, we wonder, "How shall I find him?"

How, now, do we find Saul of Tarsus? A very different man.

He Is Now "Found in Christ"

This, of course, is one of Paul's great expressions. But what is striking here is not so much his focus on union with Christ as his focus on Christ himself. The Lord Jesus is mentioned and referred to some ten times in verses 7–10. Paul's words underline the extent to which he was taken up with him. There is luxuriousness about his description of gaining Christ and enjoying "the surpassing worth of knowing Christ Jesus"—not merely the privilege of knowing him but the "surpassing worth" of this knowledge!

But surpassing *what*? Well, surpassing *everything*! All knowledge about all other things is trumped by the knowledge of Christ. Christ himself is, to borrow the title of C. S. Lewis's friend Charles Williams' novel, *The Greater Trumps*.

But there is more. Paul describes Jesus as "my Lord."

In Paul's letters, "Lord," *Kurios*, is not first of all an expression of personal devotion but a title. Many thousands of times in the Septuagint (the Greek translation of the Old Testament with which Paul was so familiar), *kurios* is used to translate the ineffable divine name *Yahweh*. So when Paul says "Jesus is Lord," he means Jesus is God; he is Yahweh.

That nuance is certainly present here. But Paul is saying more. He is speaking of his absolute, unreserved, and unrestrained devotion to the Lord Jesus.

Jesus is "*my* Lord."

Is that how you think of him? Do you speak of him in this way? Could you write of him in these words: "my Lord," renouncing all idols in your heart and life?

I do not know the etiquette for concluding a letter of thanks written to a president of the United States. But I do know what one is expected to write to the British monarch: "I have the honor to be your Majesty's most humble and most obedient servant."

Strong words of loyalty and devotion to write to an earthly monarch; but how much more appropriate they are when addressed to the Lord Jesus Christ!

Paul could say them.

Can you?

He Is "Found" Not Having His Own Righteousness

He is "found" not having his own righteousness derived from his own efforts to conform to God's law but having the righteousness that comes through faith in Jesus Christ. It is a "God-righteousness" (3:9).

This is what we call imputed righteousness—righteousness that forms the character of another is now counted to us on the basis that Christ has wrought it not for himself but for us in all he did as our representative and substitute.

In our time this idea of imputed righteousness has come under suspicion and increasingly under open attack. It is said that since "righteousness" is not a commodity but an attribute of a person, it cannot be "imputed" to anyone else. Yes, our sins may be counted ("imputed") to Christ, but his righteousness is his alone and cannot be imputed or counted to us.

The fallacy here, once observed, is egregious indeed. For sin is no more a commodity than its opposite, righteousness. It, too, is an attribute of a person. By parity of reasoning, therefore, anyone who denies the imputation of Christ's righteousness to sinners must also by the same logic deny the possibility of the imputation or counting of our sin to Christ. Thus not only is the imputation of righteousness annihilated—the imputation of my sin is rendered impossible. In pulling away the thread of imputed righteousness, the whole fabric of the gospel unravels. For if my sin cannot be counted to Christ in order for him to bear it, then my salvation becomes an utter impossibility.

Notice, here, that Paul holds together two aspects of the gospel. Union with Christ (Paul is found "in him") is coupled with justification through the imputation of Christ's righteousness! There is the sweetest harmony between them. And this naturally leads to a third aspect of the salvation in which we now find Paul.

He Is "Found" Living in Union with Christ

Here we come to the rich heart of Paul's words. Christ is everything to him. In Christ he has discovered justification; he has entered into an inexpressible union with him. He is justified in Christ. He is united to Christ.

Now Paul comes to expand on what he increasingly "found" in his union with the Lord Jesus. His deep aspiration is "that I may know him and the power of his resurrection, and may share his sufferings, becoming like him in his death, that by any means possible I may attain the resurrection from the dead" (Phil. 3:10–11).

Here, surely, if anywhere, we see how the impress of Stephen's ministry left its abiding seal on Paul's life. This was the pattern he had first encountered in perhaps the first Christian in whose life he had seen with clarity "Christiformity"—likeness to the Lord Jesus.

Notice the chiasmic construction:

(A) *resurrection* power sharing in (B) *sufferings*
(B) likeness to *death* (A) *resurrection* from the death

Notice the order. Paul came to experience Christ in his risen power on the Damascus Road. Coming to know Christ in this way, he almost immediately learned that sharing in the power of his resurrection can never be divorced from sharing in the fellowship of his sufferings. He was shown what great things he would suffer for the sake of his Savior (Acts 9:16).

Why is the Christian life marked by sharing in sufferings and in triumph like this? Because to be a Christian means to be united to Christ. And there are not two Christs, a suffering Christ and a risen Christ. There is only one Christ. We cannot tear him apart. We cannot receive him in his power and triumph but refuse him in his humiliation and suffering. And we cannot become like him if we refuse the pattern his Father employed to make him what he became in our humanity.

To be found in Christ is the pathway to justification. But it is also the pathway to transformation. The two always belong together. Christ, as Calvin loved to say, was given to us for both. And this is, ultimately, the pathway to fruitful Christian living.

Paul had first seen that in Stephen; he later taught it to others. He speaks of himself "always carrying in the body the death of Jesus, so that the life of Jesus may also be manifested in our bodies. For we who live are always being given over to death for Jesus' sake, so that the life of Jesus also may be manifested in our mortal flesh. So death is at work in us, but life in you" (2 Cor. 4:10–12).

This is the way the Master went, the *Via Dolorosa*. It is also the way the apostles went, the *Via Apostolica*. It is the way for us, too.

There is no other way. God, says Calvin, has so constituted the church that "from the beginning . . . the Cross has been the way to victory, death the way to life."[4]

Now, all this seems to be rich and glorious theology. But is it practical? How does it work out? Does it make any real difference to the way we live the Christian life?

Paul certainly thought so! For here he weaves together sublime theology with the transforming power of the gospel.

Thirdly, then, notice:

What He Became by Grace

"So soon as Christ shines forth, all those things that formerly dazzled our eyes with a false splendour instantly vanish, or at least become paltry," notes Calvin on these verses.[5]

Here Paul hints at ways in which his growth in the knowledge of Christ proved to have a life-transforming effect on him. This comes to expression in a virtually unselfconscious fashion.

Paul's heart-devotion to Christ alone produced, first of all:

4. John Calvin, *Commentary on 1 Peter, The Epistles of Paul the Apostle to the Hebrews and the First and Second Epistles of Peter*, ed. D. W. and T. F. Torrance, trans. W. B. Johnston (Edinburgh: Oliver and Boyd, 1963), 240 (ad. 1 Peter 1:11).

5. John Calvin, *The Epistles of Paul the Apostle to the Galatians, Ephesians, Philippians and Colossians*, ed. D. W. and T. F. Torrance, trans. T. H. L. Parker (Edinburgh: Oliver and Boyd, 1965), 272 (ad. Phil. 3:7).

A Holy Dissatisfaction

Paul had not arrived. He knew he needed to press on for the prize (Phil. 3:12–14). This is one of the most blessed paradoxes of gospel living. The growing Christian is like a young lover—thoroughly satisfied as he drinks deeply of the pleasures of the new companionship and the loved one to whom he gives himself with admiration and devotion. And yet he is dissatisfied until he has drunk again from the wells of her presence, seen again her face, gazed lovingly into her eyes, rested again in the knowledge that the devotion is mutual.

So it is between the soul and Christ. It presses on to make Christ its own as he has made it his own (3:12).

A Single-Minded Simplicity

Everything is put in context in verse 13: "This one thing I do."

Paul is a man of one thing.

From one perspective the statement seems almost ludicrous. What did Epaphroditus, the bearer of the letter, say as he read it over before leaving on his mission to take it to Philippi (Phil. 2:25, 28)?

"Paul, you can't say that! How can I respond when our friends say, 'But Paul is the essential multitasker! He is always writing letters; he is always praying; he never seems to stay still. He is never doing only one thing—he seems always to be doing a hundred things!'?"

But Paul meant what he said. His answer would surely have been, "But I am not *doing a hundred things*. I am *doing one thing in a hundred different ways*. There is all the difference in the world between these two ways of life! In everything I do I am getting to know Christ better, seeking to love him more ardently, to serve him more joyfully. That is what I live for! That is the one thing I do!"

Would that we all had learned this single-minded simplicity in Christ! It would simplify our inner spiritual life; it would have a profound effect on the consistency, focus, integrity, and satisfaction of our whole life!

Would that all our young Christians could learn this as early as possible, and that it might be a guiding star for the whole of their lives in this increasingly complex and complicated world in which we live!

Here, then, is a polestar by which to navigate our lives for the glory of the Savior!

But there is one more way that Christ-centeredness transformed Paul. It produced

A Genuine Spiritual Accountancy

We have already noticed the life-and-death motif that comes to expression in these verses. But there is another motif, equally obvious in verses 7–8. Paul speaks about gain, or profit, and loss. Time after time he stresses this:

- But whatever gain I had, I counted as loss for the sake of Christ (3:7).
- Indeed, I count everything as loss because of the surpassing worth ["gain"] of knowing Christ Jesus my Lord (3:8).
- For his sake I have suffered the loss of all things and count them as rubbish, in order that I may gain Christ (3:8).

"Gain" and "loss" is the vocabulary of the accountant. But in this case the accountancy is spiritual, not financial. The principle is so important to Paul that he states it in four different ways, and in an ascending order:

- He looks back on his inheritance and accomplishment "according to the flesh." This he had once counted as great gain. But now he sees it in a different light. Now it did not even constitute a neutral spiritual budget in his life. Rather, he counted it as loss. Yes. All this was treated as loss for Christ. He alone is true gain.

- He now saw everything in this light—not only religious achievements, but in fact his whole life—everything he had done, said, been, accomplished. It was all loss by comparison with knowing Christ. He is the pearl of great price, the treasure hidden in the field for which a man will sell everything he has for the one great possession.
- There is more. For Paul has actually "suffered the loss of all things" for Christ. He may well have meant the words quite literally, for the Jew who was converted to Christ placed himself in danger of destroying all his relationships at a stroke. His family might well disinherit him; his social circle would ostracize him; employment opportunities were closed to him. We need look no further than the Letter to the Hebrews for New Testament testimony to these realities. Paul was not only prepared for this. He seems to suggest that he had actually experienced it.

But there appears to be one further, even more radical statement to be made:

- By comparison with Christ, he regards everything not merely as "loss" but as "rubbish" (3:8).

"Rubbish" is the ESV's rendering of the Greek word *skubalon*. It is unexceptionable as a translation. But it is possibly a more anodyne, more hygienic idea than the one Paul had in mind.

The Greek text of Philippians was a set book for study in the university in which I studied. I still remember coming to these verses as a young man of twenty or twenty-one, and turning to my Greek lexicon to get some help on the "semantic range" of the word *skubalon*—the nuances of meaning of which it was capable.

The emotions I felt that morning as I read the concluding words to the entry "skubalon" have lingered until this day. The desk at which I sat, the dim light in the ancient library, the blue binding to my lexicon—all are there before my eyes just now, as is the "wow" that marked my inner response to reading the three final words in the entry: "Usually translated 'dung.'"

Yes, "dung."

Paul did not despise creation. But he recognized that anything fallen creation offers to us, especially to entice us from gospel grace, is—by comparison with Jesus Christ—simply this: dung, excrement.

"Let us, therefore, learn from this," writes Calvin, "what value we ought to set upon the knowledge of Christ alone."[6]

What is most fascinating about these words is that this disposition is not so much the mark of an apostle who had reached unparalleled heights of spirituality. It is the simple evidence that a person has reached Christian maturity. For, he adds, "Let those of us who are mature think this way, and if in anything you think otherwise, God will reveal that also to you" (3:15).

Hear, then, John Calvin once more:

> We lose nothing when we come to Christ naked and stripped, for those things which we once wrongly imagined that we possessed, we then really begin to obtain. He therefore shows more fully how great are the riches of Christ, because we obtain and find all things in Him.[7]

Or, as we might put it with less elegance:

6. Ibid.
7. Ibid., 274.

> The person who has everything, but does not have Christ, possesses nothing. But the person who has nothing, but possesses Christ, possesses everything.

Which are you? Saul of Tarsus was one, and became the other. All of us are one or the other. We cannot be both.

You may have reason for confidence in the flesh, in the privileges of heredity and family.

You may be resting your hopes in the contribution you have made to your church, or on the fact that you often read the Bible, or that you belong to a church utterly committed to purity of doctrine and life.

You may even be confusing knowledge of theology with saving knowledge of Jesus Christ.

But the life built on such a foundation cannot endure the searching judgment of God. These offer no safe passage to heaven and eternal life and a glorious future in the resurrection.

No, if you are to be found in heaven and then enjoy the resurrection blessedness, you must first be found in Christ and in Christ alone.

How do we find you today? Are you found in Christ?

For in Christ and Christ alone will you find everything you need in this world and for the world to come, as Calvin himself so beautifully expresses it:

> When we see salvation whole—and every single part—is found in Christ, we must beware lest we derive the smallest drop from somewhere else. For if we seek salvation, the very name of Jesus teaches us that he possesses it. If other Spirit-given gifts are sought—in his anointing they are found; strength—in his reign; and purity—in his conception. And then there's tenderness—expressed in his nativity, in which he was, in all respects save sin, like us that he might learn to feel our pain: Redemption sought? It's in his passion found; acquittal—in his condemnation lies; and freedom from the curse—is in his

cross made known to you. If satisfaction for your sins you seek—you'll find it in his sacrifice; and cleansing in his blood. And if it's reconciliation now you need —for this he entered Hades; if mortification of your flesh—then in his tomb it's laid. And newness of our life—his resurrection brings and immortality as well comes also with that gift. And if you also long to find heaven's kingdom your inheritance, his entry there secures it now with your protection, safety too, and blessings that abound —all flowing from his kingly reign The sum of all for those who seek Such treasure-trove of blessings, of blessings of all kinds, from nowhere else can now be drawn than him. For them to come to you, you must be found in Christ, in Christ alone.[8]

Delivered July 5, 2009, at St. Pierre Cathedral, Geneva, Switzerland.

8. *Institutes* (1559), 2.16.19, my translation.

3

Who Is the Wise and Faithful Servant?—Matthew 24:45–51

Henry Luke Orombi

It's so amazing that the Lord brought us together, with my chaplain, Mr. Onesimus Asiimwe, to Geneva for the first time. I had always longed to come to the mainland of Europe, and it took the Presbyterians to bring me here, and I say thank you.

I asked both Dr. Krabbendam and Dr. Hall if I could preach from that side [lectern], not because I am so tall but because of my fear of standing in this pulpit where John Calvin stood and preached many sermons. I was feeling in my heart that someday when I stand before the Lord it is going to be my weakness that "you stood in the pulpit that I preach from." Now, he has successfully gone to the Lord; I have not.

So last night, when Dr. Russell and his wife and Dr. Jack White and his wife shared a meal with me, I shared a point: I'm praying that the day I die those will be around who should put these words on my tombstone: "Henry walked with the Lord; Henry walked with the Lord." That is the passion of my heart—to walk with the Lord.

Thank you for inviting me to come and celebrate five hundred years of a faithful servant of Jesus Christ. To me, since I arrived yesterday, it was a time for stock-taking, evaluation, and a time for inspiration—stock-taking because a man who lived five hundred years ago is still being remembered by key leaders of the church in the world. This morning my heart received a deposit, a great truth, preached by a humble servant of God. I went out very inspired.

Forty-three years ago, I invited Christ into my life because I came from a nonbelieving family. My grandfather had six wives and countless aunts, uncles, nephews, and nieces; my father also had two wives—it seemed to be a very difficult marriage because I never saw those women smile to one another. I then made a decision in my heart that when I married, I would only take one wife.

I'll only have one. I have one called Phoebe. But forty-three years ago, at the age of eighteen, I gave my life to Jesus. And when he came into my life, he changed my life. He has been leading me, teaching me—I'm not a good student, but he is a patient teacher. He has encouraged me in difficult times. He has walked with me through dark days. I stand as a product of a mission enterprise of Europe.

Thirty years ago I was called into ordained, full-time ministry. Half my life, thus, I have been a full-time worker in the church. I'm a child of the Reformation. I find a kinship together with you because we believe the Word of God to be the Word of God, the only truth that mankind needs.

The message that I believe the Lord would like to speak is from the passage which has already been read to us. And let me start with the question that Jesus asks in this passage, and it is one that cuts through my heart.

The question is: who is the faithful servant whom the Master has set over his household? Who is able to give the food at the proper time? The apostles are listening. This is a teaching about the end times, so the apostles are listening.

Later this point was driven home to Simon Peter by the Galilean lake. One morning, the fishermen had gone back to fishing. A fisherman who was at the forefront of everything, who had left everything to follow Jesus for three years, who wanted to be the pastor that Jesus could depend on, making promises that he never kept, but at the time when Jesus needed him the most, he was not there.

One night Peter had fished all night but caught nothing, but the resurrected Jesus did not forget him. Thank God! He never forgets. Jesus followed him to the Sea of Galilee. Having failed all night and caught nothing, Jesus comes as a friend—not like someone who is disappointed as if his best friend deserted him. And Jesus calls, "Friends, have you caught any fish?" And they answered, "No."

You know this story. This big catch of fish and the disciples find Jesus making breakfast for them by the seashore. And he fed them. Personally, I'm encouraged that with all my mistakes, shortcomings, and failures, Jesus still has mercy on me. He fed them, and they ate in silence.

I went to John 21:15–19, and Jesus asks Peter deep, searching questions. He asked him, "Simon, Son of John, do you love me more than these? Simon, do you love me more than these?"

Three times he asks Peter; three times Peter answers, "Yes, Lord." Three times he says "Simon Peter."

The whole thing about the servant who would feed the church at the right time comes to the fore as Jesus says, "Feed my lambs; take care of my lambs; feed my sheep."

I don't know about America, but I will tell you about Uganda. My Ugandan priest wants to go to church, holding his Bible, and walking into church. He will hold it proudly, and he will like to read it as much as he can, for it has transformed his life.

But you do remember, friends, that the average Christian does not know much of the Word of God, let alone Christians teaching it to their own children.

"Feed my lambs" is a very powerful command that the church today must follow. Why do I stand here fearing and trembling today? Because the man John Calvin was a teacher of the Word; the man John Calvin fed people the Word of God. And they came. The man John Calvin was used at a time when people had a hunger for the Word of God. And he was a good chef—he cooked very well.

I would like to say that part of the difficulty today is the lack of appetite for the Word of God. I would also like to suggest that this is predominantly because of the way that the Word has been preached or even not preached. Part of the difficulty today is that the Word of God is not preached with the faithfulness of John Calvin, the faithfulness of Martin Luther, or the passion that they had, with the desire they had. They believed the Word of God. Today, the church of Christ has not believed with that passion that this is the transforming Word of God. And no wonder people may not come. And if they do come, they may want to stay two minutes or three minutes or five minutes or ten minutes and then go as soon as possible.

Instead of being fed, they are being poisoned. But when it is preached with power, and preached with such a passion, preached with faith because people believe what they are preaching, it is different.

In my context, two weeks ago I was preaching to two thousand young people in high school. One hour and twenty minutes was not enough. There was a hunger. There was a desire. "Feed my lambs." Parents, we have a duty to feed our children the Word of God, to feed it relevantly, to make it interesting, to help them love the Word of God from childhood and then they grow up into it.

My father, who never went to church regularly and did not know Jesus personally, believed that the Bible would help me. He put it in my hand, and I started reading it when I learned to read. I read it from the time I was a little boy. I read from Genesis to Revelation several times when I was a little fellow. Because he believed that the Word of God someday would bear fruit in my life. "Feed my lambs; feed them the Word of God."

I charge you, my brothers and sisters, that every moment you lose to instill the Word in your child, you are removing the bricks and blocks of foundation of true character that you would have built. "Feed my lambs." Take care of my sheep because they must be fed.

Peter is listening; he is receiving a commission; he is feeling the weight of responsibility.

May I thank Dr. Ferguson again for preaching with such passion this morning? You moved my heart. I could see it from way in the back. How I cried that the Holy Spirit will put passion in our hearts.

The Presbyterian church has been familiar with a volume of understanding of the Word. I ask God to give you passion and a deep desire that that Word be not stalled in your libraries, in your universities, in your colleges, but that it will go, and it will go out.

When Peter wrote his first letter, chapter 2, verse 2, he said, "Desire the spiritual milk of the word." Peter had come to understand the commission by the Sea of Galilee to mean his mission was to proclaim that Word. Peter believed that his mission was to spread that Word. Peter moved, preached, lived, and died believing that. This is our mission together also: to feed God's lambs.

I would like secondly to share with you, my dear friends, what God has been to us in our country in Uganda. Perhaps some of you have not been there—it does not matter; I am here now.

I would like to say to you that 132 years ago faithful missionaries from Europe—from England—faithfully proclaimed the Word of God to us in Uganda. One hundred and thirty-two years ago, the church was born there through the proclamation of the gospel. Our people there embraced the Word of God. And within ten years of starting the church, there were already martyrs who gave their lives for the sake of the gospel and the Jesus they believed in.

Forty-five could not succumb to the homosexual advances of our king back in my country, because they said, "We believe in a king who is greater than you are, and that is King Jesus." They had embraced the Word of God so deeply that they would not fear death; they were cut to pieces; they were fed to the fire, and the executioner was so amazed that people were executed for no reason and that these did not panic. Instead, they sang as they went to the fire, as they were being mutilated. Such is the value of this Word. Such is the commitment to the king who has written to us a love letter, as someone has said.

My church faced martyrdom right from the very beginning. But the faithfulness to the Word, and the faithfulness of those who believe in Jesus Christ, was such that they were willing to lay their lives down for the gospel.

In 1977 the archbishop of my country and of my church was martyred by the then-dictator Idi Amin because he stood on the Word of God and spoke with such courage against a regime that would kill at will. And he said, "No, life and human life is valuable before God." And he paid for that with his life. And when he died, the politics of my nation changed.

I now live in a house he lived in, and I sit in the office he sat in. And it is a perpetual memory of faithfulness that I am holding onto, and I ask the Lord to make me faithful just like Janani Luwum was.

I remember a bishop, Festo Kivengere, a preacher of the gospel, minister to thousands of people, a product of East African revival, a strong advocate of the Word, a man who brought hope to many Ugandans and many others, a man who stood tall in the faith that he believed in the Jesus of the Bible, and he proclaimed the Word of God.

I come from a very young church but one that has paid a heavy price for the Word and prayed for Jesus: faithful servants of the Word!

Beloved, I notice a thread that is running through: it is a fourfold thread that calls us to be faithful servants of the Lord Jesus Christ, who himself said, "I came not to be served, but to serve."

Thread number one is deep devotion, passion for the Word of God, deep devotion. I believe after Jesus' resurrection that the apostles remembered what Jesus taught. The apostles who are committed—I remember the three who were so close to him—Peter, James, and John. They were so committed to following him that they paid a heavy price. Deep devotion like theirs to the Word is what the world needs today.

I travel the world, and I look at Muslims and how they want to identify with their faith. They put us to shame. The church is in a defensive mode. The church should come out and be in the offensive mode. The church has lost her birthright. The church should come out and stand tall because Jesus is Lord. The church is hiding many times. The church needs to come out and proclaim this Word that never changes; it is what the world needs.

The news on the television and the Internet is 99 percent bad news; the world needs good news, and the church has a duty to proclaim this Word.

I speak to you because you brought us the gospel. I speak to you still because at the time when you brought us the gospel, Africa was called the "dark continent," not because the sun does not shine in Africa—the sun shines 365 days a year in Africa—but because we were in perpetual spiritual darkness. Your ancestors brought us the gospel. I'm eternally grateful for that.

But where is that passion today? Where is that faith today? Where is the love for the Word of God today? Where is that spiritually inquisitive desire that your ancestors had today? I believe with all my heart that something must be recaptured, that the whole world is waiting for the global West to rise up and follow in the steps of their ancestors.

I speak with pride in my heart that you brought the gospel to us. But I come back to challenge you. In God's economy, the seed was planted in my continent, it has borne fruit, and I am that fruit. I come back to declare to you that we must come back to the lordship of Jesus Christ and be faithful servants to the Lord Jesus Christ.

The second thread I see is boldness, boldness. One day Peter is running away denying Jesus Christ, but on the day of Pentecost, Peter is bold, strong, and he spoke as never before. Peter is declaring that Jesus Christ died and rose again. People listened to Peter. And people were convicted by the Holy Spirit because Peter knew that the Word of God had power to change. And by that Spirit of the Lord, this is the Word that will not come back empty, and three thousand souls were saved.

I challenge you, my dear brothers and sisters, how often have you reached to people who desperately need the Word and a harvest came forth? I trust God as I stand before people—declaring the greatness of God who is still relevant—I make an altar call and they stream forward, looking for Christ. This is not in Africa only.

Only last year in October, I was preaching in Virginia at a big Baptist church, and I preached the Word of God, and I made an altar call, and hundreds came forward there. The hunger is not only in Africa; the hunger is in Europe and America as well. People are hungry.

But do we have the boldness to believe in the Jesus who was and is and is to be the same? Do we take him at his word? Or do we find him the subject of embarrassment?

The third thread that I find here is a willingness to make a sacrifice. John Calvin made a sacrifice. He preached his heart out and brought us things. Today, we are so blessed because of them. The Reformers made sacrifices. Men and women who stood firm, as disciples and faithful people, made sacrifices. I don't believe that disciples aren't going to make sacrifices. If the Lord himself made a sacrifice, who am I?

Sometimes this will mean that you will be pulled out of your comfort zone. At other times it will mean that you are pulled out of your prestigious position and perhaps moved into a territory that is unbecoming, a little less attractive. Maybe sometimes it means your life is at stake as well.

Two years ago, I spoke in New York to a group of key Christians, and I was talking about some of the great challenges of our time. I asked our brothers and sisters to keep this as a family talk. They did not listen to me, and in a short time it was put on the Web, and very shortly afterwards my life was in danger. The government had to give me a plainclothes policeman to travel with me for six months.

We will be hunted down. We will be hurt. But Jesus was crucified. They did it to the chief Servant. You and I will not be excepted.

A willingness to make a sacrifice, a willingness to be able to stand and to speak to a hostile world today that is so deaf to the truth of the Word of God. They do not want to hear, especially the things that cut them surgically to the heart. We have a very unbelieving people, but we are not exempted from declaring the Word of God to them. We have a duty.

The fourth thread that I see is the sheer love for the Lord Jesus Christ, which then helps us to be obedient. "If you love me, then obey my commandments." The command we've just heard is love the Lord your God and love your neighbor as you love yourself.

Last October we were in Virginia, and someone was helping us understand about mission. And he made a comment that I would like to quote. He said, "We used to go out to Asia, but now God has brought Asians to us." Can we minister to them? You probably don't need to go far to minister. Your neighbor is in need.

Who then is a faithful and wise servant? The man John Calvin and other Reformers ask us the same question today that the disciples of Jesus Christ heard.

My heart rejoices that I can come among you. My heart also trembles that we have a witness in this man John Calvin, who has a clear testimony of faithful service to the Lord. How about us? How about you? How about the church back in America? Here in Europe? Back in my own continent of Africa?

Will you be a faithful and wise servant of the Lord Jesus?

Delivered July 5, 2009, at St. Pierre Cathedral, Geneva, Switzerland.

4

In Praise of Predestination—Ephesians 1:3–6

Bryan Chapell

I recognize the profound privilege and challenge of this moment.[1] I count it a great privilege to stand in the pulpit of the church of John Calvin as we celebrate the 500th anniversary of his birth. I also recognize the challenge of speaking on the subject of predestination, the doctrine most readily identified with Calvin, despite the fact that he confessed its depths were past finding out. "For it is not right," Calvin said, "for man unrestrainedly to search out things that the Lord has willed to be hid in himself. Understand then that through this [doctrine] he should also fill us with wonder." But more than wonder was

1. This sermon is adapted from chapter 2 of Bryan Chapell, *Ephesians*, Reformed Expository Commentary (Phillipsburg, NJ: P&R Publishing, 2009).

the object of Calvin's focus on this subject. B. B. Warfield wrote that Calvin was even more concerned to reveal God's fatherhood than his sovereignty. By this fatherly focus, Calvin also reflects his dedication to the weight of the apostle Paul's concern. As we shall see in this passage of Ephesians, so often quoted for its focus on predestination, the apostle even more closely focuses our hearts on the motivating power of a father's love.

Some years ago my oldest son, then a senior in high school, fought his way through district and regional meets to win a berth in the state wrestling championships. We were thrilled with this blessing, but our happiness was tempered by what he had to give up to go to the state tournament. The weekend of the state wrestling tournament was the same weekend that he had to be in another state to remain eligible for a prestigious college scholarship for which he also had qualified. A lot of privilege and not a little money were being jeopardized by his not going to compete for the scholarship. But what could we do? As parents we could not say to this young man who had worked so hard for his sport, his coach, and his team, "You cannot compete in a state tournament because we want to save some money." He and we would regret that all our lives. So we devised a plan: if he did well in the state tournament, we would stay there all the way; but if he did not advance very far in the early rounds, then we would get in the car—no matter the time of day or night—and drive to the scholarship competition. Whatever happened, we would consider the outcome a blessing and praise God for it.

It seemed like a fairly good plan until we got to the point where my wife and I had to consider exactly what we should pray for. Should we pray for the blessing that he win the tournament, or should we pray for the blessing that he win the scholarship? We could not pray for him to lose his wrestling matches, but we did not want him to miss the scholarship. What should we do?

There was not any question at all what we should do once the wrestling match started. When you see your own son before thousands of spectators, wrestling with all of his strength against a well-muscled foe, there is no question what a father does. He shouts as loudly as he can, "Go, Colin! Fight! Wrestle! Squeeze him! Squash him!" A father cheers as loudly as possible to encourage his son in such a match. The shouts are a father's way of saying, "I am here for you in your struggle, my son." Now, when a father is shouting that kind of encouragement to a wrestling son, those around the father may not take it so well. His words are so loud and forceful, his voice so strident, that those who are not that father's children may not understand; they may even take offense. But children who need the encouragement do understand.

When we are wrestling against spiritual forces that are challenging and sometimes overwhelming us, we may wonder, "Is my heavenly Father still here for me? Does he still want me to win? Have my compromises and weaknesses turned him away?" So, to teach us the answers, here in this passage our heavenly Father shouts his encouragement to his children who are wrestling against great evil in Ephesus. The words he uses are as strong as any in Scripture. The Father says things like, "I chose you. I predestined you. You are mine, no matter what." We cannot deny that these words are strong and even capable of causing offense, but when we see their context and their purpose of blessing and encouraging God's children who are wrestling against great spiritual foes, then we will realize that these words are cause to praise our heavenly Father.

Praise of our Father is really the focus of this passage. We should praise God because he blesses us as *our* Father. Paul highlights this theme by the praise statements that form the borders of our text: "Praise be to the God and Father of our Lord Jesus Christ who has blessed us" (Eph. 1:3); and "he predestined us to be adopted as his sons . . . to the praise of his glorious grace" (Eph. 1:5–6).[2] Between these "bookends" of praise, Paul tells us why such regard is warranted.

2. All quotations of Scripture in this chapter are from the NIV.

Blessed with Christ's Blessing (Eph. 1:3)

We should praise God because he blesses us with Christ's blessing (Eph. 1:3).

Paul says, "The Father of our Lord Jesus has blessed us in the heavenly realms with every spiritual blessing in Christ" (Eph. 1:3). We really need the last part of this verse to be able to explain the first part. The words "in Christ" remind us that our "spiritual blessing" includes several important elements.

We Are in Union with Christ (Eph. 1:3a)

Twelve times in verses 3–12, Paul refers in various ways to believers' spiritual union with Christ. The words appear so frequently that we may grow numb to their significance. However, we will not miss the impact Paul wants to make on our hearts, if we track to the end of the chapter. There Paul identifies the One with whom we are united. He is the Son whom God the Father "raised . . . from the dead and seated . . . at his right hand in the heavenly realms, far above all rule and authority, power and dominion, and every title that can be given, not only in the present age but also in the one to come. And God placed all things under his feet and appointed him to be head over everything for the church, which is his body, the fullness of him who fills everything in every way" (Eph. 1:20–23). Paul says that we are united to the One who is above every earthly power and authority in this age and the age to come. He is Lord. Yet we share his honor and blessings by being united to him.

Paul spells out the blessings: Christ is risen from the grave with power over sin and death; he is seated in the heavens with the Father; his power and privileges exceed anything on earth; and we share his glory. He is head of all things, and all that is precious in the church and the world is filled with him. All of these blessings we share by the marvelous grace of being united to Christ.

We struggle fully to apprehend all the goodness and glory of our union with Christ. The beauty of a sunset, the power of a storm, the purity of a child's prayer, the majesty of a hero's glory, the wonder of love's passion, and the hope of eternal glory when such earthly blessings fail—all these are of him, all are under him, all are by him, all reflect the wonder, majesty, purity, power, and beauty of who he is. And because we are in union with him, they are ours, too.

We Are in Heaven with Christ (Eph. 1:3b)

If such wonder is ours to enjoy, then a song may come to mind: "Heaven, I'm in heaven." And that is just the point that the apostle makes in the first part of verse 3. There he reminds us the blessings of Christ involve not only being in union with Christ but, through that union, being in heaven with Christ.

Paul says that God "has blessed us [past tense] in the heavenly realms with every spiritual blessing" (Eph. 1:3). Does that mean that God is in the heavenly realms—up there—blessing us down here? Yes, but it means more, also. Paul will later remind us with these same words that God raised Jesus "from the dead and seated him at his right hand in the heavenly realms" (Eph. 1:20). Jesus is in the heavenly realms; believers are united to him. So where are we? It is clear: we are also blessed with every spiritual blessing in the heavenly realms. This is precisely what Paul says in the following chapter: "God raised [past tense] us up with Christ and seated [past tense] us with him in the heavenly realms in Christ Jesus" (Eph. 2:6).

Because we are in union with Christ, who is in heaven, then we are in heaven with God. The apostle urges praise for God, not so much because the Father is in heaven blessing us but because we are there with him being blessed by him. As hell is total, conscious separation from the blessings of God, so the spiritual dimension of heaven is total and conscious union with God. In our union with Christ, we are already partakers of this spiritual reality, even though it is not fully realized until we are in our glorified state, freed of our mortal bodies and the constraints of our temporal existence. This means we are already experiencing aspects of heaven, although we are not yet there.

The benefits of this "already and not yet" Paul has already stated—grace and peace (Eph. 1:2). I recognized how John Calvin reflected these benefits when walking through his Auditoire earlier today, and there read a copy of a letter he wrote to John Knox, upon learning of the death of the Scottish Reformer's wife. Calvin wrote to his friend, "Since you know well from whence consolation comes when we are overwhelmed with grief, I have no doubt that you will be able to endure with patience." In earthly pain, the peace that allows patience with all God's providences comes from the certainty of the graces already ours, though they are not yet fully experienced. We yet face difficulty, danger, and the deceit of our own hearts, but heaven and all its benefits are already and most certainly ours.

The difference the "already and the not yet" makes can be compared to an experience our family had some time ago. On our family vacations, we enjoy going to a cabin that adjoins a deep set of woods. At certain times of the year, the woods are so dense that when we have been out hiking, it is difficult to find the path back to the cabin. As night closed in during one such hike, we knew that we would not be able to spot our regular landmarks. So we began to angle through the woods in the direction we thought the cabin was. It got darker and darker; no familiar landmarks came into view. The children assumed that we were lost. I kept a brave face, as if I knew where we were, but ultimately I turned around to tell them the real situation. But just as I turned, a light from the cabin caught my eye. In the dark and dense woods we had actually walked past the cabin, but seeing the light, I knew we were safe. We were not *yet* inside, but the light meant that we were *already* safe and secure. What was my reaction to being "home"? Relief and peace.

It is a similar reaction that Paul intends for us. He does not promise that we will never have to walk through the dark and dense woods. Trials are still here, disease still comes, finances are still hard, jobs and relationships remain difficult, and next steps may remain uncertain, but in Christ we are already home. We do not have to worry that there will be no place for us or that our God will not receive us, because he has already united us to his household through his Son and included us in his purposes. This gives us the confidence to be courageous in the face of opposition, whether inside or outside the church. We say with the psalmist, "The LORD is with me; I will not be afraid. What can man do to me?" (Ps. 118:6). Such confidence enables us to be less worried about the dollars and cents of a troubling bill and more willing to consider how God is calling us to be faithful, less concerned with the wrath of a godless boss and more willing to entrust ourselves to God's care. Because we have eternal security that the depravations of this world cannot deny, we are able to stand for truth when peers demand compromise or to stand up to a child who claims that our discipline will erase his love for us. The reality of our heavenly status in Christ makes earthly challenges less intimidating, even if they are not less real.

But what if we do not feel worthy of such honor, or capable of earning such blessing? What if we face the same trials and temptations as did the Ephesians?

Blessed with Christ's Status (Eph. 1:4–5)

We should praise God not only because he has given us Christ's blessings, but because he gives us Christ's status. Spiritual blessings are ours because through our union with Christ, we have his sanctity and his sonship.

Christ's Sanctity (Eph. 1:4)

The apostle says that God "chose us in him before the creation of the world to be holy and blameless in his sight" (Eph. 1:4). Paul's wording reveals God's purpose. God chose us to be "holy and blameless in his sight." This dual description relates to us the tandem benefits of our union with Christ in terms of our sanctification before God. We have something *removed* from us and something *supplied*.

By virtue of our union with Christ, we have our blame *removed*. What shames us and justly condemns us is not held against us any longer. As Christ is without spot, so also we are "blemishless" (i.e., the origin of the word *blameless*) by virtue of his work on our behalf. Paul will explain this process later in the chapter, but for now he identifies the results of the Savior's work: our guilt and shame are taken away; we are made blameless.

The effects of shame and blame can be amazingly real and long-lasting. Recently a pastor confided that he discovered that he was great at doing funerals—but he added a strange confession. He said, "I have a knack for being able to distill the character of a person and tie it to the gospel, but I hate visiting the family afterwards. The visit cannot be scripted, and I know that I ran the risk of looking bad. This discovery made me realize that I am more concerned with impressing people than helping them."

The discovery of his need to impress led the pastor to seek wise counsel. And in the course of that confidant's conversation the pastor said, "The need to impress people became acute in my life after fourth grade. I was always the best student in class, but in fourth grade I got sick and missed material needed for a math quiz. I did poorly on the math quiz, and the teacher wrote my name on the blackboard as one who needed remedial work. When she wrote my name on the board, I got physically sick. My teacher had to take me home, thinking that I was ill, but the problem really was that I blamed myself for being unprepared, and I worked never to be so shamed again."

Life will not allow any of us to be free of shame. Our weaknesses, the world's uncertainties, and our sin all have the potential to shame us before those in earth and heaven. But the glory of the gospel is that our heavenly Father has erased our names from the blackboard—the handwriting that was against us, he took away and nailed it to the cross (cf. Col. 2:14). He no longer blames us for what shames us.

Not only does our union with Christ remove our blemishes; it also *supplies* his righteousness. We are "holy" and blameless before the Father. The righteousness that was Christ's through his perfect obedience is imputed to us. The holiness that God requires, he also supplies, not by our works but by our union with his holy Son, who shares with us his own status of holiness. This is cause for amazement: God sees me as holy as his own Son. Not only do I have my debt wiped away; I have the riches of Christ's righteousness applied to my account (see also 2 Cor. 5:21). God does not pay our debt and then leave us with a zero balance. Rather than have us destitute, he opens the vaults of heaven to give us the benefits of the storehouse of his grace made full by Christ's obedience. The Bible says, "He who did not spare his own Son, but gave him up for us all—how will he not also, along with him, graciously give us all things?" (Rom. 8: 32). Having removed our sin, God also supplies whatever is needed out of his entire creation—present or future—to bless us in the best way possible with the riches of the righteousness of his Son. But we question how this could be, since we are so unworthy of such riches. The answer is that God not only gives us the benefits of Christ's sanctity, but also gives us the status of Christ's Sonship.

Christ's Sonship (Eph. 1:5)

The Father "predestined us to be adopted as his sons through Jesus Christ, in accordance with his pleasure and will" (Eph.

1:5). This sentence explains the goal of God's predestination of us. It was God's will and pleasure to adopt us as members of his own family through the work of Jesus. We should not miss the remarkable statements of verses 2 and 3. First, we are told that grace and peace come from God *our* Father (Eph. 1:2), and then we are told to praise the God and Father of our Lord Jesus Christ. If God is the Father of Jesus and of me, then I am Christ's brother and also a son of the heavenly Father. Through no work of my own, I have the status of my Lord Jesus; I am a child of the Father. What this means is beautifully articulated in an account in theologian Robert Peterson's book on adoption. A woman named Lisa writes:

> Adoption is attractive to me because it is the perfect antidote to legalism. . . . [Legalism] was the driving force in my life. I kept trying to be good enough for God but despaired at how impossible the task was. At the very heart I was afraid of one thing. At some point I would do something terrible and consequently lose my salvation. Although the church I was raised in preached assurance of salvation, I often wondered if I believed it mostly because I wanted it to be true. The confusion came from the fact that although the churches I attended said they believed in the assurance of salvation, they preached a list of things one had to do to be a "good Christian." I got the feeling that if you failed in any of those areas you probably were not saved to begin with.
>
> The study of adoption has clarified the confusion I once felt. Adoption is a legal procedure that secures a child's identity in a new family. . . . God didn't choose to be our *foster* parent. We don't get kicked out of the family because of our behavior. We don't have to worry day to day whether or not we are good enough to be part of the family. In his infinite kindness, God made us a permanent part of his family. . . . Nothing can undo the legal procedure that binds me to Christ. He died to redeem me. He signed the adoption papers, so to speak, with his blood.

Nothing can cancel the work he did for me. I am free from the fear of falling away. Hallelujah![3]

God loves us because we are in union with the Son that he loves. United to Christ, we are also adopted by the Father, and as such have all the rights, privileges, and affection that the Son of God himself receives from God. Adoption in the Roman world emphasized the rights and privileges of sonship, and the analogy to our spiritual lives was one of Paul's favorites (cf. Rom. 8:15, 23; Gal. 4:5). In Paul's day the head of a family would adopt a son (often a grown man) in order to pass on the family name and inheritance. Note how the saints' inheritance is also important later in the opening chapter of Ephesians (1:11, 14; cf. 1:18).

These blessings are truly amazing to our ears: Christ's sanctity and sonship are ours. The status that he has before God, we have by virtue of our union with him. Because God makes provision for us to receive Christ's blessing and status, we have much reason to praise him. Yet the question remains, how do we get these blessings and this status that God arranges to lavish upon us?

Blessed through Christ Alone (Eph. 1:5–6)

How do we get the blessings and status of Christ from the Father? Paul answers when he repeats his goal of having us praise the Father. "He predestined us. . . through Jesus Christ, in accordance with his pleasure and will—to the praise of his glorious grace, which he has freely given us in the One he loves" (Eph. 1:5–6).

Salvation Comes without Human Cause at All (Eph. 1:5)

How much do these blessings of grace cost? Paul says the blessings of salvation are "freely given," and what that really means is

3. Robert A. Peterson, *Adopted by God: From Wayward Sinners to Cherished Children* (Phillipsburg, NJ: P&R Publishing, 2001), 76–78.

the primary message of this passage. God alone is to be praised for our salvation because it comes to us without any human cause.

Over and over in this passage, Paul makes this point of divine cause alone: God chose us *in Christ* (Eph. 1:4), not because of anything *in us*. It was his choice to put us in union with his Son. In fact, human initiative seems to be purposely undercut when we also are told that God chose us before creation (Eph. 1:4). Before we could do anything of merit, God chose to love us (cf. Rom. 8:26–39, esp. 29–30, 33; 2 Tim. 1:9;). This divine initiative undercuts the prejudices of that day (and ours), as Paul places the origin of God's love before the world's origin and, consequently, before any human cause. God chose his people before any national, family, or personal achievements would warrant his love (see also Rom. 16:13; Col. 3:12; 1 Thess. 1:4; 2 Tim. 2:10; Titus 1:1).

Some commentators debate whether the election in Ephesians 1:4–6 is corporate (a group is elected) or individual (each person is chosen). While a corporate dimension should not be ruled out, to insist that the election is merely corporate would be to overlook the way that the personal blessings of being "chosen" and "predestined" (Eph. 1:4–5) are part of the larger picture of spiritual blessings Paul describes in Ephesians 1:3–14, and these other spiritual blessings undoubtedly have individual dimensions (e.g., redemption, forgiveness, sealing of the Holy Spirit).

Modern events may help us understand why God would reveal his everlasting love to believers in a place like Ephesus. Like all cities, Ephesus was full of wickedness, and the pervasive evil was as discouraging as it was tempting. The message of God's prevenient love must have been vital to this fledgling church that included supposedly "unworthy" Gentiles. I understood more of the vital nature of such love when I recently listened to a church planter describe his experience of planting a church in downtown New Orleans. The downtown church had only two intact families. The struggling congregation of forty people was facing the likelihood that fifteen of them would move away because they wanted to get out of the troubled city. Alcoholism is rampant in the community (he said that nursery-school parties for his children have been hosted with kegs of beer available for adult attendees). The stranglehold of poverty grips generations. Corruption remains too common to be news. The last Fortune 500 company left town years ago—long before Hurricane Katrina ravaged what remained. The Christians in the city struggle to maintain any vision of God among them and any hope of change. Their situation should remind us of the seemingly hopeless plight of believers in Ephesus. Sensing that helplessness helps explain why Paul would seek to supply hope by writing of God's eternal and unchanging love. Were he able to join us in this Cathedral today, he would gleefully proclaim to us that God's love is deeper, higher, stronger, and more lasting (Jer. 31:3) than any aspect of creation. Longer than there have been fish in the ocean or stars in the heavens, and long before the foundations of this earth were laid, your Lord loved you, treasured you, and made provision for your eternal welfare. The apostle intends for our knowledge of this divine love that is longer than our fathoming to give us endurance beyond our strength for trials beyond our understanding.

Wouldn't it make a difference to your heart, to your zeal, to know that God loved you forever, even when you as a church were wrestling to survive? The message of God's eternal and unwavering love for his church is as powerful an encouragement for struggling churches today as it was for the baby churches in Paul's day.

Paul uses the assurances of predestination to strengthen the church for her struggles against evil and discouragement. This perspective does not solve all our logical questions about predestination; however, understanding Paul's purpose helps us properly contextualize our presentation of this precious doctrine when we talk to others. Predestination was never meant to be a doctrinal club used to batter people into acknowledgments of God's sovereignty. Rather, the message of God's love preceding our accomplishments and outlasting our failures was meant to give us a profound sense of confidence and security in God's love so that we will not despair in situations of great difficulty, pain, and shame.

Salvation Comes through Divine Love Alone (Eph. 1:6)

This relational focus is most clear where the word *predestination* is actually used. Paul wants us to understand that salvation comes through divine love alone. So he says that God predestined us to be adopted as his sons in accordance with *his* pleasure and will, not based on *our* pleasure and will (Eph. 1:5).

We have already heard this language of God choosing someone by divine will in the preceding verses introducing this letter. There Paul said that he was an apostle of Jesus Christ according to the will of God (Eph. 1:1). What could be more obvious to this apostle formerly named Saul? He was going one direction to arrest and kill Christians, with his heart and mind bent on hostility to Christ, when suddenly on the road to Damascus, Christ turned Paul around. Paul knows that it was not his own pleasure and will to become a light to the Gentiles. God did something in and to Paul that the apostle recognized was beyond his own desire or choosing. Now Paul turns this language of what made him Christ's apostle to what makes believers God's children.

Paul's turnabout reminds me of a winter when we had a sixteen-inch snow that kept us in the house for days. Finally, getting cabin fever, my wife and I ventured out in the snow in our vintage Ford Pinto. We tried to drive down the two-lane main street of our little town. The street had been plowed but still had a healthy topping of ice. I discovered one of the ice patches as we were heading north on the road. The car shuddered, and suddenly without any planning or effort on my part, we were traveling south in the other lane. My wife said, "What did you do?" I said, of course, "I didn't do anything." We went right on home. There was a force beyond my actions and intentions that sent us another way than we had planned.

Think how often we hear the same sort of thing from those whom God has saved from deep sin. I think of the good friend of mine whom God saved from a life of hard living and anger at the church. When he became a Christian, he wanted to stand in church and tell how God had saved him. But he was so new a Christian that he did not know what he was supposed to say. So, in a speech laced with profanity, he said that it was a darn (but he didn't say *darn*) good thing that God had gotten a hold of him because he was on the sure road to hell. There were a few gasps in the congregation at the language that was used, but the really mature Christians were thrilled. They said to each other, "Look what God did. He plucked a brand from the fire and saved a man who obviously could not save himself, because it was God's will and pleasure to do so. Isn't God's love great?"

This explanation of God's need to choose us because we cannot save ourselves obviously does not answer questions about why some are plucked from spiritual danger and others are not. Those are hard questions, but Paul has not yet come to the point of addressing them in this letter. He is simply saying that God makes us his own and loves us, even though we know that we are not good enough and do not merit his affection. In fact, knowing that we are not good enough or able to save ourselves is one of the marks of God putting his Spirit in us. Salvation is not about earning; it is about grace. We need to know this so that when we fall short of God's love in our own eyes, we can remember that we never were God's because of what we did. God "graced us" (v. 6, literally); we did not gain him by the merit of our doing, background, or choosing. "In love he predestined us to be adopted as his sons through Jesus Christ . . . to the praise of his glorious grace, which he has freely given [lit., *graced*] us" (Eph. 1:4b–6).

Paul is using the doctrine of predestination not to separate believers, not to instill pride in our being chosen, nor to vaunt any special knowledge of how God works, but simply to assure hard-pressed believers that God has loved them and does love them apart from any merit of their own. In other words, predestination is meant to bless believers' hearts. It is *not* meant for endless argument; it is *not* an excuse not to evangelize; it *is* our basis of comfort when we face the limitations of our actions, will, and choices. We can make predestination the source of our pride in our doctrine rather than the basis of assurance for those wrestling with their sin and the world's trials. To such God says, "I loved you before the world began, so don't doubt me now." Predestination is the heavenly Father's shout of eternal love that echoes in our songs of thankful praise as our strength is renewed by the assurance of his care. When predestination is properly taught, it accomplishes what Paul says is his goal: praise to God for his glorious grace and peace to his people (vv. 3, 6).

An alumnus of Covenant Seminary who has a special heart for evangelism tells of a man who came to his office after attending a worship service. The man had been in the church for years, but confessed that though he "knew" everything about the gospel, he was not a believer. He said that what had kept him from faith was his fear that he was not predestined. My pastor friend responded with great wisdom: "That is just like the evil one to place that fear in your heart. He confounds us by putting what should be your last concern first. You are worried about predestination even though you are not a believer. Predestination is for those who already love Jesus to assure them that their failures do not destroy his love." This is plainly Paul's point as he writes to "the saints in Ephesus." The pastor continued, "The goal of predestination is not to raise questions in unbelievers; it is to bring peace to believers. What you need in this moment is simply to respond in faith, to confess that you need Jesus and to love him. Later on God will confirm to your heart the wonder that he loved you first."

Whether or not you agree that predestination is for saints more than unbelievers, discerning the motive of Paul's writing reveals the wisdom of this pastor's comments. Before we answer all the questions of why some are predestined and why not others, we need to discern why Paul spoke to these saints wrestling in such a difficult circumstance. God shouts to them, "I have loved you with an everlasting love. Before the world was made I called you my own. You are mine." No doubt you will continue wrestling with the logic of predestination, as everyone does from time to time; but the next time you are wrestling with sin, difficulty, or your own failure, may you hear this shout from heaven: "You always have been in my heart, no matter what happens. I have chosen to love you since before the world began. You are mine." Although such a shout may offend some, those who are children of the Father hear it as the greatest encouragement possible that brings grace and peace.

Our son did not make it past the first few rounds at the state tournament, so we went to the college, and there he won the scholarship. It was a head-spinning weekend. Yet afterward my son was able to say, "It's amazing, Dad. God had it all planned from the beginning." How good for my son to know that his heavenly Father had it all planned. We did not, and do not, know all the reasons why the events unfolded as they did, but knowing that the heavenly Father had it all planned from beginning to end gives us a sense of peace not only about those events but also about the unknown events ahead. As my son prepares to wrestle with other issues that are sure to come in his life, the knowledge that his heavenly Father is always there for him, is always in control, and always loves is a wonderful source of grace and peace. We should praise God that in all the wrestling that he (and we) will do, the Father is still shouting to us in his Word that his love is higher, deeper, and more lasting than anything in all of creation, and in this love we discover the strength and peace he provides for all of life.

Delivered July 5, 2009, at St. Pierre Cathedral, Geneva, Switzerland.

5

A Great Door for Spreading the Gospel—1 Corinthians 16:5–9

Philip Graham Ryken

It is strange to say, but somehow the idea persists that because Calvinists believe in the absolute sovereignty of God, they are not very committed to evangelism or enthusiastic about the missionary work of the church. Nothing could be further from the truth. John Calvin's faith in the sovereignty of God and his commitment to God's merciful grace in the gospel compelled him to promote the global proclamation of the cross and the empty tomb. The Geneva Reformer believed that God had given his church a wide-open door for spreading the gospel.

Worshipers in Geneva would have sensed Calvin's keen interest in gospel outreach virtually every week, at least from the prayers that typically closed his expositions of Scripture. Calvin prayed for the success of missionary work at the end of almost every sermon. In fact, Richard Muller estimates that his parishioners must have heard the following prayer or its rough equivalent more than two thousand five hundred times. Calvin typically prayed for God:

> To grant this grace, not only to us, but to all people and nations of the earth, bringing back all the ignorant souls from the miserable bondage of error and darkness, to the right way of salvation, for the doing whereof it may please him to raise up true and faithful ministers of his word, that seek not their own profit and vainglory, but only the advancement of his holy name, and the welfare of his flock . . . to the intent that his glory may shine over all, and the Kingdom of our Lord Jesus Christ be increased and advanced more and more.[1]

The Church Plant in Ephesus

Calvin's prayers have been answered millions of times over the last five hundred years through the missionary work of the church. The Holy Spirit will answer them again as we consider one of the biblical texts that Calvin considered a compelling motivation to spread the gospel, and which included one of his favorite images for evangelism: the open door. In Calvin's text, the apostle Paul wrote:

> I will visit you after passing through Macedonia, for I intend to pass through Macedonia, and perhaps I will stay with you or even spend the winter, so that you may help me on my journey, wherever I go. For I do not want to see you now just in passing. I hope to spend some time with you, if the Lord permits. But I will stay in Ephesus until Pentecost, for a wide

1. John Calvin, *Sermons on Galatians*, 925–26, quoted in Richard A. Muller, "'To Grant This Grace to All People and Nations': Calvin on Apostolicity and Mission," in *For God So Loved the World: Missiological Reflections in Honor of Roger S. Greenway*, ed. Arie C. Leder (Belleville, Ontario: Essence Publishing, 2006), 230.

> door for effective work has opened to me, and there are many adversaries. (1 Cor. 16:5–9)[2]

The place to begin opening this text is by considering its context. The apostle Paul was writing to the church in Corinth, a troubled congregation with so many troubles like our own. In the church itself there were sharp conflicts over matters of theology and practice, including some petty disagreements. The surrounding culture was awash with the worldviews of many religions. Corinth was a sex-crazed, money-loving city; its wealthy citizens reveled in moral degradation. So Paul wrote to the believers in Corinth about their unity in Christ, about the holy gospel of the cross and the empty tomb, about all the controversies that were killing their church, and at the end of his epistle, about his plans for future ministry.

Paul hoped to visit the Corinthians again soon and to speak with them in person. He had planted their church by the preaching of the gospel. On his second missionary journey, Paul had stayed in Corinth for a year and a half, teaching the Word of God, and by the end of that time he had built up a church. Now he wanted to see the Corinthians again, like a good pastor would. "I will visit you after passing through Macedonia," he said, "and perhaps I will stay with you or even spend the winter" (1 Cor. 16:5–6). Paul also hoped that the visit would be a long one: "I do not want to see you now just in passing. I hope to spend some time with you, if the Lord permits" (1 Cor. 16:7).

In the meantime, the apostle had some work to do. It was the same work that he was always doing—the missionary work of preaching the gospel, with the explicit purpose of planting a new church. We think of Paul as a missionary, but he was also a serial

2. I am grateful to the Reverend Randall Grossman, minister of the Grace Bible Fellowship Church in Reading, Pennsylvania, for suggesting this text and recommending many useful resources on Calvin's commitment to missions, evangelism, and church planting.

church planter. Once a church was well underway, he would go somewhere new, not building on someone else's foundation (see Rom. 15:20) but breaking new spiritual ground, bringing people to faith in Christ and then gathering them into a worshiping, witnessing community. Now Paul was doing that work in the great city of Ephesus. So he said, "I will stay in Ephesus until Pentecost, for a wide door for effective work has opened to me, and there are many adversaries" (1 Cor. 16:8–9).

This text contains at least three simple, practical truths about the high calling of church planting and the missionary work of the kingdom. These spiritual lessons are for the pastors who are called and ordained to this great work, but not for them alone. They are really for the whole people of God.

The Constraint of the Call

Notice first the constraint of the call. As we have seen, it was Paul's sincere and personal desire to spend more time with the Corinthians. But the apostle was not at liberty to do what he might have chosen to do as the expression of his own personal will. Instead, his life was submitted to the sovereignty of the Lord Jesus Christ. He was totally committed to doing what Jesus wanted him to do, not what *he* wanted to do. This is clear from the end of verse 7, where he says "if the Lord permits." This was not a cliché or a concession but the commitment of Paul's entire life. Just at the moment, his commitment to doing God's will constrained him to remain in Ephesus and plant a church.

Every servant of the gospel is constrained by his or her calling. When we say, as Calvin said, "My heart, I give you, O Lord, promptly and sincerely," from then on we are duty-bound to do whatever God tells us to do and to go wherever God sends us to go. If we have plans of our own, these plans must be surrendered to God's sovereign will, so that even "in the inward affection of the mind, we submit to God and his providence, whatever we resolve upon."[3]

In this respect, Calvin practiced what he preached, for he experienced divine constraint in his own life. Calvin never wanted to go to Geneva. All he really wanted to do was to sit in his study and write more books like his famous *Institutes*. But when the Catholics came to power in France, Protestants like Calvin were given six months to leave the country or else submit to Rome—this was according to the Edict of Lyon. So Calvin and his family set off for Strasbourg in Switzerland. While they were on their way, local troop movements forced them to make a detour through Geneva, where they only intended to stay for a single night.

That night someone told the Reformer William Farel that the famous John Calvin was staying at the local inn. Farel knew that Calvin was just the preacher he was looking for to make a difference for Christ in Geneva. So he went to the inn, banged on Calvin's door, and begged him to stay in the city and serve as their pastor. At first Calvin refused, telling Farel that he was a scholar, not a shepherd, and that he wanted nothing to do with the burdens of pastoring a church. Finally, Farel said something to Calvin that all but forced him to stay. Here is how Calvin described their conversation:

> Wherever else I had gone, I had taken care to conceal that I was the author [of the *Institutes*]; and I had resolved to continue in the same obscurity, until at length William Farel detained me at Geneva, by a dreadful curse, which I felt to be as if God had from heaven laid his mighty hand upon me to arrest me. . . . I had resolved to pass quickly by Geneva, without staying longer than a single night in that city. . . . Farel, who burned with an extraordinary zeal to advance the gospel, immediately strained every nerve to detain me. And after learning that my heart was

3. John Calvin, *Commentary on the Epistles of Paul the Apostle to the Corinthians* (Grand Rapids: Baker, 1999), 2:71.

> set upon devoting myself to private studies, he proceeded to utter the imprecation that God would curse my retirement and the tranquility of the studies which I sought, if I should withdraw and refuse to help, when the necessity was so urgent. By this imprecation I was so terror-struck, that I gave up the journey I had undertaken.[4]

So Calvin came to Geneva, constrained by the call of God. Later, in the providence of God, Calvin was called away from Geneva for a season. This may have been due to the enmity of the Consistory. From the perspective of divine providence, it may also have been because Calvin needed to be humbled. These are two of the many reasons why God often moves us out of one ministry situation or prevents us from entering another. But ultimately it is all under God's sovereign control.

Eventually, by the will of God, Calvin was also called back to Geneva. As hard as it was for him to leave, in many ways it was even harder for him to return. The great Reformer had never wanted to go to Geneva in the first place, and once he left, he never wanted to return. Calvin even went so far as to describe his time in Geneva as a kind of crucifixion: "Rather would I submit to death a hundred times than to that cross on which I had to perish daily a thousand times over."[5] Yet Calvin was constrained by his calling—not just his general calling to serve as a minister of the gospel but his more specific calling to serve a particular people in a particular place.

Every follower of Christ has begun to answer that call. We have answered God's call to be a minister of the gospel, or a teacher, or a counselor, or a missionary, or a worker in some other calling that has the blessing of God. At the very least, each of us has received the call of every disciple to witness for Jesus Christ. Now

4. John Calvin, preface to *The Psalms*, quoted in T. H. L. Parker, *John Calvin: A Biography* (London: J. M. Dent, 1975), 53.

5. Calvin, quoted in Parker, *John Calvin*, 79–80.

our calling constrains us to continue in ministry by the grace of God the Father, in the name of Christ the Son, and through the power of the Holy Spirit.

How is God calling you to serve, and what will he call you to do in days to come? Is your life still open to the sovereign direction of God? For a believer in Christ, the answer must always be "yes" to God's calling. When we gave our lives to Christ, it was not just for the forgiveness of our sins; it was also for everything that Jesus would call us to do for the rest of our lives.

Are you still following the call? Are you able to say—as Calvin said to his friend Farel—that you have set aside all considerations of self and have no other desire than to look "most for the glory of God and the advantage of the church"? If so, then you can also say what Calvin said next: "I submit my will and my affections, subdued and held fast, to the obedience of God."[6]

The Openness of the Door

As we answer God's constraining call, we should seize the opportunities that God is giving us for gospel work. So consider, in the second place, the openness of the door. As he looked at the situation in Ephesus, with all its possibilities, Paul said, "A wide door for effective work has opened to me" (1 Cor. 16:9; cf. 2 Cor. 2:12). This is why the apostle could not come to the Corinthians but was constrained to stay in Ephesus: it was because the Holy Spirit was opening a wide door for him to preach the gospel and to plant a new church—what Calvin called "a great door,"[7] thinking perhaps of the huge wooden portals to the castles and cathedrals of France and Switzerland.

6. John Calvin, *Letters of John Calvin* (Carlisle, PA: Banner of Truth, 1991), 66.

7. Calvin, *Corinthians*, 2:71.

The Corinthians knew something about open doors. On his first trip to Corinth (see Acts 18), Paul met some fellow tentmakers who became some of his dearest friends in ministry. Aquila and Priscilla were part of the core group for his church plant, and eventually they became founding members of the first church in Corinth. So did some of the other people that Paul met in those days: Crispus, the ruler of the local synagogue, and Titius Justus, who lived next door. The Scripture says that in those days "many of the Corinthians hearing Paul believed and were baptized" (Acts 18:8). Whether they were Jews or Gentiles, neighbors or strangers, God was opening a door to their hearts.

This door would continue to remain open. Thus when Jesus spoke to Paul in the night, he gave him this promise: "Do not be afraid, but go on speaking and do not be silent, for I am with you, and no one will attack you to harm you, for I have many in this city who are my people" (Acts 18:9–10). God was opening a great door for effective ministry. By God's sovereign grace, people would come to Christ through Paul's ministry. He stayed in Corinth for the next eighteen months, proclaiming the crucifixion and the resurrection, bringing people to faith in Christ, and planting a new church.

Now Paul was telling the Corinthians that he was finding a wide-open door in Ephesus as well (see Acts 19). It started with twelve men who were baptized and received the Holy Spirit. It continued in the local synagogue, and then later at the Hall of Tyrannus, where Paul preached the gospel every day for two years (Acts 19:9–10). He also went out in the marketplace to perform healing miracles that confirmed the truth of his message. Thus what Paul wrote to the Corinthians was true: God had indeed opened "a wide door for effective work" (1 Cor. 16:9).

This is what God always does. By the power of the Spirit, there is always an open opportunity for the ministry of the gospel. Calvin saw this in Geneva. "A door has been opened for us by the hand of God," he wrote, "in order that we might introduce Christ."[8] As Calvin preached the Bible, faithfully expounding the Scriptures as many as twenty times a week, he saw people come to saving faith in Christ and then grow in practical godliness. Through the preaching of the Word, reformation came to Geneva— a reformation not just of the church but also of daily life. Poor refugees were welcomed in the name of Christ. The sick received medical care. Children were educated for Christ, including girls as well as boys.

This gospel work spread from Geneva to the rest of the French-speaking world. Calvin believed the promise of the gospel: Jesus has been given all authority in heaven and earth. He believed further that by the power of the Holy Spirit God's Word would always do its work. On the basis of these promises, Calvin opened doors for the gospel in his beloved France. Although he may have lost his country, he never stopped loving it. Eventually, his burden for his countrymen was embraced by his congregation, and they sent scores of missionaries to every part of France. In the words of one church historian, "Geneva became a dynamic center or nucleus from which the vital missionary energy it generated radiated out into the world beyond."[9] This was in keeping with Calvin's firm belief that God had commanded "the ministers of the gospel to go a distance, in order to spread the doctrine of salvation in every part of the world."[10]

Many of Geneva's missionaries and church planters were refugees who first came to the city for asylum and then received training for ministry under Calvin's leadership before going back home to preach the gospel. The results of their work, as recorded in

8. John Calvin, *Commentary on 1 and 2 Corinthians*, quoted in John Calhoun, "John Calvin: Missionary Hero or Missionary Failure?" *Presbyterion* 5, 1 (Spring 1979): 26.

9. Philip E. Hughes, "John Calvin: Director of Missions," in *The Heritage of John Calvin: Heritage Hall Lectures, 1960–1970*, ed. John H. Bratt, (Grand Rapids: Eerdmans, 1973), 40–54 (45).

10. John Calvin, *Calvin's Commentary: Harmony of Matthew, Mark, and Luke* (Grand Rapids: Baker, 1979), 384.

The Register of the Company of the Pastors and in other places, were staggering.[11] In 1555 there were only five evangelical and Reformed churches in France. By 1559 there were over a hundred, and by 1562 there were more than two thousand! There were churches and house churches in Paris, Lyon, Aix-en-Provence, Montpellier, Villefranche, Toulouse, Nerac, Bordeaux, La Rochelle, Nantes, Bourges, Orleans, Rouen, Paris—the list goes on and on. One congregation, pastored by Pierre Viret, had more than eight thousand members. It was all because Calvin and other Calvinists had faith in the God of the open door.

By the grace of God, there is also an open door for us. Do you see the gospel opportunities that God is giving the church now and in the coming days? The meaning of Paul's metaphor, wrote Calvin,

> is that an opportunity of promoting the gospel had presented itself. For as an opportunity of entering is furnished when the *door is opened*, so the servants of the Lord make advances when an opportunity is presented. The *door is shut*, when no prospect of usefulness is held out. Now as, on the door being shut, it becomes us to enter upon a new course, rather than by farther efforts to weary ourselves to no purpose by useless labour, so where an opportunity presents itself of edifying, let us consider that by the hand of God a door is opened to us for introducing Christ there, and let us not withhold compliance with so kind an indication from God.[12]

What opportunities is God presenting today? Who are our neighbors, and how much do they need the gospel? What opportunities do we have for ministry in the church, on the campus, with internationals, in prison, on the streets of the city, or to the far

11. See, for example, the account provided by Errol Hulse in "John Calvin and His Missionary Enterprise," http://www.errollhulse.com/wp-content/uploads/2009/01/calvin-and-mission.pdf.

12. Calvin, *Corinthians*, 2:155.

places of the world? Our call is to go through the open door. This means praying that God will give us a faithful, fruitful ministry. It means sharing the gospel through our personal witness with people outside the church. It means praying for the Lord of the harvest to send more workers. It means proclaiming the gospel of Jesus Christ, both in his atoning crucifixion and in his triumphant resurrection. It may well mean suffering for the sake of the gospel. It certainly will mean persevering in times of trial. It means fulfilling all the duties of our ministry, whatever God calls us to do.

There is still so much work to be done. What Calvin said in the sixteenth century remains true today: "the Kingdom of God was only begun in the world, when God commanded the Gospel to be everywhere proclaimed . . . At this day its course is not as yet completed."[13] Just as the gospel went out from Geneva to the world, so now it goes out to the world from the many places where the church is already established. Our hope, our prayer, and even our expectation by faith is that the God of the wide-open door would, as Calvin also said, "show himself by his grace to dwell not only in one city, or in a little handful of people, but that he would reign over all the world, that everyone may serve him, and worship him as he deserves."[14]

The Strength of the Opposition

It would be nice to stop there, celebrating the openness of the door that God has given us for ministry. However, the Scripture goes on to say something very sobering. Yes, the door is open for the efficacious work of the gospel. But Paul also says this: "there are many adversaries" (1 Cor. 16:9). Thus we should consider, briefly and finally, the strength of the opposition.

13. John Calvin, *Commentary on Micah*, quoted in Muller, "Grace," 221.

14. John Calvin, *Sermons of M. John Calvin, on the Epistles of S. Paule to Timothie and Titus*, trans. L. T. (London: G. Bishop, 1579), 321.

If anyone knew the strength of the opposition, it was the apostle Paul. He had suffered Satan's attacks all over the Mediterranean world, as he faced trouble, hardship, and distress. Paul was frequently imprisoned and often on the run. He was whipped, beaten, stoned, and left for dead (2 Cor. 6:4–10; 11:23–27). "To the present hour," he wrote, "we hunger and thirst, we are poorly dressed and buffeted and homeless . . . We have become, and are still, like the scum of the world, the refuse of all things" (1 Cor. 4:11, 13).

When Paul said that there were many adversaries, therefore, he knew what he was talking about. The Corinthians had seen it for themselves, in the hatred of the Jews who put Paul on trial in their own city. The same thing would happen in Ephesus, and worse. Ephesus was the scene of a famous riot, when the merchants who made idols of the goddess Diana sent the whole city into an uproar against Paul and his gospel of the one true God (see Acts 19:23–41). There is something about church planting that always arouses the hatred of the devil.

Yet the strength of the opposition neither discouraged nor dissuaded the apostle Paul. On the contrary, this was one of the very things that constrained him in his calling. It was just because there were many adversaries that he knew he had to stay in Ephesus and keep doing the work of church planting. When a missionary is constrained by the gospel, he or she does not give up in the face of difficulty but remembers that this is the very reason why he or she was called: to take the mighty sword of the Word of God and raise it against the spiritual forces of evil.

Here again, John Calvin is an ideal example. Like the apostle Paul, he knew the strength of the opposition. In his commentary on Genesis, Calvin offered a frank assessment of what the church was up against: "Today, when God wishes His gospel to be preached in the whole world, so that the world may be restored from death to life, He seems to ask for the impossible.

We see how greatly we are resisted everywhere and with how many and what potent machinations Satan works against us, so that all roads are blocked."[15] Calvin might well have been thinking of the roadblocks in his own city, for it took him many years to persuade his congregation to engage in missionary work. It also took him many years to raise up men who were ready and willing to give their lives for the gospel. Up until 1555 there was only a trickle of church planters going out from Geneva. But eventually that trickle became a mighty flood, with as many as a hundred men going out in a single year, from a city with a population of only twenty thousand.

These church planters did not have a very good life expectancy. When they went to France and preached the gospel, it was always at the risk of their very lives. In fact, when Calvin wrote to encourage the churches in France, he did not mention their true locations or use the real names of their church planters. We take similar precautions today when we send people to China or Turkey or Saudi Arabia. How real was the danger in Reformation France? According to Philip Hughes:

> It would be hard to exaggerate the extremely hazardous nature of the assignment undertaken by those who sallied forth from Geneva as missionaries. The unbridled hostility to the Reformation meant that the utmost secrecy had to be observed in sending out these evangelical emissaries. . . . Their lines of infiltration were along perilous paths through the mountains, where they were dependent on friendly cottagers for food and hiding in case of necessity. Nor did the danger end when they arrived at their various destinations, for there too the utmost caution had to be observed lest they should be discovered and apprehended, with all the dire consequences that would be involved. Where a congregation was mustered, services were

15. John Calvin, *Commentary on Genesis*, quoted in Calhoun, "John Calvin," 25.

> conducted in a private home behind locked doors or in the shadows of a wooded hillside.[16]

Despite these precautions, the worship of the Protestant churches was sometimes discovered and persecuted. On one occasion, Calvin received a letter from Paris informing him that a Reformed congregation had been raided by enemies; almost two hundred people were being held captive and threatened with imminent harm.[17] Then there were the martyrs, at least nine of them, including five young theology students from Lausanne who were seized in Lyon, thrown into prison, and then put to death because they professed their faith in Christ. Nevertheless, their enemies did not triumph. As Calvin wrote in his famous letter to these five beloved brothers, "Let enemies do their utmost, they shall never be able to bury that light which God has made to shine in you. . . . As He has commenced this work in us, so He will complete it, to the end that all glory may be given to Him, and that whether we live or die, all may be to His honor and glory, to the edification of his poor Church, and to the advancement of our salvation."[18]

Gospel work is an unpredictable enterprise. There is never any way to tell for certain how well a church will begin, how well a mission will do, or how effective one's own ministry will turn out to be. But if there is one thing that we can always count on, it is for all hell to break loose. I mean this in a serious and literal way. The last thing that Satan wants to see is another Spirit-filled, gospel-believing, Bible-preaching, God-worshiping congregation of the Lord Jesus Christ. What Paul experienced in Ephesus is what every church planter, missionary, evangelist, pastor, and disciple experiences: there are many adversaries.

16. Hughes, "John Calvin," 46.

17. Ibid., 51.

18. John Calvin, *Letters of John Calvin*, ed. Jules Bonnet (Philadelphia: Presbyterian Board of Publication, 1858), 2:406.

A Final Charge

Understand that when God called us to serve him, therefore, he was really sending us into spiritual battle. Therefore, we will need all the help of the Holy Spirit to fulfill our ministry. May the Lord bless us, and keep us, and help us to know the blessed constraint of God's call to kingdom service. May God help us to see the doors that he has opened for us in ministry. May we believe that his Spirit will enable us to walk through these doors and into the lives of people who need the gospel. We should not be surprised by the opposition we face, but we should not be afraid of it, either. Let us preach and teach in the power of the Holy Spirit. Let us love and serve in the strength of the Lord.

As we do whatever gospel work that God has called us to do, let us also remember the saving work of the Lord Jesus Christ. He too was constrained by his call—the call of his Father to serve and to save his people. Jesus came to deliver men and women and children of all nations from their spiritual prison. To open the door to salvation, Jesus first had to suffer the deadly cross and the dark tomb. Only then could he walk through to the other side, with the stone rolled away and the glory of his resurrection shining in all its splendor. In doing this life-giving work, Jesus had to overcome the opposition in all its diabolical strength. Satan did everything he could to tempt and to murder Jesus, to destroy him forever. But God was victorious in the fight: "He disarmed the rulers and authorities and put them to open shame, by triumphing over them" (Col. 2:15).

Now we are called to follow Jesus through all the open doors he gives us for spreading the gospel, no matter what hardships we face. The words of John Calvin can give us courage. Consider the following charge, prayer, and benediction from a letter he wrote to a church plant on an island just off the coast of France. Calvin's letter was carried by the man who would become their first pastor, Philibert Hamelin. Pastor Hamelin was faithful to his calling—faithful unto death, for he suffered martyrdom just four years later. Here is what Calvin wrote to encourage Hamelin, his church, and every faithful follower of Christ:

> Take courage and dedicate yourselves wholeheartedly to God who has purchased you through His own Son at such cost, and surrender both body and soul to Him, showing that you hold His glory more precious than all that this world has to offer. May you value the eternal salvation which is prepared for you in heaven more than this fleeting life. Therefore, and in conclusion, most dear brethren, we shall pray the good Lord to complete what He has begun in you, to advance you in all spiritual blessings, and to keep you under His holy protection.[19]

May the Lord Jesus Christ, who purchased the church at the cost of his own blood, give us grace to be faithful in our calling and fruitful in our ministry, from now until the day that he calls us to enter the great door to paradise.

Delivered July 6, 2009, at St. Pierre Cathedral, Geneva, Switzerland.

19. John Calvin, writing under the pen name Charles d'Espeville, in a letter from the Company of Pastors of Geneva to "the believers of certain islands in France" (October 12, 1553), as quoted in Hughes, "John Calvin," 49. The islands are off the coast of Saintonge, near La Rochelle.

6

All the Glorious Offices of Christ—1 Corinthians 1:29–31

Peter A. Lillback

You've probably said each of the following:

- "We're having an *office* Christmas party!"
- "I gave at the *office*."
- "Criticize the person (replace *person* with *president, pastor, teacher*, as appropriate) but respect the *office*."

The person you criticize, whose office you are to respect, is usually in the corner office!

The word *office* is a word that is a bit ambiguous, since an office is both a room with a title and a position with a title. *Office* connotes both a place and a person who occupies that place. A new American president, for example, has the privilege to move into the Oval Office precisely because he's been elected to the office of president.

Christ also holds office; in fact, we should say *offices* in the plural. If you are familiar with the Westminster Shorter Catechism, you will recognize questions 23–26, where Christ's redeeming work is described by the three offices of prophet, priest, and king.

Question 23 asks, "What offices doth Christ execute as our Redeemer?" Answer: "Christ, as our Redeemer, executeth the offices of a prophet, of a priest, and of a king, both in his estate of humiliation and exaltation."

Question 24 queries, "How doth Christ execute the office of a prophet?" Answer: "Christ executeth the office of a prophet in revealing to us, by his word and Spirit, the will of God for our salvation."

Question 25 probes deeper, asking, "How doth Christ execute the office of a priest? Answer: "Christ executeth the office of a priest, in his once offering up of himself a sacrifice to satisfy divine justice, and reconcile us to God; and in making continual intercession for us."

Question 26 reaches the climax when it asks, "How doth Christ execute the office of a king?" Answer: "Christ executeth the office of a king in subduing us to himself, in ruling and defending us, and in restraining and conquering all his and our enemies."

I would like us to consider the idea of the "offices" of Christ. But as we do, we will not simply focus on the traditional catechetical offices of prophet, priest, and king.[1] Instead, we will also reflect on Christ's offices as taught by the apostle Paul and explained by Calvin in his comments on 1 Corinthians 1:29–31. This text says:

> so that no one may boast before him. It is because of him that you are in Christ Jesus, who has become for us wisdom from God—

1. Calvin develops Christ's threefold office of prophet, priest, and king in *Institutes*, 2.15.1–6.

> that is, our righteousness, holiness and redemption. Therefore, as it is written: "Let him who boasts boast in the Lord." (NIV)

Let us study this text under these heads:

- The Glory of "Office"
- The Glorious Offices of Christ
- Christ's Glorious Offices and Our Salvation
- Christ's Glorious Offices Should Bring Him Glory

The Glory of "Office"

The glory of a physical office is in its size, its location, and its furnishings. But the glory of a positional office is in its authority. The positions of authority become more glorious as more authority is associated with them. Most would agree that the office of Chief Justice of the Supreme Court of the United States is a more glorious office than the office of Chief Dog Catcher of Washington, DC, even though each may have a physical office in the same important city, with both often trying to address cases of misconduct!

Furthermore, an officeholder becomes even greater when he unites multiple offices in one. An extraordinary example would be a person who simultaneously held the offices of Supreme Court Justice, Speaker of the House, and President of the United States. Such a person might euphemistically be called a plenipotentiary, but more likely be called a dictator! Perhaps even a tyrant. For after all, only an absolutely perfect being can have absolute power and be absolutely good at the same time.

Consider then the glory of Christ. For at the same time he holds the glorious office of Messiah, the anointed one, he also possesses and joins together three additional glorious offices. These three offices are identified in the catechism as prophet, priest, and king. Each reflects his messianic office.

Let us not forget that *Messiah* means "anointed" in Hebrew. The occupants of the offices of prophet, priest, and king were all installed, ordained, or crowned by anointing with oil in the Old Testament.[2]

As we turn our attention specifically to 1 Corinthians 1:29–31, let us see how Calvin develops this great passage about the glorious offices of Christ. On this text Calvin remarks: "You will scarcely meet with another passage of Scripture that more distinctly marks out all the offices of Christ."[3]

The Glorious Offices of Christ

While the "offices" of Christ have a traditional sense as defined by the Shorter Catechism, nearly a century before it was composed, Calvin, too, had wrestled with the concept of "office" in relation to Christ's saving work.

But the offices of Christ that Calvin identifies here are not literally identified as prophet, priest, and king as he does elsewhere.[4] Instead, following Paul he speaks of Christ's offices as "righteousness, holiness, wisdom, and redemption."

Indeed, to use Calvin's words, "You will scarcely meet with another passage of Scripture that more distinctly marks out all the offices of Christ." These are not just mere titles for the offices of Christ; these terms describe his exclusive, glorious role in the accomplishment of our salvation. Calvin adds:

2. "If we seek salvation, we are taught by the very name of Jesus that it is 'of him' (1 Cor. 1:30). If we seek any other gifts of the Spirit, they will be found in his anointing" (*Institutes*, 2.16.19).

3. All citations of Calvin used here, unless otherwise noted, are from the Calvin Translation Society, *Commentary on 1 Corinthians* (Grand Rapids: Baker, 1979), 92–95.

4. "Therefore, in order that faith may find a firm basis for salvation in Christ, and thus rest in him, this principle must be laid down: the office enjoined upon Christ by the Father consist of three parts. For he was given to be prophet, king, and priest" (*Institutes*, 2.15.1).

> In fine, of all the blessings that are here enumerated we must seek in Christ not the half, or merely a part, but the entire completion. For Paul does not say that he has been given to us by way of filling up, or eking out righteousness, holiness, wisdom, and redemption, but assigns to him exclusively the entire accomplishment of the whole.

Summarizing, Calvin says Paul "ascribes here to Christ four commendatory titles, that include his entire excellence, and every benefit that we receive from him."

Christ the Redeemer

The connection between Paul's four offices with the catechism's traditional threefold office of prophet, priest, and king can readily be seen. First, remember the catechism begins its discussion of Christ's offices with Question 23, which asks, "What offices doth Christ execute as our *Redeemer?*" It is as Redeemer that Christ executes his threefold offices. Significantly, the fourth office listed by Calvin in 1 Corinthians 1:30 is "redemption."

Prophet of Wisdom

Yet we also can see the connection with Christ's offices of prophet and priest as well.

Paul uses the word "wisdom" as one of "the four commendatory titles" that present Christ's "entire excellence." Surely, the message of a prophet is the communication of divine wisdom:

> In the *first* place, he says that *he is made unto us wisdom,* by which he means, that we obtain in him an absolute perfection of wisdom, in as much as the Father has fully revealed himself to us in him, that we may not desire to know any thing besides him. There is a similar passage in Col. ii. 3—*In whom are hid all the treasures of wisdom and knowledge.*

Priest of Righteousness and Holiness

Moreover, Paul's words "righteousness and holiness" describe the work of a priest. Calvin sees Christ as the one who provides righteousness by his sacrifice:

> For when he calls Christ, our *righteousness*, a corresponding idea must be understood—that in us there is nothing but *sin*.
>
> *Secondly*, he says that he *is made unto us righteousness*, by which he means that we are on his account acceptable to God, inasmuch as he expiated our sins by death, and his obedience is imputed to us for righteousness. For as the righteousness of faith consists in remission of sins and a gracious acceptance, we obtain both through Christ.
>
> Christ's work as priest is also reflected in his provision of holiness:
>
> *Thirdly*, he calls him our *sanctification*, by which he means that we who are otherwise unholy by nature, are by his Spirit renewed unto holiness, that we may serve God.

King of Glory

But we can also find here Christ's office of king. This is seen in the focus of verse 31, where Paul declares, "*He that glorieth let him glory in the Lord.*" Calvin explains this text as follows: "Mark the end that God has in view in bestowing all things upon us in Christ—that we may not claim any merit to ourselves but may give him all the praise."

Is not such exclusive glory the prerogative of a king, indeed, the King of kings? Thus in this context Calvin declares the Reformation's motto of *soli Deo gloria*—"to God alone be the glory. Simply put, the redemptive offices of Christ underscore his unique glory as Savior.

Having seen that Christ occupies these glorious redemptive offices of the Messiah, let us next consider how this fact impacts our salvation.

Christ's Glorious Offices and Our Salvation

Calvin's interpretation of Christ's four offices emphasizes the exclusive and glorious nature of the redeeming work of Christ. Calvin asserts:

> For when he calls Christ, our *righteousness*, a corresponding idea must be understood—that in us there is nothing but *sin*; and so as to the other terms. Now he ascribes here to Christ four commendatory titles, that include his entire excellence, and every benefit that we receive from him.

Righteousness and Salvation

As we engage Calvin at this point, we should emphasize that Calvin was greatly influenced, as were all the Reformers, by Luther's seminal theological insight of justification of the sinner by faith alone, in Christ alone, according to the Scriptures alone. Thus here he emphasizes that Christ's four offices are directly connected with our saving faith:

> Now as you will scarcely meet with another passage of Scripture that more distinctly marks out all the offices of Christ, you may also understand from it very clearly the nature and efficacy of faith. For as Christ is the proper object of faith, every one that knows what are the benefits that Christ confers upon us is at the same time taught to understand what faith is.

Holiness and Salvation

Along with the critical point of our righteousness through faith in Christ, we also find here another significant insight of Calvin's theology. This is the inseparability of righteousness and holiness—of justification and sanctification. To put it another way, Christ's office of "righteousness" must not be separated from his office of "sanctification." This Calvin describes as *duplex gratiae*, or the double graces, of the new covenant as seen in Jeremiah 31.[5]

Luther's motto was "justification by faith alone." Calvin and his theological heirs agreed. However, they augmented his motto by saying, "We are justified by faith alone, but the faith that justifies is never alone but is ever accompanied by all saving graces." For example, the Westminster Confession of Faith declares:

> Faith, thus receiving and resting on Christ and His righteousness, is the alone instrument of justification: yet is it not alone in the person justified, but is ever accompanied, with all other saving graces, and is no dead faith, but worketh by love. (WCF 11.2)

Thus Calvin emphasizes the inseparability of Christ's offices of righteousness and sanctification.[6] Calvin underscores Paul's connection of Christ's office as justifier with his office as sanctifier. He explains:

> From this, also, we infer, that we cannot be justified freely through faith alone without at the same time living holily. For these fruits of grace are connected together, as it were, by an indissoluble tie, so that he who attempts to sever them does in a manner tear Christ in pieces. Let therefore the man who seeks to be justified through Christ, by God's unmerited goodness, consider that this cannot be attained without his taking him

5. See Peter A. Lillback, *The Binding of God* (Grand Rapids: Baker, 2001), 180n83.

6. "But another much clearer argument now offers itself. Since faith embraces Christ, as offered to us by the Father (cf. John 6:29)—that is, since he is offered not only for righteousness, forgiveness of sins, and peace but also for sanctification (cf. 1 Cor. 1:30) and the fountain of the water of life (John 7:38; cf. 4:14)—without a doubt, no one can duly know him without at the same time apprehending the sanctification of the Spirit" (*Institutes*, 3.2.8).

at the same time for *sanctification*, or, in other words, being renewed to innocence and purity of life.

This in Calvin's mind was a critical point in answering the Roman Catholic charge that the Reformers' doctrine of justification by faith alone leads to an abandonment of good works. He declares:

> Those, however, that slander us, as if by preaching a free justification through faith we called men off from good works, are amply refuted from this passage, which intimates that faith apprehends in Christ regeneration equally with forgiveness of sins.

Justification and Sanctification Are Different

Nevertheless, the interconnection of these two offices of Christ does not mean the equality of the two! In no way does he want to be misunderstood. He explains:

> Observe, on the other hand, that these two offices of Christ are conjoined in such a manner as to be, notwithstanding, distinguished from each other. What, therefore, Paul here expressly distinguishes, it is not allowable mistakenly to confound.[7]

7. "Yet you could not grasp this without at the same time grasping sanctification also. For he 'is given unto us for righteousness, wisdom, sanctification, and redemption' (1 Cor. 1:30). Therefore Christ justifies no one whom he does not at the same time sanctify" (*Institutes*, 3.3.19). "Accordingly, they must be reborn if they would enter the Kingdom of Heaven. Forgiveness of sins is preached when men are taught that for them Christ became redemption, righteousness, salvation, and life (1 Cor. 1:30), by whose name they are freely accounted righteous and innocent in God's sight. Since both kinds of grace are received by faith, as I have elsewhere proved, still, because the proper object of faith is God's goodness, by which sins are forgiven, it was expedient that it should be carefully distinguished from repentance" (*Institutes*, 3.11.6). "Yet Scripture, even though it joins them, still lists them separately in order that God's manifold grace may better appear to us. For Paul's statement is not redundant: that Christ was given to us for our righteousness and sanctification (1 Cor. 1:30). And whenever he

It is true, Calvin insists, that justification and sanctification are inseparable. Yet he equally insists that they must be carefully distinguished!

The Redeemer's Exclusive Work of Salvation

Having considered Christ's offices of wisdom, righteousness, and holiness, we must now see Christ in his office as Redeemer. Calvin explains: "If it is asked in what way Christ is given to us for *redemption,* I answer—'Because he made himself a ransom.'"

For Calvin, redemption is both the first and the last blessing of our union with Christ.

> *Fourthly,* he teaches us that he is given to us for *redemption,* by which he means, that through his goodness we are delivered at once from all bondage to sin, and from all the misery that flows from it. Thus *redemption* is the first gift of Christ that is begun in us, and the last that is completed.

Theologians have often spoken of the "already-and-not-yet" character of salvation. Here we see Calvin's expression of that reality when he writes: "For the commencement of salvation consists in our being drawn out of the labyrinth of sin and death; yet in the meantime, until the final day of resurrection, we groan with desire for *redemption* (as we read in Rom. 8:23.)"

Because Christ occupies all the glorious offices of our salvation, he alone is our Redeemer. Salvation is his work alone. It is not our work. Accordingly, he alone should receive the glory for our salvation. Next and lastly, we now follow Calvin's insight into the Reformers' motto *soli Deo gloria* "to God alone be the glory"!

---

reasons—from the salvation purchased for us, from God's fatherly love, and from Christ's grace—that we are called to holiness and cleanness, he clearly indicates that to be justified means something different from being made new creatures" (*Institutes,* 3.16.1).

Christ's Glorious Offices Should Bring Him Glory

We have reviewed Calvin's view of Paul's "four commendatory titles" for Christ, which Calvin also refers to as "all the offices of Christ" in his interpretation of 1 Corinthians 1:29–31. But in this context, Paul and Calvin would surely be comfortable with our speaking of these as "all the *glorious* offices of Christ." For Calvin recognizes how Paul sandwiches these four offices of Christ in verse 30 between his strong statements on God's glory in Christ in verses 29 and 31.

Thus on verse 29 Calvin declares the glory of God:

> *That no flesh should glory. . . .* It is a sentiment that is worthy to be kept in remembrance—that there is nothing left in us which we may justly glory. . . . By this expression all mankind are put to silence when they come into the presence of God; as Habakkuk says—*Let all flesh keep silence before God* (Hab. 2:20). Let every thing, therefore, that is at all deserving of praise, be recognized as proceeding from God.

In verse 30, he continues to emphasize the theme of God's glory in Christ alone:

> You have your beginning from God, who *calleth those things which are not,* (Rom. 4:17,) passing by those things that appear to be; and your subsistence is founded upon Christ, and thus you have no occasion to be proud. Nor is it of creation merely that he speaks, but of that spiritual existence, into which we are born again by the grace of God. . . . For when he calls Christ, our *righteousness,* a corresponding idea must be understood—that in us there is nothing but *sin* . . . He ascribes here to Christ four commendatory titles, that include his entire excellence, and every benefit that we receive from him.

Then he brings the theme that God alone is to receive glory for the exclusive saving work of Christ as Redeemer to a crescendo and climax in verse 31:

> *He that glorieth let him glory in the Lord.* Mark the end that God has in view in bestowing all things upon us in Christ—that we may not claim any merit to ourselves but may give him all the praise. For God does not despoil with the view of leaving us bare, but forthwith clothes us with his glory—yet on this condition, that whenever we would glory we must go out of ourselves. In short, man, brought to nothing in his own estimation, and acknowledging that there is nothing good anywhere but in God alone, must renounce all desire for his own glory, and with all his might aspire and aim at the glory of God exclusively.

To know Christ as wisdom, righteousness, holiness, and redemption is to know that he alone is worthy of our praise.[8] Wouldn't this insight alone make all the difference in our so-called "worship wars"? What would our worship look like if our all-consuming concern was the glory of God alone in Christ alone instead of the pleasure of the worshiper? In our worship wars, Christ's exclusive glory is all too often the casualty! Sadly, in the very throne room of God, the lowly office of believers usurps and displaces all the glorious offices of the King of kings,

8. "In these things are parts of the true knowledge of God—to be stricken by the awareness of our own iniquity and to reflect that he benefits us, unworthy as we are—why do we attempt, to our great harm, to filch from the Lord even a particle of the thanks we owe his free kindness? Likewise, when Jeremiah proclaims, 'Let not the wise man glory in his wisdom, or the rich man in his riches, or the mighty man in his might' (Jer. 9:23, order changed, cf. Vg.), but 'let him who glories, glory in the Lord' (1 Cor. 1:31, Vg.; cf. Jer. 9:24), does he not imply that God's glory is somewhat diminished if man glories in himself? Surely Paul accommodates those words to this use when he teaches that every part of our salvation rests with Christ that we may glory in the Lord alone (1 Cor. 1:30–31). His meaning is this: whoever thinks that he has anything at all of his own rises up against God and casts a shadow upon his glory" (*Institutes*, 3.13.1).

Lord of lords, Priest of priests, and Prophet of prophets. *To God alone be the glory* is too often exchanged for "To my taste alone be the worship!"

Conclusion

Thus our study of all the glorious offices of Christ connects the three offices of prophet, priest, and king with the four offices of Christ in 1 Corinthians 1:29–31. At the same time we also see the connection between the mottoes of the Reformation. *Sola fide* means *soli Deo gloria*. Faith alone requires that to God alone be the glory!

We have also seen in Calvin that faith alone is affirmed but augmented by the truth that while faith alone justifies, the faith that justifies is never alone but is always accompanied by all the glorious offices of Christ. As our Redeemer, Christ brings wisdom, righteousness, and holiness that are inseparably connected. Union with Christ in all his glorious offices brings the inseparable union of justification and sanctification in the believer. Nevertheless, these offices and their gifts to the believer must be distinguished, for that is what Paul himself does.

Calvin's understanding of "all the offices of Christ" leads us to the conclusion that all glory belongs to God in Christ. Calvin's teaching on the glorious offices of Christ underscores the doxological motto of the Reformation—*soli Deo gloria*.

As Calvin expounds Paul's words, he with the apostle declares our duty to glorify God. But in doing so, he also reminds us that Paul in 1 Corinthians 1:31 is also quoting from Jeremiah 9:23–24, where Jeremiah also calls forth the theme of *soli Deo gloria*:

> This is also more clearly apparent from the context in the writings of the prophet, from whom Paul has borrowed this testimony; for in that passage the Lord, after stripping all mankind of glory in respect of strength, wisdom, and riches, commands

> us to glory only *in knowing him*, (Jer. 9:23, 24). Now he would have us know him in such a way as to know that it is *he that exercises judgment, righteousness, and mercy*. For this knowledge produces in us at once confidence in him and fear of him. If therefore a man has his mind regulated in such a manner that, claiming no merit to himself, he desires that God alone be exalted; if he rests with satisfaction on his grace, and places his entire happiness in his fatherly love, and, in fine, is satisfied with God alone, that man *truly* "glories in the Lord."[9]

In saying this, Calvin reminds us of the true duty of another office—the office of the Christian. Christ's exclusive glory, his being chief in our salvation, calls to mind our chief end. The Shorter Catechism, question 1, asks:

"What is the chief end of man?"

9. See Calvin's *Commentary on Jeremiah*, 9:23–24: "He afterwards adds, 'in understanding and knowing me.' Though by these two words the Prophet means the same thing, yet they are not used without a design; for as men despised the knowledge of God, it was necessary to remind them, that to know God is the chief part of perfect wisdom. He therefore intended to correct the mischievous error under which almost the whole world labours; for while all attend to various pursuits, the knowledge of God is neglected. We see with what ardour every one pursues his own fancies, while hardly one in a hundred deigns to spend half an hour in the day in seeking the knowledge of God. And there is also another evil, a false opinion, which proceeds from pride—that to know God is a common thing. We hence perceive why the Prophet has employed these two words to designate the same thing; it was to rouse more fully the attention of men; for he saw that almost all were torpid and indifferent on a subject which is justly entitled to the labour of a whole life; nay were a hundred lives given us, this one thing would be sufficient to engage our attention. But, as it has been said, what ought to be preferred to all other things is despised and neglected."

In *Institutes*, 1.10.2, he writes: "In Jeremiah, where God declares in what character he would have us know him, he puts forward a less full description but one plainly amounting to the same thing. 'Let him who glories, glory in this,' he says, 'that he knows that I am the Lord who exercise this,' he says, 'that he knows that I am the Lord who exercise mercy, judgment, and justice in the earth.' (Jer. 9:24; 1 Cor. 1:31). Certainly these three things are especially necessary for us to know: mercy, on which alone the salvation of us all rests, judgment, which is daily exercised against wrongdoers, and in even greater severity awaits them to their everlasting ruin; justice, whereby believers are preserved, and are most tenderly nourished."

Answer: "The chief end of man is to glorify God and to enjoy him forever."

We truly honor Christ our Redeemer's offices of prophet, priest, and king as well as his offices as our wisdom, our righteousness, our holiness, and our redemption, when we seek to know him by his Word, and when we seek to glorify him with our lives. All the glorious offices of Christ call on us to glorify him and to enjoy him today and forever. Paul's, Jeremiah's, and Calvin's command found in 1 Corinthians 1:31 says it so very well: *He that glorieth let him glory in the Lord.*

Indeed, *Soli Deo Gloria*!

Delivered July 6, 2009, at St. Pierre Cathedral, Geneva, Switzerland.

7

Calvin's Cherished Text—John 17:3

W. Robert Godfrey

John Calvin, as far as I know, never explicitly declared that he had a favorite verse in the Scriptures. But as one reads widely in his writings and becomes familiar with his theology, one verse recurs again and again and seems a most apt summary of his deepest conviction about the Christian faith. That verse is John 17:3, "And this is eternal life, that they know you the only true God, and Jesus Christ whom you have sent."

Those who are not well acquainted with Calvin might have expected that his favorite verse would be found in Romans or Ephesians or some other text where the doctrine of predestination is taught. But the heart of Calvin's teaching is wonderfully expressed in this rather simple verse where Jesus summarizes his gospel in what has often been called his high-priestly prayer. As Calvin said of this verse, "Almost every one of the words has its weight."[1] For Calvin, the heart and foundation of Christianity is the gospel of free grace, of salvation in Jesus Christ, expressed in this verse.

Something of the importance of this verse to Calvin can be seen in his citing it explicitly five times in the *Institutes* and several times throughout his commentaries on several books of the Bible. Its importance to Calvin for the basic presentation of the Christian message can also be seen in its presence twice in his Genevan Catechism, once near the beginning and once toward the end.

Near the beginning (questions 13 and 14) the catechism discusses the love of God:

> Q. Where will this [God's love] be apparent to us?
> A. In his Word, where he reveals his mercy to us in Christ, and testifies of his love towards us.
>
> Q. Then the foundation and beginning of faith in God is to know him in Christ? (John 17:3)
> A. Quite so.[2]

Toward the end of the catechism in the section on the sacraments (question 300), Calvin wrote:

> Q. What are we to conclude from the matters that have been treated by us?
> A. What truth itself teaches and I proposed at the beginning: this is life eternal, to know the one true God as Father and Jesus Christ whom he sent (John 17:3). I say to know him, in order that we may offer to him the honour and worship that is due, so that he be not only Lord to us, but also Father and Saviour

1. Calvin, *Commentary on the Gospel according to John*, trans. William Pringle (Grand Rapids: Baker, 1979), 2:166 (ad 17:3).

2. John Calvin, "The Catechism of the Church of Geneva" (1545), in *Calvin: Theological Treatises*, ed. J. K. S. Reid, (Philadelphia: Westminster, 1954), 92.

> (Matt. 1:21), that we on our side be his children and servants, and accordingly dedicate our life to display his glory."[3]

John 17:3 teaches the importance of knowing the truth. Calvin in his teaching stressed the foundational character of knowledge to Christianity. The centrality for Calvin of the knowledge of God in Christ to the true religion is clear in the way Calvin organized his *Institutes of the Christian Religion*. He begins that book stating that we must know God and ourselves in order to know the truth.

Ultimately, that knowledge must not be just a matter of information but a matter of faith and trust. The knowledge Calvin writes about is not only in the head but also in the heart. As he commented on John 17:8, "he shows that nothing which relates to God can be known aright but by *faith*, but that in *faith* there is such certainty that it is justly called *knowledge*."[4] Calvin preached this knowledge and called his hearers to believe. This verse still calls us to believe and know today.

As a preacher, Calvin followed a simple expositional style, reflecting verse by verse on God's message for his people. He was not a preacher who divided his sermons into three points and certainly never concluded with a poem. Yet this text, John 17:3, neatly provides three points for our consideration today. Jesus encapsulates the gospel he preached by calling us to know the life that is eternal, to know the God who is true, and to know the Christ whom God has sent.

First, Then, the Gospel Is to Know the Life That Is Eternal

Calvin and Calvinists have often been portrayed as life-denying, joyless ascetics. Calvin would have vigorously denied such

3. Ibid., 129.
4. Calvin, *Commentary on John*, 2:172 (ad 17:8).

a charge. He once observed, for example, that we are nowhere forbidden to smile or enjoy good wine. But his deeper conviction and more serious response to this charge would be to ask what life is. The life of this passing world is necessarily short and full of trouble, however good that life might be. The life that should concern us is eternal life, which for those in Christ begins now but lasts beyond this life into eternity.

Christianity is about this eternal life. As Jesus said, "I came that they [the sheep] may have life and have it abundantly" (John 10:10). Calvin commented on this text: "He declares that *life* is continually increased and strengthened in those who do not revolt from him. And, indeed, the greater progress that any man makes in faith, the more nearly does he approach to the fullness of *life*, because the Spirit, who is *life*, grows in him."[5] Growing in God is growing in life.

The life that Jesus promises stands in sharp contrast to the death in which humanity finds itself. Though our bodies are alive, our souls are bound and dead in rebellion against God. As Calvin wrote: "We ought first to know that we are all in death, till we are enlightened by God, who alone is life."[6]

Those outside Christ do not recognize the dead state in which they live. As Calvin commented on Psalm 49, "These infatuated enemies of God . . . cannot fail to perceive that death is the universal lot of mankind, that the wise are equally liable to it with the foolish; and yet they persist in the imagination that they will remain here always, and will live as if they were never to quit with this world!"[7] Today, even more so than in Calvin's day, our world seeks to deny the reality of death, whenever possible avoiding the very use of the word *death* or *dying*.

5. Ibid., 1:402 (ad 10:10).

6. Ibid., 2:166 (ad 17:3).

7. John Calvin, *Commentary on the Book of Psalms*, trans. James Anderson (Grand Rapids: Baker, 1979), 2:243 (ad 49:10).

The foolishness of this world is nowhere more manifest than in believing that our material possessions are what is really important in life: "For surely it is the height of folly in any man for a mere momentary happiness—a very dream—to abdicate the crown of heaven, and renounce his hopes for eternity."[8] It really is true that "you can't take it with you."

Although the life of Christians in this world is often difficult, God promises to his own people eternal rewards in comparison with which the attractions of this world will indeed seem pale. "There is a higher lesson still inculcated by the Psalmist—that, as God's providence of the world is not presently apparent, we must exercise patience, and rise superior to the suggestions of carnal sense in anticipating the favourable issue. That it is our duty to maintain a resolute struggle with our afflictions, however severe these may be, and that it were foolish to place happiness in the enjoyment of such fleeting possessions as the riches, honours, or pleasures of this world."[9]

The eternal life that God promises begins with a life lived now out of faith, filled with love for God and the neighbor. The life of faith looks always to the promises of Christ, interpreting all of the experiences of life in terms of them. The life of love remembers that we are not the center of our lives but that God and those who bear his image must temper our self-love, drawing us out of our self-love to a fuller life.

This eternal life culminates in the blessings of the new heaven and earth in which there will be no tears, no hunger, no sin, and no death. There, God will be forever present in his glory with his glorified people. There will be a world of righteousness in which the Lamb of God will be the light. While we cannot begin to imagine the full splendor of it, by faith we do have a foretaste.

8. Ibid., 2:248 (ad 49:14).
9. Ibid., 2:235 (ad 49:1).

To cultivate a confidence in the eternal life that Christ promises, Calvin recommended the discipline of meditating on the future life. We are all so caught up in the work, frustrations, and pleasures of the present life that often the promise of eternal life in a new heaven and earth ceases to attract or move us. As Calvin recognized, "Such is the weakness of our minds that we rise with difficulty to the contemplation of his glory in the heavens."[10] Because of this weakness, he recommends that we regularly take time to ponder the joy of the world to come in order to reset our values and priorities. "If Heaven is our country, what can earth be but a place of exile? If departure from the world is entrance into life, what is the world but a sepulcher, and what is residence in it but immersion in death? . . . Thus when the earthly is compared with the heavenly life, it may undoubtedly be despised and trampled underfoot."[11] The practice of such a discipline will refocus our priorities and our faith.

Second, the Gospel Is to Know the God Who Is True

Calvin recognized that in the history of the world there had been a very small number of committed atheists. He responded to their arguments in book 1 of the *Institutes of the Christian Religion*, but was rather dismissive of theoretical atheism as intellectually untenable. For Calvin, the two great problems of mankind were, first, what we might call practical atheism, and second, idolatry. Practical atheists give formal assent to the existence of God, but that assent has little if any impact on most of their thinking and living. Practical atheism is a life where the focus of trust, concern, and love is on the self or something else in this world, rather than on the true God.

10. Ibid., 4:52.

11. John Calvin, *Commentary on Second Corinthians*, cited by Ronald S. Wallace, *Calvin's Doctrine of the Christian Life* (Grand Rapids: Eerdmans, 1959), 91 (ad 4:17).

Others in this world, who are not practical atheists, live their lives in the service of false gods. As Calvin wrote, "The mind of man, I say, is like a work place of idolatrie."[12] Humans are incurably religious, often inventing gods to fulfill their religious needs.

Christ calls us away from godlessness and all false gods to the one true God revealed in the Bible and taught by Jesus. He calls us to know the one true God through his Word and Spirit. This is the God who is the God of Abraham, Isaac, and Jacob, the God who is the Holy One of Israel, the God who has now fulfilled his promises to send a Messiah and Savior for his people in the incarnation of his own eternal Son, Jesus. This is the God against whom mankind rebelled, and this is the God in whom alone sinners can find forgiveness and life. This is the true God and the God of truth.

Truth is an important theme in the Gospel of John, and Jesus teaches that truth is liberating: "You will know the truth and the truth will set you free" (John 8:32). But the truth that liberates is not a philosophical abstraction. Rather, it is the truth of being a follower of the true God. Jesus' whole teaching in John 8 states: "If you abide in my word, you are truly my disciples, and you will know the truth, and the truth will set you free" (vv. 31–32). In Christ we are free to live in and for the true God.

For Calvin, knowing the true God sets the believer free from idolatry, liberates for true worship, and leads to personal growth in holiness. False conceptions of God inevitably lead to false worship. Calvin saw the reform of worship as one of the great tasks to which he was called. He dedicated himself to the reform of worship in Geneva.

If Calvin were to visit most Reformed churches today for a worship service, he would be surprised and appalled by how far we have moved away from the simplicity and Word-

12. Cited by T. Brienen, *De Liturgie bij Johannes Calvijn* (Kampen: De Groot Goudriaan, 1987), 145, from a sermon by Calvin on Deuteronomy 11.

centeredness that he saw as the heart of worship. He would surely not approve the drift into entertainment and excitement that informs the worship of many today, focusing not on God but on us, either to amuse us or to stimulate us to action. Today, he would rightly call those who know the true God to worship him in Spirit and in truth. In particular, he would recall us to strictly Word-centered worship, where the Word is not only read and preached but also sung, prayed, and seen in the sacraments.

For Calvin, knowing the true God was also foundational to any growth in the mortification of the flesh and progress in holiness: "And therefore there is no other remedy for subduing this lawless desire than *the knowledge of God*. We see how the Prophet again makes the government of Christ to rest on faith and the doctrine of the gospel, as indeed he does not gather us to himself (Eph. i. 10) in another way than by enlightening our minds to reveal the heavenly life, which is nothing else, as he himself declares, than *to know the only true God, and Jesus Christ, whom he hath sent*."[13]

A commitment to the true God also means for the Christian a lifetime of continuing to learn: "Whatever progress any of us has made in the gospel, let him know that he needs fresh additions. The reward that Christ bestows on their perseverance is to make them more familiar with Himself. But by doing so, He merely adds another gift to the former, so that no man may think that he is repaid anything by way of reward. For He who puts His Word in our hearts by His Spirit is the same who daily chases from our minds the clouds of ignorance which obscure the brightness of the Gospel."[14] As servants of the true God, we are continually growing in the truth.

13. Calvin, *Commentary on the Prophet Isaiah*, trans. William Pringle (Grand Rapids: Baker, 1979), 1:387 (ad 11:10).

14. Calvin, *Commentary on John*, 1:221 (ad 8:32).

Third, the Gospel Is to Know the Christ Whom God Has Sent

Who is Jesus and what is his mission? Is he the troublemaker and impostor that the political and religious leaders of his day thought him to be? Is he simply a fallible human teacher who is at times insightful and helpful, as many would say today? Or is he, as he claimed, the only one who can reveal the true God and reconcile sinners to him as their heavenly Father? Jesus clearly and audaciously makes this last claim—a claim that Calvin and all Christians have believed.

Jesus is the only Son who is God come in the flesh and makes the Father known. As Jesus said in his prayer to his Father, "For I have given them the words that you gave me, and they have received them and have come to know in truth that I came from you; and they have believed that you sent me" (John 17:8). As Calvin said: "There is no other way in which God is known but in the face of Jesus Christ, who is the bright and lively image of him."[15] He expanded on this thought, in the context of referring to John 17:3, writing: "For, as he is the only true image of the invisible God, as he is the only interpreter of the Father, as he is the only guide of life, yea, as he is the life and light of the world and the truth, as soon as we depart from him, we necessarily become vain in our own devices."[16] The only way to know God is in and through Jesus.

In particular, Calvin insisted that the great work of Christ was to make God known as the loving Father of his people. Calvin laid this point out remarkably and powerfully in the short sixth chapter of his second book of the *Institutes of the Christian Religion*. In that chapter he picked up again the truth that he had

15. Ibid., 2:166 (ad 17:3).

16. John Calvin, *Commentaries on the Catholic Epistles*, trans. John Owen (Grand Rapids: Baker, 1979), 273 (ad 1 John 5:20).

discussed in the first book, namely, that God is revealed in the creation. But the natural revelation of God is limited in what it communicates. He wrote: "We cannot by contemplating the universe infer that he [God] is Father."[17] We can know that there is an almighty, eternal God, but we cannot know that he cares for us as a father does for his children. And natural revelation cannot make known the way of salvation. Salvation is known and accomplished only in Jesus: "God is comprehended [as Father] in Christ alone."[18] All the assurance of salvation must be found in Christ: "Unless God confronts us in Christ, we cannot come to know that we are saved."[19]

The Christ who teaches and saves us so that God becomes our Father is the Christ who fills and surrounds us with the Father's love. For many, Calvin may not be thought of as a great teacher of the love of God, but he is. Consider this remarkable statement of the love of God from his commentary on Hebrews: "Then let us first remember that the Gospel is here compared with the Law; and secondly, that there are two parts in this comparison—that God's glory displays itself more illustriously in the Gospel than in the Law—and that his invitation is now full of love, but that formerly there was nothing but the greatest terrors . . . The Gospel contains nothing but love, provided it be received by faith."[20]

Jesus makes eternal life ours, reconciling us to the Father by his saving work: "I give them eternal life, and they will never perish, and no one will snatch them out of my hand" (John 10:28). The work of Christ is our salvation, as Calvin makes clear in this comment (again just before citing John 17:3):

17. John Calvin, *Institutes of the Christian Religion*, ed. J. T. McNeill (Philadelphia: Westminster, 1960), 2.6.1.

18. Ibid., 2.6.4.

19. Ibid.

20. Calvin, *Commentary on Hebrews*, cited in part by Iain Murray, *The Cross—the Pulpit of God's Love* (Edinburgh: Banner of Truth, 2008), 4 (ad 12:18–19).

"Christ is called our Righteousness, because he was the only purging sacrifice, and hath reconciled the Father to us by his death, and did rise again afterward, that, having overcome death, he might purchase for us eternal life. Therefore the whole substance of our salvation is in Christ's person."[21] Jesus is our Savior.

Indeed, Christ is our Savior in his great work as our king and priest: "The confession [Peter's confession: 'You are the Christ'] is short, but it embraces all that is contained in our salvation; for the designation *Christ*, or *Anointed*, includes both an everlasting Kingdom and an everlasting Priesthood, to reconcile us to God, and, by expiating our sins through his sacrifice, to obtain for us a perfect righteousness, and, having received us under his protection, to uphold and supply and enrich us with every description of blessings."[22] Jesus is the Priest-King Messiah promised in the Old Testament and now fully revealed among us.

John 17:3 is indeed a wonderful text, summarizing for us the gospel of our Lord Jesus Christ. It also provides a clear window into some of the basic elements of Christianity that were most central and most dear to John Calvin. On the 500th anniversary of his birth, Calvin would be little interested in the attention we have given to him. As his favorite text makes so clear, he would rather be interested in making the gospel of Jesus Christ known.

As we have gathered for a conference of scholars, preachers, and believers to remember the life and work of a great scholar and preacher, I know of no better way of concluding this sermon than quoting Calvin one last time, to direct

21. John Calvin, *Commentary on the Acts of the Apostles*, ed. Henry Beveridge (Grand Rapids: Baker, 1979), 1:553 (ad 13:47).

22. John Calvin, *Commentary on a Harmony of the Evangelists, Matthew, Mark, and Luke*, trans. William Pringle (Grand Rapids: Baker, 1979), 2:289 (ad Matt. 16:16).

scholars, preachers, and all listeners to Christ: "Where Christ is not known, men are destitute of true wisdom, even though they have received the highest education in every branch of learning; for all *their* knowledge is useless till they truly 'know God' (John 17:3)."[23]

Delivered July 6, 2009, at St. Pierre Cathedral, Geneva, Switzerland.

23. Calvin, *Commentary on Isaiah*, 3:17 (ad 33:6).

8

John Calvin and Guarding the Gospel— Galatians 1:6–10

Steven J. Lawson

> To know what are the leading points of the gospel, is a matter of unceasing importance. When these are attacked, the gospel is destroyed.[1]
>
> —John Calvin

In every generation, spiritual leaders in the church are charged by God to fight for the purity of the gospel of Jesus Christ. Amid the many truth wars, true shepherds will find themselves in ongoing conflict with those who pervert the saving message of the gospel. John Calvin understood this. The

1. John Calvin, "Galatians," *Calvin's Commentaries* trans. William Pringle, (Grand Rapids: Baker, 2003), 21:1.31. All citations to *Calvin's Commentaries* are taken from this series.

Genevan Reformer asserted, "The church cannot stand, except false teachers be prevented from turning truth into falsehood."[2] It was absolutely necessary that he wage war against these enemies of the cross if the church was to stand strong.

Calvin asserted, "The pastor ought to have two voices, one for gathering the sheep, and another, for warding off . . . wolves."[3] A faithful teacher, he believed, must instruct the flock in the truth and protect it from vicious attacks. "To assert the truth is only one half of the office of teaching." The other half of his calling requires that "all the fallacies of the devil be also dissipated."[4] In other words, a leader must feed the congregation *and* fend off its enemies. They must build up the saints *and* beat down the false teachers. As Nehemiah labored with a trowel in one hand and a sword in the other, Calvin did the same during his twenty-five-year pastorate in Geneva, both building up God's work and beating off its enemies.

Recognizing the sovereign power of the gospel, Calvin maintained: "Christ's gospel is the scepter of His kingdom."[5] This message contains, he wrote, "the remission of sins and the grace of eternal salvation."[6] Nothing is of greater value to the church. Insisting upon the centrality of the gospel, he maintained, "Our salvation consists in the doctrine of the cross."[7] He added: "The whole accomplishment of our salvation, and all the parts of it, are contained in His death."[8] "There is no part of our salvation which may not be found in Christ."[9] Thus Calvin believed that

2. Calvin, "Zechariah-Malachi," *Calvin's Commentaries*, 15:5.380.

3. Calvin, "Titus," *Calvin's Commentaries*, 21:9.296.

4. Calvin, *Commentaries on the Book of the Prophet Jeremiah and the Lamentations*, 3:423.

5. Calvin, "Synoptic Gospels," *Calvin's Commentaries*, 1:447.

6. Calvin, "Genesis," *Calvin's Commentaries*, 1:1.178.

7. Calvin, "Matthew," *Calvin's Commentaries*, 17:3.275.

8. Calvin, "John," *Calvin's Commentaries*, 18:2.235.

9. Calvin, "Acts," *Calvin's Commentaries*, 18:2.247.

guarding the gospel *is* a battle worth fighting, one that must be defended at all costs.

Fighting the Good Fight

One of the most powerful expository series that Calvin preached in Geneva was his exposition of the book of Galatians, in which he gave unflinching defense of the gospel. From November 14, 1557, to May 8, 1558, this French-born Reformer preached forty-three sermons from this polemic epistle,[10] presenting an airtight defense of the saving gospel of Jesus Christ. Especially memorable were his two sermons on Galatians 1:6–10,[11] in which he valiantly fought for the absolute truth of the salvation that is found exclusively in Jesus Christ.

In Galatians 1:6–10, the apostle Paul waged war to protect the purity of the gospel against the mounting attacks by the false teachers known as Judaizers. Mixing law *and* grace, and mingling works *and* faith, these erroneous men claimed that salvation must be earned by human efforts, specifically by keeping the Mosaic Law. In so doing, they corrupted the very gospel of God that alone can save and sanctify. In response, the apostle Paul fired back with the Letter to the Galatians.

This was normative for Paul's *entire* ministry. He fought Jewish legalism in Galatia, incipient Gnosticism in Ephesus, strict asceticism in Colossae, fanaticism in Thessalonica, and a denial of the resurrection in Corinth. The constant refrain of his ministry came back to a simple truth: "There is only one pure gospel, as also there is only one Jesus Christ

10. T. H. L. Parker, *Calvin's Preaching* (Louisville, KY: Westminster/John Knox Press, 1992), 150–59.

11. John Calvin, *Sermons on Galatians*, trans. Kathy Childress (Edinburgh; Carlisle, PA: Banner of Truth, 1563, 1574, 1997), 34–63.

on whom it is founded."[12] The struggle for the gospel would prove to be one of the most demanding contests of his apostolic ministry.

The Same Battle Calvin Fought

Soldiers of the cross come and go, but the battle remains the same. Calvin fought the very same battles as Paul over the pristine nature of the gospel. For a quarter century, the great Reformer confronted many foes—the sacredotalists of Rome, the antinomian Libertines, the Unitarians such as Michael Servetus, and many others. Calvin noted, "In our own times, the Papists, choosing to have a divided and mangled Christ, have none, and are therefore 'removed from Christ.' They are full of superstitions, which are directly at variance with the nature of Christ."[13] And again, "at the present day, the Papists describe in the strongest terms the sacredness with which they regard the gospel, and kiss the very name with the deepest reverence, and yet, when brought to the trial, are found to persecute fiercely the pure and simple doctrine of the gospel."[14] For Calvin, guarding the gospel was no time to mince words.

Galatians 1:6–10 was emblazoned upon Calvin's soul and distinguished his ministry as a guardian of the true gospel of Jesus Christ. May it be so with Christ's servants today. May God raise up a new generation of preachers in this hour who will fight for the gospel against its many attacks. Let us now consider what Paul wrote to the Galatians in his fiery defense of the gospel. Let us remember how Calvin did the same in his day—and how we must do the same in ours.

12. Ibid., 35.
13. Calvin, "Galatians," *Calvin's Commentaries*, 21:1.29.
14. Ibid., 21:1.31.

Paul's Amazement

Paul begins this section by expressing his astonishment over the Galatians' desertion of the true gospel. The apostle writes: "I am amazed that you are so quickly deserting Him who called you by the grace of Christ for a different gospel" (v. 6).[15] He is "amazed" at them, a strong word (*thaumazo*) that means "to be astounded, bewildered, astonished, shocked, or extraordinarily disturbed." Paul is absolutely dumbfounded at what he learns of their spiritual departure. He is shocked that they are "deserting" the gospel, a military term (*metatithethe*) for a soldier abandoning his position or post. The Galatians have defected from the gospel and turned a traitor of grace.

A Deserting of God Himself

Addressing their departure, Paul states that abandoning the gospel equates to abandoning God *himself*. To depart from the gospel is to depart from "him." No one can separate God and his gospel—God *is* the gospel. An indissolvable bond exists between God and his saving truth because the gospel is the greatest revelation of the glory of God. The gospel is the ultimate theater in which the spectacle of God's glory is put on display. Every attribute of God is most vividly seen in the saving truth of Jesus Christ. All lines of theology proper intersect at the gospel message.

In the gospel, we see the *holiness* of God. The cross reveals that an infinite chasm separates holy God from sinful men. In the gospel, God makes known his *wrath*, which he poured out upon Christ, who bore the sins of his people. The cross manifests the *righteousness* of God, which is imputed to believing sinners. The gospel displays the *grace* of God that provides salvation freely apart from any human merit. The cross showcases the *immutability* of God, testifying that it is, forever, the only way

15. All quotations of Scripture in this chapter are from the NASB.

of salvation. The gospel makes clear the *eternality* of God, that Christ is the Lamb of God slain before the foundation of the world who saves forever. In the gospel, we see the *omnipotence* of God, that he possesses the right to save even the chief of sinners. In the gospel, we see the *truth* of God, that here is the genuine reality of his saving purposes. In the gospel, we see the *sovereignty* of God, that he possesses supreme authority to rescue the elect out of the grip of Satan.

In this dramatic departure, the Galatians were abandoning God who effectually "called" them "by the grace of Christ." Paul charges them with turning from the very One who had effectually summoned them to himself. Could anything be more alarming for them to hear than this? They had turned from darkness to light, from sin to righteousness, from error to truth, from idols to the living God, only now to become spiritual deserters.

Turning to a Different Gospel

In this abandonment, the Galatians were turning to "a different (*heteros*) gospel"—that is, *another* gospel of a totally different kind. This *different* gospel was entirely deficient, unable to save sinners or sanctify saints. They were embracing a counterfeit message with fraudulent forgiveness and bogus benefits. This mongrel message brought *no* salvation whatsoever. To be sure, there are only two gospels—the *saving* gospel and one that is *nonsaving*—the latter being entirely bankrupt of any saving grace. Tragically, the Galatians were leaving the true gospel for a false one. But a different gospel is *no* gospel.

In verse 7, Paul maintains that a different gospel "is really not another." In no uncertain terms, he asserts there is *not* another saving gospel. There is only *one* gospel that redeems sinners, reconciles enemies, regenerates unbelievers, imputes righteousness, gives life, converts souls, cleanses iniquity, frees captives, justifies unbelievers, sanctifies saints, and preserves forever. There is only *one* gospel that satisfies God's wrath and presents defiled sinners faultless before the throne of God. Any other message plunges the wicked into the fiery flames below. Salvation comes only *by* grace alone, *through* faith alone, *in* Christ alone.

The Exclusivity of Salvation in Christ

The entire Bible speaks with one voice on this matter. Jesus declared that salvation is entirely in *himself*: "I am the way, and the truth and the life; no one comes to the Father but through Me" (John 14:6). Equally emphatic, Peter announced, "And there is salvation in no one else; for there is no other name under heaven that has been given among men by which we must be saved" (Acts 4:12). Without any equivocation, Paul claimed, "For there is one God, and one mediator also between God and men, the man Christ Jesus" (1 Tim. 2:5). There are *not* many ways to God. There is only *one* way, and it is through the gospel of Jesus Christ. To desert *this* gospel is to forfeit the only way of salvation.

Why, we ask, is Jesus the only way of salvation? The answer is clear. No one else has been born of a virgin, lived a sinless life, and died in the place of the ungodly. No one else has suffered the full wrath of God, borne the sins of men, or given his perfect righteousness to sinners. No one else has reconciled an infinitely holy God to his filthy creatures. No one else has rescued sinners out of their bondage to sin, Satan, and self. No one else has washed away their sins, leaving them as pure as white wool. No one else has been raised from the dead for their justification and seated them in heavenly places. No one else has done *all* this—only Jesus Christ.

Paul's Adversaries

The problem the Galatians were facing originated with these corrupters of the true gospel. Paul "charges them with the additional crime of doing an injury to Christ, by endeavoring to subvert his gospel."[16] He writes: "only there are some who are disturbing you and want to distort the gospel of Christ" (v. 7). These subversive shepherds, the Judaizers, were throwing the Galatians into spiritual disorder.

Those Who Distort the Gospel

The false teachers, Paul writes, "want to distort the gospel of Christ" (v. 7). "Distort" (*metastrepho*) carries the idea of "amending or altering." This Galatian heresy categorically distorted the true gospel, modifying the very essence of its message. Calvin affirmed: "the doctrine of the false apostles was not entirely contrary, or even different, from that of Paul, but corrupted by false additions."[17] These false teachers perverted the grace of God by changing it. By tampering with the message, they neutered its saving power.

Specifically, these Judaizers added law to grace, deeming the death of Christ to be an insufficient atonement by itself to save sinners. They claimed the law of Moses, when added to the message of the cross, brought a supposed salvation. They insisted that observing holy days and circumcision redeemed sinners, that religious effort earned acceptance with God, and that, therefore, the cross by itself was of no effect. Combatting this works-righteousness was precisely Paul's point when he wrote, "If righteousness comes through the Law, then Christ died needlessly" (Gal. 2:21). Furthermore, he wrote, "For as many as are of the works of the Law are under a curse; for it is written, 'Cursed is everyone who does not abide by all things written in the book of the law, to perform them'" (Gal. 3:10).

Ravenous Wolves, Bad Trees, Rotten Fruit

Jesus warned about such deception. He explained that many religious deceivers stand next to the narrow gate, flagging unsus-

16. Ibid., 21:1.31.
17. Ibid., 21:1.34.

pecting people to turn onto the broad path: "Beware of the false prophets, who come to you in sheep's clothing, but inwardly are ravenous wolves" (Matt. 7:15). Religious impostors, like wolves in sheep's clothing, defraud many by appearing to be true shepherds, but instead teach lies. They promise heaven, but deliver hell. What makes them so deceiving is that these fraudulent men are standing immediately beside the narrow gate, flagging people onto the broad road. They are standing between the two gates, exerting all of their influence to dupe, deceive, distort, and delude.

Jesus continued, "You will know them by their fruits" (Matt. 7:20). That is, the fruit of their character and converts reveals their true identity. He stated, "Grapes are not gathered from thorn bushes nor figs from thistles, are they? So every good tree bears good fruit, but the bad tree bears bad fruit. A good tree cannot produce bad fruit, nor can a bad tree produce good fruit" (vv. 16–18). Jesus is teaching the consistency between a tree and its fruit. A bad tree will always produce bad fruit. In other words, people must look past these slick-talking religious hucksters and actually examine their fruit. Jesus said that believers must open their eyes and examine the life, converts, and message produced by these charlatans. Jesus said, "So then, you will know them by their fruits" (v. 20).

Similarly, Paul warned the elders at Ephesus that false teachers would arise from within the church. "I know that after my departure, savage wolves will come in among you, not sparing the flock; and from among your own selves men will arise, speaking perverse things, to draw away the disciples after them" (Acts 20:29–30). These pretenders are like hidden reefs and wandering stars, who shipwreck and misdirect the faith of many (Jude 12–13).

Many such false teachers were prevalent in Calvin's day, and they persist today. These pretenders acknowledge the cross, but deny that the death of Christ is sufficient to make guilty sinners right with a morally perfect God. These blind leaders of the blind claim that one earns salvation by faith *and* good works. They demand faith *and* religious rites, faith *and* rituals, faith *and* religious routines such as baptism, church membership, Mass, last rites, the treasury of merit, and indulgences. In so doing, they corrupt the gospel and condemn souls.

Paul's Anathemas

Because the Judaizers contributed to the damnation of the deceived, Paul *had* to respond swiftly and boldly. He *must* denounce these heretical foes. For the apostle, the glory of God was at stake, as was the purity of the gospel and the salvation of souls. So, the apostle writes, "But even if we, or an angel from heaven, should preach to you a gospel contrary to what we have preached to you, he is to be accursed!" (v. 8). These are the strongest words that Paul ever wrote.

Let Him Be Accursed

Verse 8 reads, "even if we . . . preach . . . a gospel contrary." "We" includes Barnabas, his traveling associate—as well as Paul himself. Not even his inner circle was exempt. Not even "an angel from heaven" was off-limits, whether Michael the archangel, or Gabriel the chief angel, or any ruling angel, guardian angel, seraphim, cherubim, or *any* elect angel. Calvin declares, "Though his argument is derived from an impossibility, it is not superfluous. This exaggerated language must have contributed greatly to strengthening the confidence in Paul's preaching. His opponents, by employing the lofty titles of men, attempted to press hard on him and on his doctrine. He meets them by the bold assertion, that even angels are unable to shake his authority."[18] If

18. Ibid., 21:1.33.

any messenger—human or angelic—should preach a different gospel, Paul says, "he is to be accursed!"

To be "accursed" (*anathema*) means to be "devoted to destruction." Paul says such a false messenger is already judged and denounced by God, ready to be consigned to the flames of hell. Put bluntly, a false teacher should go to hell *now* before he takes others with him, lest their blood be on his hands.

Seething with emotion, Paul is consumed with holy jealousy for God's honor. If any pretender should preach a message contrary to the gospel, he is to be eternally damned. If anyone denies the divine person and saving work of Jesus Christ, he is to be consigned to the lake of fire. If anyone adds human works to pure grace, he is to be sentenced to perdition. Selah.

No Room for Neutrality

Martin Luther commented: "Here Paul is breathing fire. His zeal is so fervent that he almost begins to curse the angels themselves."[19] The German Reformer left *no* room for neutrality. James Montgomery Boice adds, "How can it be otherwise? If the gospel Paul preaches is true, then both the glory of Jesus Christ and the salvation of men are at stake. If men can be saved by works, Christ has died in vain (Gal. 2:21); the cross is emptied of meaning. If men are taught a false gospel, they are being led from the one thing that can save them and are being turned to destruction (cf. Matt. 18:6)."[20] Calvin thought no differently: "Paul . . . demands such unhesitating belief of his preaching, that he pronounces a curse on all who dared to contradict it."[21] Those who corrupt the one saving gospel must be silenced and singed.

19. Martin Luther, *Luther's Works, Lectures on Galatians 1535, Chapters 1–4 vol. 26*, ed. Jaroslav Pelikan (Saint Louis: Concordia Publishing, 1963), 55.

20. James Montgomery Boice, "Galatians," in *The Expositors Bible Commentary, vol. 10*, ed. Frank E. Gaebelein (Grand Rapids: Zondervan, 1976), 429.

21. Calvin, "Galatians," *Calvin's Commentaries*, 21:1.32.

In order to drive his point home, Paul emphatically repeats what he previously said. "As we have said before, so I say again now" (v. 9). This references his prior visit in Galatia on his first missionary journey. At that time, he warned them of this very danger: they were prone to depart from the gospel. Yet despite this caution, the Galatians nevertheless fell for the deception of the Judaizers. Paul had forewarned the Galatians that men would arise after he left and pervert the gospel. Yet they *still* were duped.

A Clear and Present Danger

Lest there be any misunderstanding, Paul repeats the severity of his words: "if any man is preaching to you a gospel contrary to what you received, he is to be accursed!" (v. 9). It makes no difference if the messenger is an apostle, angel, or self-appointed teacher. If anyone preaches another gospel, he is to be *damned*. So threatening is this danger to the Galatians that Paul uses the present tense ("is preaching"), indicating an immediate crisis at that very moment. This addresses the seriousness of tampering with the truth of the gospel. Such a false teacher should be consigned to hell before he takes others with him into the pit below. The hottest place of hell is reserved for those deceiving ministers who distort the gospel and usher people to eternal destruction.

Rather than issuing his usual words of thanksgiving at this point of the epistle, Paul issues these fiery words here. Normally, he opens with "I thank my God through Jesus Christ for you all" (Rom. 1:8), "I thank my God in all my remembrance of you" (Phil. 1:3), "We give thanks to God . . . , praying always for you" (Col. 1:3), or "I thank God . . . as I constantly remember you in my prayers" (2 Tim. 1:3). But there is none of that here. At this moment, Paul is *not* thankful. Rather, he is indignant, consumed with holy zeal because the gospel has been corrupted. Instead of pastoral platitudes, he has only stinging rebuke. Because the gospel itself is at stake, he is burning with righteous indignation—and so should we.

Paul's Aim

As Paul concludes this section, he reaches the essential bottom line: "For am I now seeking the favor of men, or of God? Or am I striving to please men?" (v. 10). Who is the apostle trying to please? Is he seeking approval with God or popularity with men? Is he striving for approval in heaven or accolades on earth?

Pleasing God, Not Men

If Paul was seeking the favor of *men*, he would have certainly toned down his rhetoric. But he was not courting the approval of men. Rather, he was seeking the approbation of *God*. This confrontational language was hardly calculated to win the support of men, least of all false teachers. Men-pleasers do not hurl anathemas against those who proclaim false gospels. Simply put, Paul *must* please God. If he pleased God, it did not matter whom he displeased. And if he displeased God, it did not matter whom he pleased.

The apostle concludes: "If I were still trying to please men, I would not be a bond-servant of Christ" (v. 10). Paul admits that he cannot have it both ways. He could please men, *or* serve Christ—but *not* both. The two are mutually exclusive. Guarding the gospel is an either/or proposition, never both/and. Men-pleasers displease God, and God-pleasers displease men. To this point, one cannot be popular *and* faithful.

Serving Only One Master

Jesus had already established the same ultimatum: "No one can serve two masters; for either he will hate the one and love the other, or he will be devoted to one and despise the other. You cannot serve God and wealth" (Matt. 6:24). This is the unavoidable decision before every person. Every individual must decide where his highest allegiance lies. Will it be God, or man? Paul wrote that he speaks "not as pleasing men, but God who examines our hearts" (1 Thess. 2:4). An individual can only have *one* master.

All too tragically, many preachers are men-pleasers. Paul warned against this trap: "For the time will come when they will not endure sound doctrine; but wanting to have their ears tickled, they will accumulate for themselves teachers in accordance to their own desires, and will turn away their ears from the truth and will turn aside to myths" (2 Tim. 4:3–4). Paul knew he was sovereignly chosen, irresistibly called, and commissioned by *God*. He was graciously saved, set apart, redeemed, enlightened, instructed, and appointed by *God* himself. Why would he suddenly please *men*, knowing that he would stand before *God* at the judgment seat of Christ (2 Cor. 5:10)? Thus it is *God* whom he must please, and that necessitated preaching the pure gospel.

Guardians of God's Glory

This fight to maintain the purity of the gospel was a demanding battle that Paul fought throughout the entirety of his ministry. So did John Calvin. The Genevan Reformer was vigilant in his defense of the saving message of Jesus Christ. What Paul said of himself can be attributed to Calvin, that he "fought the good fight, . . . finished the course, . . . [and] kept the faith" (2 Tim. 4:7). True to his calling, this Genevan pastor guarded the gospel during his hour of history. A case in point follows.

Defending the Gospel Truth

After Calvin was expelled from Geneva in 1538, Cardinal Jacopo Sadoleto, Bishop of Carpentras, France, sent a letter to the officials and people of Geneva, urging them to return to the Roman Catholic Church. Despite having removed Calvin, the city fathers nevertheless looked to him for help. He responded by writing his "Reply to Sadoleto," in which he affirmed the Protestant faith and denounced the errors of Rome. At the heart of controversy was the nature of the gospel.

Calvin wrote to Sadoleto: "It is not very sound theology to confine a man's thoughts so much to himself, and not to set before him as the prime motive of his existence zeal to show forth the glory of God. We are born, first of all, for God and not for ourselves. As all things flowed from him and subsist in him, as Paul says (Rom. 11:36), they ought to be related to him."[22] This Magisterial Reformer saw the attack on the gospel for what it is—an assault on the glory of God. Calvin added: "You . . . touch upon justification by faith, the first and keenest subject of controversy between us . . . Wherever the knowledge of it is taken away, the glory of Christ is extinguished, religion abolished, the Church destroyed, and the hope of salvation utterly overthrown."[23] *This* was a hill worth dying on.

The Chief Issue in Everything

In its denial of justification by faith *alone*, Calvin charged Rome with displacing the glory of God for that of man. He viewed every attack on justification by faith alone—whether it be by priestly abuses, transubstantiation, prayers to saints, and papal authority—as being not merely doctrinal deviations, serious as that is. Rather, he saw this as a frontal assault on the primacy, majesty, and supremacy of God's own perfect glory. Calvin saw the chief issue in *every* matter, but especially in the gospel, as being the magnification of the glory of God.

22. John C. Olin, ed., *A Reformation Debate: John Calvin and Jacopo Sadoleto* (Grand Rapids: Baker Books, 1966), 58.

23. Ibid., 66.

Where are such valiant men as John Calvin today? Where are those servants of God who will preach the pure gospel with boundless energy? Where are those defenders of the faith who will defend it in the face of much opposition? Where are such soldiers of the cross?

May God grant a new generation of guardians of the gospel, who are zealous to uphold the truth of God's saving message. May the Lord give this generation pure vessels who preach a *pure* gospel.

Delivered July 7, 2009, at St. Pierre Cathedral, Geneva, Switzerland.

9

Three Great Intercessions—Romans 8:26–34

Iain D. Campbell

Likewise the Spirit helps us in our weakness. For we do not know what to pray for as we ought, but the Spirit himself intercedes for us with groanings too deep for words. And he who searches hearts knows what is the mind of the Spirit, because the Spirit intercedes for the saints according to the will of God. And we know that for those who love God all things work together for good, for those who are called according to his purpose. For those whom he foreknew he also predestined to be conformed to the image of his Son, in order that he might be the firstborn among many brothers. And those whom he predestined he also called, and those whom he called he also justified, and those whom he justified he also glorified.

What then shall we say to these things? If God is for us, who can be against us? He who did not spare his own Son but

> gave him up for us all, how will he not also with him graciously give us all things? Who shall bring any charge against God's elect? It is God who justifies. Who is to condemn? Christ Jesus is the one who died—more than that, who was raised—who is at the right hand of God, who indeed is interceding for us. (Rom. 8:26–34)

Although several attempts have been made to identify a central and overarching theme to Calvin's writings, it is surely beyond dispute that at the center of all his activity, both theological and practical, was the person and work of Jesus Christ. Gaspar Olevian summed up the *Institutes* in the following line:

> Man, being first created upright, but afterwards being not partially but totally ruined, finds his entire salvation out of himself in Christ.[1]

The centrality of Christ in the *Institutes* sustains its twofold polemic against salvation through works of our own on the one hand, and salvation through the intercession of saints and of other created beings on the other:[2] "Condemned, dead and lost in ourselves," Calvin writes, "we must in [Christ] seek righteousness, deliverance, life and salvation" (2.16.1). All the themes that Calvin addresses are like streams from this central fountain. If man is to be saved at all, "he must go beyond himself" (3.20.1) and find in Christ the fullness of the salvation that alone can make him free.

But if these are the themes that are central to the life and work of the one whose birth we commemorate in these days, it was not because of a desire to be polemical, but rather because of a desire

1. Olevian's "Epitome of the Institutes," quoted in John Calvin, *Calvin's Institutes* (Florida: Macdonald Publishing Company, n.d.), 6.

2. See, for example, Calvin's comments on 1 John 2:1, where he says that since Christ continually intercedes for us, we ought to beware lest we transfer this honor to any other, in John Calvin, *Commentaries on the Catholic Epistles* (Grand Rapids: Baker, 2009), 172.

to be *biblical* that this is so. The centrality of Christ in Calvin is merely a reflection of the centrality of that theme in Scripture. Calvin's conversion, in the words of B. B. Warfield, did not mean that he ceased to be a man of letters any more than he ceased to be a man, but "all his talents and acquisitions were henceforth dedicated purely to the service of God and His gospel."[3]

It was as a student of the gospel of Christ that Calvin became "the theologian of the Holy Spirit," as Warfield describes him.[4] Calvin discovered from his New Testament that it is the work of the Holy Spirit to magnify Christ in the gospel, objectively, and in the heart of the believer, subjectively. These are the themes that occupy the apostle Paul constantly and not least in Romans chapter 8. Opening with the assertion of "no condemnation in Christ," it climaxes with the affirmation of "no separation from Christ." God did for us what we could not do for ourselves, and he keeps us when we are unable to keep ourselves.

These Pauline emphases draw our attention to what we might call the three great intercessions of Romans 8. The word "intercession" is used to translate two related Greek words in verses 26 ("the Spirit himself intercedes") and 34 ("Christ Jesus is the one who . . . is at the right hand of God, who indeed is interceding"). But there is another emphasis on our own intercession, as we shall see.

Indeed, we want to look at the outworking of this great salvation that is ours in Christ in three directions.

Intercession for Us

First, we want to emphasize *the intercession that is going on within the veil*. That is the climax of Paul's argument, drawn

3. B. B. Warfield, "The Man and His Work," in *The Works of Benjamin B. Warfield* (Grand Rapids: Baker, 2003), 3:4.

4. Ibid., 3:21.

from the great indicatives of salvation. In Christ we have been predestined, called, justified, and glorified. Our salvation is secure while we are in Christ. While we are united to him, God is for us, and none can be against us. Lest we should think that this is all very well but that there remains the possibility of our falling out of Christ, Paul strenuously closes the door on this reasoning. No one can raise a valid charge against God's elect people. No one can condemn. No one can separate us from Christ.

The basis of this confidence is what Christ has done and continues to do for his people. "Christ Jesus is the one who died—more than that, who was raised—who is at the right hand of God, who indeed is interceding for us" (Rom. 8:34). Our confidence of nonseparation is grounded not merely in what Christ accomplished on earth but in what he continues to achieve for us in heaven. He died, and now he lives to make intercession.

These twin actions of Christ—death on the one hand and intercession on the other—are the concomitant actions of Christ as our great high priest. Intercession, says Calvin, commenting on Hebrews 7:25, "teaches us . . . that he is performing his office as a priest; for it belongs to a priest to intercede for the people."

The great Scottish Calvinist Hugh Martin (1822–85) explored the relationship between atonement and intercession in his classic work, *The Atonement*. "Christ," he says, "entered into heaven as an intercessor."[5]

> The Atonement is real—real sacrifice and offering and not mere passive endurance, because it is in its very nature an active and infallible intercession; while on the other hand, the intercession is real intercession—judicial, representative, and priestly intercession, and not a mere exercise of influence, because it is essentially an atonement or substitutionary oblation, once

5. H. Martin, *The Atonement in Its Relations to the Covenant, the Priesthood, the Intercession of Our Lord* (Edinburgh: Lyon and Gemmell, 1877), 113.

> perfected on Calvary, now perpetually presented and undergoing perpetual acceptance in Heaven.[6]

Martin enlarges this thought with reference to the tabernacle worship of the Old Testament, with its two altars, one of brass in the outer courtyard, and one of gold within the veil:

> The two altars of sacrifice and of incense were combined and correlative instruments of official action to the priest in the one complete office of his priesthood; and they constituted component and indispensable factors of one complete act of sacrificial worship. The same functionary, or office-bearer, transacted at both: he transacted for the self-same person or persons; the blood of the self-same sacrifice that he had slain and offered on the one altar, he sprinkled or put upon the horns of the other. To dislocate or derange this co-ordination would be to negative his official action in its intrinsic import, to annihilate the gracious results of his priestly intervention, and indeed to divert his office utterly. His action at the altar of Atonement was pre-requisite to his approach to the altar of Incense; and the successful achievement which signalized his action at the latter revealed beyond the possibility of doubt the nature and efficacy of the services which he had accomplished at the former; while only in virtue of the two, in their combination and synthesis, was Aaron's priesthood a real priesthood at all.[7]

Calvin draws on the same Old Testament ritual regarding the action of the priest: "if the priest reconciled God to the whole people or to himself," he says, "in order that the intercession might be more efficacious, he entered the sanctuary to pour out blood on the opposite side of the veil."[8]

6. Ibid., 115.
7. Ibid., 116–17.
8. Calvin on Leviticus 6:30, in John Calvin, *Commentaries on the Four Last Books of Moses Arranged in a Harmony* (Grand Rapids: Baker, 2009), 2:367.

The salvation of God's people is grounded, therefore, in the successful priesthood of Jesus Christ. He offered himself in a public arena, before the eyes of a watching world, as a sacrifice once to bear away our sins forever. When he said, "It is finished" (John 19:30), Jesus did not mean that he had performed the final action necessary for the salvation of his people. His dying at Calvary was not the end; it was merely the end of the beginning. In his self-offering, Jesus had completed the preliminary action necessary for the secondary action to begin: to enter heaven itself, and to officiate as our priest at the golden altar of incense. There, hidden from the eyes of the world, and ever present before the eyes of God, Jesus makes continual intercession for us.

He does so by his very presence in glory as our mediator. He has not entered the Holy Place without blood but with his own blood, thus sustaining his eternal priesthood, as Calvin puts it in his comments on Hebrews 9:25, on the unfailing virtue of his sacrifice on earth. The ascension is the ultimate commentary on the completion of his work on earth. Now he enters heaven as he had never occupied it before: in human nature, the God-man.

But we must not think of his intercession merely in terms of bare presence. He is our advocate. As Calvin points out, "Christ was indeed our advocate when he was on earth, but it was a further concession made to our infirmity that he ascended into heaven to undertake there the office of an advocate."[9]

As an advocate, Christ presents a case. And the case is, first, that his work was completed on behalf of his people; and, second, that it has been specifically applied to each one of them: "he appears before God for this end, that he may exercise towards us the power and efficacy of his sacrifice . . . The intercession of Christ

9. Commentary on Hebrews 9:24, in John Calvin, *Commentaries on the Epistle of Paul the Apostle to the Hebrews* (Grand Rapids: Baker, 2009), 216.

is a continual application of his death for our salvation."[10] We are sustained in our personal faith by the continued application of that death. Our sacrifices could only profane heaven's sanctuary, but in Christ we have One who offers a perfect sacrifice on our behalf: "hence it appears how needful for us is the intercession of Christ; for, if his perfect cleanness did not wash away our impurity, no oblation could proceed from us except what would be foul and unsavory."[11]

All our hope and confidence, therefore, are grounded in what Jesus is and has done and in what he continues to be and do for us in heaven itself. We are called today to look to the cross, not as something that must be continuously offered but as something that is continually presented before heaven's throne as the basis of our salvation. We look up to where Jesus is, to the place from which we expect him to return.

Intercession by Us

Second, we want to emphasize *the intercession that is going on within the church*. There is an unmistakable emphasis in Romans 8 not only on Christ's interceding before the Father but on our crying to him. We have received the Spirit of Christ, which for us is not a Spirit of bondage but a Spirit of adoption, and its evidence is that we cry to our Father in heaven. For this reason, Calvin makes prayer a chief evidence of piety: "words fail," he says, "to explain how necessary prayer is."[12] It is "the chief exercise of faith and hope; and it is in this way that we obtain from God every blessing."[13]

10. Commentary on 1 John 2:1, in Calvin, *Commentaries on the Catholic Epistles*, 171.

11. Commentary on Leviticus 21:16ff., in Calvin, *Commentaries on the Four Last Books of Moses*, 2:240.

12. *Institutes*, 3.20.1.

13. Commentary on Ephesians 6:18, in John Calvin, *Commentaries on the Epistles of Paul to the Galatians and Ephesians* (Grand Rapids: Baker, 2009), 340.

Even if it is true that "we do not know what to pray for as we ought" (Rom. 8:26), we know that we ought to pray. Indeed, we are commanded in 1 Timothy 2:1 to make "supplications, prayers, intercessions, and thanksgivings" for all people. While Calvin confesses that he does not know the precise nuances of Paul's use of these different words, he argues that Paul heaps them together "in order to recommend more warmly, and urge more strongly, earnest and constant prayer. We know how sluggish we are in this religious duty; and therefore we need not wonder if, for the purpose of arousing us to it, the Holy Spirit, by the mouth of Paul, employs various excitements."[14]

Christians are people who pray. Not to put too fine a point on it, they are people who *intercede*. "Christ does not by his intercession hinder us from pleading for one another in the church."[15] Indeed, there is a deep and intimate connection between our intercession and Christ's. Were he not in heaven interceding for us, Calvin argues in his great sermon on the ascension of Christ, our prayers for one another would be in vain:

> When we presume to pray to God we shall be rejected unless Jesus Christ is there in our name. Since he is there, he is our intercessor and presents our prayers there and causes us to be answered, as if we had the privilege of saying what we have to do and to pour out our heart before God.[16]

This is why, says Calvin, we pray in Christ's name. God will be satisfied with us if we have this single advocate, "who so fre-

14. Commentary on 1 Timothy 2:1, in John Calvin, *Commentaries on the Epistles to Timothy, Titus and Philemon* (Grand Rapids: Baker, 2009), 50.

15. *Institutes*, 3.20.19.

16. Sermon 15: "Fourth Sermon on the Ascension of Christ, Sermons on the Deity of Christ," accessed via Ages software, "Sermons of John Calvin," John Calvin, *The Deity of Christ and Other Sermons*, trans. Leroy Nixon (Audubon, NJ: Old Paths Publications, 1997), 236–73.

quently and so kindly offers to us his labours on our behalf."[17] Apart from this we have no access to God: "God can listen to no prayers without the intercession of Christ";[18] "there is no other way of praying aright, but by approaching God with reliance on the Mediator."[19]

But through that advocacy, what limitless access we have! The treasures of the covenant have been pointed out to us in the gospel, and we can go to dig them up.[20] In Christ, God has come to us in the great gospel realities of a complete atonement, an exalted priest, and a perpetual intercession; in Christ we can come to God, boldly and without reserve. There is no doubt as to the openness of that access, "for when Christ receives us under his protection and patronage, he covers with his goodness the majesty of God, which would otherwise be terrible to us, so that nothing appears there but grace and paternal favor."[21] To put it otherwise, it is the intercessory work of Christ alone that can "change the throne of dreadful glory into the throne of grace."[22]

So we pray in confidence, with thankfulness; we pour out our hearts, delighting in God's gifts. Amid all the events of our lives and the circumstances of our providence, we are invited to deal with God as suppliants, keeping God's glory before our eyes before we descend to our own affairs and pray for daily bread, for forgiveness of our sins, and for protection from evil. We persevere in our intercession, learning through the discipline of

17. Commentary on John 16:24, in John Calvin, *Commentary on the Gospel according to John* (Grand Rapids: Baker, 2009), 154.

18. Commentary on Exodus 29:38–46, in Calvin, *Commentaries on the Four Last Books of Moses*, 2:295.

19. Commentary on the Lord's Prayer, in John Calvin, *Commentary on a Harmony of the Evangelists, Matthew, Mark and Luke* (Grand Rapids: Baker, 2009), 317–18.

20. *Institutes*, 3.20.2.

21. Commentary on Hebrews 4:16, in Calvin, *Commentaries on Hebrews*, 111.

22. *Institutes*, 3.20.17.

prayer the difference between what we want and what we need. Our encouragement to come to our Father is that he knows what we need before we ask, but often it is through being denied what we want that we discover what we need. "How prone are we to fret and to murmur," says Calvin, "when it has not pleased God immediately to grant us our requests! Our discontent may not be openly expressed, but it is inwardly felt when we are left in this manner to depend upon his naked promises."[23] In this way, however, prayer becomes a means of grace to us. Through petitioning the king, we obtain much more than we could ever ask or even think.

So we are called today to look out on a church and on a world that need us to intercede; we are called to come to the throne of the King as suppliants and to our Father as his children, sanctifying ourselves in prayer for the sake of others, as Christ sanctified himself for our sakes. By prayer we express our confidence in the sufficiency of God's grace. As Calvin puts it, commenting on the prayers of the Philippian believers for himself and for one another, "he who depends for help on the prayers of the saints, relies on the promise of God."[24] Prayer is only a way by which we claim these promises for ourselves and for those on whose behalf we plead before God.

Perhaps we need to remember this in these days of financial insecurity and political instability in which we live. It is to God we must come, interceding for our nations, lest the charge be laid to us as it was in Ezekiel's day, when God said: "I sought for a man among them who should build up the wall and stand in the breach before me for the land, that I should not destroy it, but I found none" (Ezek. 22:30). Those who have trusted to the work

23. Commentary on Psalm 60:4, in John Calvin, *Commentary on the Book of Psalms* (Grand Rapids: Baker, 2009), 350.

24. Commentary on Philippians 1:19, in John Calvin, *Commentaries on the Epistles of Paul the Apostle to the Philippians, Colossians and Thessalonians* (Grand Rapids: Baker, 2009), 40.

of Christ as their priest in heaven are of the best use to earth, because they have learned to intercede.

This is the point that the great Puritan Richard Sibbes makes in his sermon on "The Spiritual Favourite at the Throne of Grace." He says that:

> Any good Christian may be a good statesman in one good sense. What is that? A good Christian hath credit in heaven, and he hath a spirit of prayer, and his prayer can set God on work; and God can set the king on work; and he can set his subjects on work. Now, he that can prevail with God to prevail with the gods upon earth here, surely such a man is a profitable man in the state. And you know, God can alter all matters, and mould all things: it is but a word of his mouth. And what God can do, prayer can do; for prayer binds God, because it is the prayer of faith; and faith, as it were, overcomes God. Now prayer is the flame of faith, the vent of faith; and faith is a victorious, triumphant grace with God himself. If it be any, it is Christians that can prevail with God for a blessing upon a state. Then certainly there is no good Christian but is of excellent service in the state.[25]

For the same reason, we might say, there is no good Christian but that is of excellent service in the church as well. It is no accident to find Paul in this great Epistle to the Romans, in which he emphasizes the importance of intercession, appealing to his brothers in Rome "to strive together with me in your prayers to God on my behalf" (Rom. 15:30). Listen to Calvin's comment on these words:

> Since then it is so great a favour from God to be helped by the prayers of the faithful, that even Paul, a most choice instrument of God, did not think it right to neglect this privilege, how

25. "The Spiritual Favourite at the Throne of Grace," in *The Works of Richard Sibbes* (Edinburgh: James Nichol, 1863), 6:106–7.

> great must be our stupidity, if we, who are abject and worthless creatures, disregard it?[26]

By intercession we are the helpers of each other. "If our strength is derived from prayer to God," says Calvin, "we can in no better way confirm our brethren, than by praying to God for them."[27] We are intercessors of one another, *striving* together for each other, as Paul puts it. This, says Calvin, shows "how the godly ought to pray for their brethren . . . They are to assume their person, as though they were placed in the same difficulties."[28]

Yet even when all of this is said, we face another problem. We may not be so stupid (to use Calvin's terminology) as to disregard prayer, but we are ignorant as to what the proper content of that intercession ought to be. We do not know what to pray for as we ought. For this reason we want to note the third great intercession of the chapter.

Intercession in Us

Third, we want to emphasize *the intercession that is going on within our hearts*. It is Paul's assertion that "the Spirit helps us in our weakness. For we do not know what to pray for as we ought, but the Spirit himself intercedes for us with groanings too deep for words" (Rom. 8:26). Our weakness is manifest nowhere as it is here. We can be so overburdened by the cares and concerns of daily Christian living that we are ready to fall under the cross. But, says Calvin, "we are taught by the same Spirit how to pray, and what to ask in our prayers. And appropriately has he annexed prayers to the anxious desires of the faithful; for God does not afflict them with miseries, that they may inwardly feed on hid-

26. Commentary on Romans 15:30, in John Calvin, *Commentaries on the Epistle of Paul the Apostle to the Romans* (Grand Rapids: Baker, 2009), 539.
27. Ibid., 540.
28. Ibid., 539–40.

den grief, but that they may disburden themselves by prayer, and thus exercise their faith."[29]

The life of prayer is one of the ways God encourages us as we "suffer with him" (Rom. 8:17) in this world. The burdens we carry are heavy ones. But when Paul says that the Holy Spirit "helps" our infirmities, he uses a striking idea. As Calvin rightly points out, the Greek word for "helps us" is strong—it means that "the Spirit takes on himself a part of the burden . . . He not only helps and succours us, but lifts us up, as though he went under the burden with us."[30]

Perhaps we have too long overlooked the intimate, personal, helping nature of the Holy Spirit of God in the lives of his people. There is a level of help here that only God can give, and only he is qualified to give it. One of my routine responsibilities as a pastor is to write references for people, usually women, who apply to work as home-care health workers or residential-home workers. Often there is a question about the suitability of the applicant to deliver "personal and intimate care"—the kind of care that only a particular kind of person could give, the kind of care that is sensitive to personal needs, that understands personal feelings, and that can be given discreetly, confidently, and with such thoroughness that no one else even knows it has been provided.

That is the kind of help the people of God have in their burdens, when they are so weighed down that prayer itself is a difficulty. The supreme caregiver of our souls steps in to enable us to raise our cry heavenward, toward the throne of God. With personal groans and sighs, our prayers ascend like the incense from the altar toward God, and he is only receiving back from us what he gave in the first place.

That means that our prayers are given by God before they are heard by God! That, says Calvin, is the cardinal difference

29. Commentary on Romans 8:26, in ibid., 312.
30. Ibid., 311.

between the prayers of the ungodly and the prayers of believers: "The unbelieving," he says, "do indeed blab out their prayers, but they only trifle with God; for there is in them nothing sincere, or serious, or rightly formed." How different is the case with the believer.

> The Spirit is said to *intercede,* not because he really humbles himself to pray or to groan, but because he stirs up in our hearts those desires which we ought to entertain; and he also affects our hearts in such a way that these desires by their fervency penetrate into heaven itself. And Paul has thus spoken, that he might more significantly ascribe the whole to the grace of the Spirit. We are indeed bidden to knock; but no one can of himself premeditate even one syllable, except God by the secret impulse of his Spirit knocks at our door, and thus opens for himself our hearts.[31]

"The children of God have two divine intercessors," says that other eminent Scottish Calvinist, Professor John Murray (1898–1975). "Christ is their intercessor in the court of heaven. The Holy Spirit is their intercessor in the theatre of their own hearts. Too seldom has the intercessory activity of the Holy Spirit been taken into account. The glory of Christ's intercession should not be allowed to place the Spirit's intercession in eclipse."[32]

Nor, I suggest, should we overlook the coordination between these intercessions. As Christ intercedes for me in heaven, I intercede on earth, and the Holy Spirit intercedes in my heart. And the Holy Spirit intercedes only in the hearts of those for whom Christ intercedes in glory. Limited intercession is coordinate with limited atonement. The hearts of unbelievers are like the ruins of the Acropolis—striking monuments to the religion of a lost age;

31. Ibid., 313.

32. John Murray, *The Epistle to the Romans,* NICNT (Grand Rapids: Eerdmans, 1959), 311–12.

but the hearts of believers are like the Holy Place in Jerusalem's temple, always infused with the fragrance of the divine presence, and bringing heaven to earth, fulfilling the promise of the Savior in respect of the Father and the Son: "we will come to him and make our home with him" (John 14:23).

The Spirit's intercession is with groanings; these are "the media"—to use Professor Murray's language—"of the Holy Spirit's intercession." These groanings ascend to heaven with an incoherent eloquence that is lost on us but is perfectly attuned to the mind of our heavenly Father. More is said in these inarticulate groanings that rise from earth to heaven than in the polished liturgies of formal, spiritless religion. In utter dependence on the triune God, this threefold intercession goes on continually: prayers authored by the Spirit, uttered by the believer, and carried by the Savior into the presence of the Father.

Perhaps when we realize this, we get close to understanding what Paul meant when he said that we have been called by the Father into the fellowship of the Son (1 Cor. 1:9). We are caught up in the dialogues of heaven, which now extend to earth. Now we are face to face with God, as the Son, who is God, was eternally face to face with God. We are in the heavenlies. Little wonder that Octavius Winslow can talk about "the inconceivable preciousness of a throne of grace."

> To have a God to go to, who knows the mind of the Spirit, a God who can interpret the groan and read the language of desire; to have promise upon promise inviting the soul to draw near—how precious this is . . . Let this encourage you, when you feel you cannot pray by reason of the weakness of the flesh, or the depth of your feeling; if the Spirit is interceding in you, your heavenly Father knows the mind of the Spirit, and not a sigh or a groan can escape His notice.[33]

33. O. Winslow, *The Work of the Holy Spirit* (Edinburgh: Banner of Truth, 1961), 188–89.

Here, then, are the three great intercessions of Romans 8—an intercession going on *for us*, in heaven; an intercession going on *by us*, on earth; and an intercession going on *in us*, by the Holy Spirit. All of this fills out what it means for us to cry "Abba," and to direct our prayers to "our Father, who is in heaven."

Calvin's written prayers are sometimes the most weighty and glorious elements of his published work. It seems fitting to conclude with one, and to make it our own:

> Grant, Almighty God, that since thy Son has been made known to us, through whom is brought to us the perfection of all blessings and of true and real glory,—O grant, that we may continue settled in him, and never turn here and there, nor fluctuate in any way, but be so satisfied with his kingship and priesthood, as to deliver up ourselves wholly to his care and protection, and never doubt but that we are so sanctified by his grace as to be now acceptable to thee, and that relying on him as our Mediator, we may offer ourselves as a sacrifice to thee with full confidence of heart, and thus strive to glorify thee through the whole course of our life, that we may at length be made partakers of that celestial glory which has been obtained for us by the blood of thy only-begotten Son.—Amen.[34]

Delivered July 7, 2009, at St. Pierre Cathedral, Geneva, Switzerland.

34. Commentary on Zechariah 6, in John Calvin, *Commentaries on the Twelve Minor Prophets. Volume Fifth: Zechariah and Malachi* (Grand Rapids: Baker, 2009), 164.

10

The Christian Life—Philippians 2:12–13

J. Ligon Duncan

In June of 1917, on the eve of the American entrance into the Great War (World War I), when General John J. "Black Jack" Pershing (head of the American Expeditionary Force) arrived at Gilbert du Motier, the tomb of the legendary Marquis de Lafayette (French commander and ally of the Patriot Cause in the American War of Independence), he is said to have uttered, "Lafayette, we are here."[1] These words evoked a man remembered, a debt owed, and a readiness to repay that debt. The memory and debt owed was the crucial contribution of Lafayette to American freedom. The words mean that Pershing, on behalf of a grateful United States, had not forgotten Lafayette's (and France's) critical aid in a time of need, and reckoned it as a national obligation. And

1. In fact, the words belong to Pershing's aide, Colonel Charles E. Stanton, but they were widely attributed to Pershing and have been reckoned so ever since.

more, that America was ready for her own sons to shed blood to aid in the cause of French freedom.

We are gathered here, in St. Pierre Church, in Geneva, Switzerland, in July of 2009, five hundred years after the birth of another Frenchman—one who is generally reckoned the greatest Protestant Reformer of the sixteenth century and one of three greatest Christian theologians in history, one to whom the whole Reformed and Protestant world is indebted. We are here to remember, to acknowledge a debt owed, and to indicate a desire to repay it. So on behalf of grateful, Bible-believing, Christ-exalting, gospel-loving Christians from the Americas, Africa, Asia, Australia, and Europe, I say, "Jean Cauvin, *nous sommes ici*."

It is almost certain that John Calvin would be horrified by our celebration of the anniversary of his birth, just as he would have been mortified at the sight of his looming statue on the Reformation Wall. After all, this was a man who insisted on being buried in an unmarked grave (and we have never quite figured out exactly where), because the whole thrust of his life and ministry was to give all praise and glory to God. "We are not our own, we are God's," he would say. "Let us therefore live for him and die for him and take none of the honor or credit for ourselves but give all to him." Hence, there is no better way we could adorn his memory than to live lives consumed with a passion for God's glory and animated by gratitude for his sovereign, saving love.

Calvin on the Christian Life

That makes the subject of this message one of particular importance. In Philippians 2, Paul's concern is to articulate a key truth about the living of the Christian life, about growth in grace. Modern theologians often refer to this subject as "sanctification." Calvin sometimes called it "regeneration," meaning not (as we often do) simply the Spirit's initial renovation of us in our conversion but the Spirit's transformation of us over the whole course of life, so that we grow in grace and become conformed to the image of God's own Son, Jesus Christ.

This transformation was a particular concern of Calvin's. He valiantly contended for the truth of justification by grace alone through faith alone in Christ alone. But he also emphasized the importance of the progressive, moral life renovation that always and invariably accompanies our free justification. I think I can very safely say that the only tribute to his memory that he would have desired would have been that of the congregations of Christians in his home city, and those who embrace his exposition of the Scripture around the world, living lives, individually and corporately, that bear witness to the transforming work of the Spirit, or, to use Paul's language in Philippians, walking "in a manner worthy of the gospel." He would have desired no flowing banners strung from the massive classical columns of the St. Pierre facade, no billboards advertising exhibits of a day in his life, no museums, no conferences, no plaques, no monuments of stone, just Christians living out the gospel, personally and congregationally, glorifying God in life and doctrine.

Timely and Problematic

Calvin's emphasis on "progressive sanctification," or the whole-life, lifelong regeneration of the Christian, is timely because it is so problematic in our own day. Three reasons come immediately to mind. As urgent as is the need for the church to live consistently with its profession and experience of the gospel, (1) some view sanctification as legalism; (2) some misunderstand and misconstrue the nature of sanctification; and (3) some have given up on sanctification.

Is Sanctification Legalism?

First, many well-meaning Christians in our time equate an emphasis on sanctification, consecration, holiness, and piety with legalism. Very often those who have come from backgrounds that are moralistic and legalistic, and have for the first time come to appreciate the freedom of grace and justification by an alien righteousness, become suspicious of any emphasis on the imperatives of the Christian life. "Free from the law, O happy condition, I can do as I please, now that I have remission" becomes their attitude, and woe to the preacher who calls them to self-denial (a pervasive aspect of Calvin's thought), to strive for holiness, to be not conformed to this world but transformed.

In fact, very often ministers who call upon the flock to embrace any of the hundreds of New Testament directives and commands relating to the Christian life are accused of "not understanding grace" or of "not understanding the gospel." Meanwhile, some prominent Protestant preachers teach that now being justified, "if we are not free to sin, then we are not really free." Calvin would have called this view "libertinism" ("I can do whatever I want now that I'm justified").

It should be needless to say that this kind of teaching is unbiblical and unhelpful. Calvin's exposition of the Christian life offers a needful corrective.

Is Sanctification Self-Help, and Is Perfection Possible?

Second, the biblical doctrine of the Christian life is often misunderstood and misconstrued, in different directions. On the one hand, there are those who view sanctification as fundamentally our work. God forgives us, but now we are on our own. Justification is God's work, but sanctification is ours, and we need to just pull ourselves up by our own bootstraps and get on with it. In other words, they relate the gospel to justification, but fail to relate it to sanctification. This error fails to understand that both justification and sanctification are of God's grace. Justification is a one-time act of God's grace, and sanctification is an ongoing work of God's grace. Yes, we are called to obey, to do, and to "stretch every nerve and press with vigor on," but all in humble reliance upon God's grace.

On the other hand, there are those who teach that Christians can, and should, attain complete victory over sin in this life. They use different terms to express this thought: we ought to attain to "the higher life," "perfect love," or "entire sanctification." The idea is that we get to a point in this life that the fight with sin within is over and victory is won. This is a theological error called perfectionism (the great Princeton theologian B. B. Warfield wrote a massive two-volume historical, exegetical, and theological critique of it!).

When I was a new professor at Reformed Theological Seminary, a godly young couple, headed for the mission field, came to my office one day. I had said something in class that had encouraged them about the Christian life and their vocation, but they were deeply troubled by what they had been taught in Bible college, so they wanted to hear more from me on the subject, and wanted to ask questions about teaching they had received to the contrary. It seems that the president of their institution had said in chapel their last semester that he had "not sinned in several years," and that they, too, should strive to experience this victorious life. This had confused and discouraged them—even made them question their calling to and suitability for missions work. Although they were truly godly and devoted (indeed, I saw evidences of Christian maturity and self-sacrifice in them beyond my own), they knew that they were still sinners. They knew that they were not perfect, not even close. They felt the dread power of sin in their lives and questioned their qualification for ministry. They had fallen prey to a false teaching about the Christian life, and it was my joy to show them what the Bible actually says.

The fight with sin within, the warfare that we experience against the flesh, is not a sign of death but a sign of life! It is an evidence that the Spirit is at work in us, waging battle against besetting sin. That fight ought to encourage us. It is the absence of a fight with sin within that ought to scare us.

Here again, over against both mistaken directions, self-help ("God has forgiven my sins, the rest is up to me") and perfectionism ("sinlessness is achievable in this life"), Calvin's biblical exposition offers a better way.

Is Sanctification Futile?

Third, many dear folk, overwhelmed by besetting sin and the ongoing fight with the world, flesh, and devil, begin to question the reality of their experience of grace or to doubt the very possibility of change, growth, and progress in the Christian life.

Maybe that is where some of you are. You have been a Christian for a long time. You have served the Lord in the home and in the church and in your vocation. Those who know you best see every evidence of God's grace at work in you, but there are areas in your life that still haunt you. There are abiding sins that harass you. You have warred against them; you have pleaded against them; you have wanted to kill them (or to die yourself), but still they remain as an ever-present, deeply painful thorn in the flesh.

You are tired of them. So tired, you do not know how to go on in the fight, and you are beginning to wonder if change is really possible, or if it is hopeless. Some are counseling you to come to terms with this tension by "giving up on trying to be good," while others are telling you that you have never really believed in the first place, if you are having this kind of struggle. What are you to think? What are you to do?

Well, once again, Calvin is waiting for you, to point you to the Scriptures, to give you encouragement and hope by the robust exposition of the Word of God. Let us go with him to Philippians and scan the middle section of that great letter, from Philippians 1:27–2:18.

Philippians and the Christian Life

Paul's letter to the Philippians has as its central concern a joyful exposition of the Christian life. Indeed, the first major exhortation in the letter is "conduct yourselves in a manner worthy of the gospel of Christ" (Phil. 1:27 NASB). Paul is urging us to *live a life that fits the gospel.* This is, in fact, the theme of the entire middle section of Philippians (1:27–2:18). It is a call to holy conduct, to the pursuit of godliness.

Once again, in Philippians 2:5 Paul presses, "Have this mind among yourselves, which is yours in Christ Jesus." This is a call to emulate, with the help of God's Spirit and by God's grace, Jesus' humility, obedience, and servanthood. Paul is fostering humility and service in the congregation. He is asking us to manifest, congregationally, humble service of one another, in obedience to and emulation of the example of Christ. He wants to see humble, willing, tangible, self-displacing, serving, gospel love to others, grace-wrought service in which the interests of the other take priority over our own interests, and in which our service is rendered with humility.

A Crucial Text on the Christian Life

The passage we are going to concentrate on is Philippians 2:12–13 (esp. 12b–13). It is *one of the most important passages in all of the Bible about "sanctification,"* which means growing in Christian maturity, becoming more like Christ, growing in godliness. There, Paul says:

> Therefore, my beloved,
> as you have always obeyed,
> so now, not only as in my presence but much more in my absence,
> *work out your own salvation with fear and trembling,*
> *for it is God who works in you, both to will and to work for his good pleasure.*

Paul is telling us here that it is only a Spirit-wrought realization of our utter need for God's grace in living the Christian life, and of

God's infinite supply of grace for the living of the Christian life, that can cultivate humility (by crushing pride) in us, challenge spiritual laziness within us, comfort the discouraged among us, and move us to gospel-enabled Christian growth and life. As Calvin says, it is only in realizing the truth that it is "God who works in us" that "is the true artillery for destroying all haughtiness; this is the sword for killing all pride, when we hear that we are utterly nothing, and can do nothing, except through the grace of God alone. I mean supernatural grace, which comes forth from the Spirit of regeneration."[2]

The reason that this is so crucial is because growth in grace is always accompanied by a temptation to pride. When we experience growth in grace and victory over particular sins, we are sometimes tempted to think that such victory is, fundamentally, the result of our efforts, and we are tempted to impatience toward those still struggling with sins that we have already mastered. This truth that it is God who is at work in us reminds us that there is no aspect of our sanctification for which we in the final analysis can take the credit, and therefore there is every reason to be patient with and charitable to others struggling with sin—because whatever growth we have experienced is all due to the Lord's gracious work in us.

And so I want to look at this passage with you briefly to see how it (1) *cultivates humility* by crushing pride, (2) *challenges indolence* in the pursuit of holiness, and (3) *comforts the discouraged* who are struggling with besetting sin.

Something to Bear in Mind

Before we look at these three things, because so many come to this text and read the language "work out your own salvation"

2. John Calvin, *The Epistles of Paul the Apostle to the Galatians, Ephesians, Philippians and Colossians* (1548), ed. David W. Torrance and Thomas F. Torrance trans. T. H. L. Parker, (Grand Rapids: Eerdmans, 1963), 253–54.

and thus think that Paul is teaching that we must save ourselves by our own efforts, it is important for us to be disabused of that notion. Paul, emphatically, does *not* mean that we must somehow save ourselves by our own works, or own efforts, or own doings, or own goodness? No! Not at all. Look at the context of the verses. What is it about? It is about our following Jesus' example—not so that we will be forgiven, accepted, converted, or justified but so that we will be more like Jesus! In other words, Paul is not saying, "work so that you will be saved," but "work out the salvation you have received." He is not saying, "save yourself by your own works," but "work out, live out, the gracious salvation you have received."

It is the same message he has given so clearly in Philippians 1:27 and 2:5. Live a life consistent with the gospel; live, walk, and work in a manner worthy of the gospel; in your conduct and behavior, follow the example of Jesus. Paul (and Peter, and the author of Hebrews) repeatedly makes this same point with different language elsewhere in the New Testament.

Ephesians 2:8–10: "For by grace you have been saved through faith. And this is not your own doing; it is the gift of God, not a result of works, so that no one may boast. *For we are his workmanship, created in Christ Jesus for good works, which God prepared beforehand, that we should walk in them.*" Notice that Paul makes it clear here that we are not saved by our works but for good works. We did not become Christians by our works but in order to do good works. In other words, our works do not save us, but our salvation does enable us to do good works, which God has planned for us to do from before the world was made

Romans 6:17 (NASB): "But thanks be to God that though you were slaves of sin, you became obedient from the heart to that form of teaching to which you were committed." Since Paul thanks *God* that the Romans became obedient from the heart, it is obvious that God is the one who worked to bring about this obedience in their hearts! God was at work in them both to will and to work for his good pleasure (see Phil. 2:13).

2 Thessalonians 1:11–12 (NASB): "We pray for you always, that our God will . . . fulfill every desire for goodness and the work of faith with power, so that the name of our Lord Jesus will be glorified in you." Paul prays here that Jesus will get all the glory, every time we desire to do good things, or to do works that spring from faith, since, after all, it is God who gives us the power to do them in the first place. Thus Christ gets the glory when it is manifest that God has enabled us to fulfill our good resolves and desires through him.

Hebrews 13:20–21 (NASB): "Now the God of peace . . . equip you in every good thing to do His will, working in us that which is pleasing in His sight, through Jesus Christ, to whom be the glory forever and ever. Amen." It is God who equips us to do his will (not our doing his will that causes him to save us). Again, notice that since God enables us to do what is pleasing in his sight "through Jesus," it is Jesus who gets the glory and credit, not us.

1 Peter 4:11 (NASB): "Whoever . . . serves is to do so as one who is serving by the strength which God supplies; so that in all things God may be glorified through Jesus Christ, to whom belongs the glory and dominion forever and ever. Amen." The giver of strength to the one who serves gets the glory, not the one who serves by the strength of the giver. Because God is the one who enables us to "serve" him, he gets the credit for the service. He is at work in us to do his good pleasure!

Galatians 5:22–23: "The fruit of the Spirit is love, joy, peace, patience, kindness, goodness, faithfulness, gentleness, self-control; against such things there is no law." Christian attitudes, behaviors, and deeds are the fruit of the Spirit, not ultimately the fruit of our own efforts. Our efforts are essential, but not finally decisive. As Augustine said, "whatever good I do is due to you, O Lord, the rest is my fault."

So what does "work out your own salvation" mean? It means *that we are to pursue godliness because God is at work in us for godliness*. Philippians 2:12–13 is giving us an encouragement from God that we *can* and you *will* make progress in driving sin from our lives. Paul's teaching is not "God accepts you, therefore no change is necessary in your life," but rather "God accepts you, therefore change is now possible in your life."

Paul's flow of logic in Philippians 2:12–13 is simple and clear: (1) continue to obey; (2) live out your salvation; (3) do this in reverent humility; (4) because God is at work in you. Five truths can be deduced about "progressive sanctification," or growth in the Christian life, from this short passage: (1) Obedience is a vital and essential part of the Christian life. (2) We are to be active in living the Christian life. (3) We are to be humble/God-fearing in our living of the Christian life. (4) We are to be encouraged that God is at work in us. (5) God's work in us is not to lead us to laziness/inactivity/passivity but to exertion.

The sovereignty of God in our salvation and sanctification is not permission for passivity but a reason to hope. The sovereignty of God makes us hopeful that change is possible, not passive as if no change were necessary.

Something Else to Bear in Mind

Relating sanctification to two other great benefits of Christ's work on our behalf may help us better understand this passage and what it teaches. When God saves us, he does three things. He accepts us, he adopts us, and he changes us. Theologians call these three things *justification*, *adoption*, and *sanctification*. This is all part of the salvation that God is accomplishing on our behalf.

So when Paul says "work out your own salvation" in 2:12b, he is talking about sanctification (not justification, or adoption). Now, as I said, when God saves us, he does at least three things for us (he does more, but he does not do less!). Let us think about those three things for a moment, and how they relate to one another, and how they relate to this passage.

God Accepts Us

When I say that he accepts us, I mean that he pardons us and forgives us, and he accepts us as righteous—not because we are righteous but because Jesus is righteous, and his righteousness is imputed to us. We are acquitted and declared not guilty, and justified, and accepted, and pardoned. Our God accepts us.

This is what theologians call justification. It is a very precious truth that God accepts us not because of something in us, not because we deserve to be accepted, not because we have done good things, not because we have done enough good things to outweigh our bad things; but he accepts us not for anything in us, but for Christ alone. "In Christ alone, our hope is found." The reason is because God accepts us in Christ alone. Whenever a person is saved, when God's work of salvation comes to bear on his or her life, he or she is accepted by God.

God Adopts Us

But that is not all. We are also adopted by God. Our gracious heavenly Father not only accepts us and forgives us and pardons us, but welcomes us into his own family. He makes us to be his children, and he makes us inheritors of his estate and brothers and sisters of his only begotten Son, Jesus Christ. Because he welcomes us into his very family, he no longer calls us "servant," but "friend" and "child."

This is what theologians call adoption. God gives to us all the privileges of his own children. He accepts us, and he adopts us. These things God does without our contributing anything to them. The apostle Paul in the whole New Testament is emphatic that we contribute nothing to our being accepted by God. We contribute nothing to our being adopted by God. They are acts of God's free grace. He does them all by himself.

God Changes Us

But that is not all God does. He not only accepts us and adopts us, but changes us. The Lord God is desirous not only that we would be pardoned for our sin and welcomed into his family but that we would begin to look in our character like his children. The heavenly Father would have us to fellowship with him forever, and he cannot fellowship with sin, and so he is in the business of eradicating sin.

This process will never be finished in this life. We will always wrestle with sin until we breathe our final breath. But our God is actively, powerfully, and sovereignly at work changing us so that we die to sin and become more and more like Christ, so that we are matured in the faith, so that we grow up, so that we are not just always drinking the milk that babies would drink but growing up to eat strong meat, like adults.

This is what theologians call sanctification. It is all part of the salvation that God is accomplishing on our behalf. God accepts us, he adopts us, and he changes us. He is sanctifying us, and he is transforming us. Calvin sometimes called this "regeneration." God is changing us, transforming us, maturing us, growing us, and making us holier.

So What

If we bear all this in mind, it is apparent that Paul is talking in Philippians 2:12–13 about God changing us, not God justifying or adopting us. The topic of the verses and their whole context is not how we are forgiven and accepted by God, or how we are welcomed into his family and numbered among his children, but rather about how we grow to be more like him (having already been justified and adopted).

Hence, "work out your own salvation" does not mean that we must somehow save ourselves from God's judgment by our works, efforts, doings, and goodness. But rather that having been saved from God's judgment (not by our own works, but by God's grace, through the work of Christ), we are now to follow Jesus' example (in our sanctification), not so that we will be saved but so that we will be more like Jesus! So that we will manifest the great and gracious salvation we have received.

All that having been said, how in this passage does Paul *cultivate humility in us, challenge our indolence,* and *comfort our discouragements* in our sanctification? Let us see.

By Ascribing the Whole of Our Progress in Holiness to the Sovereign, Gracious Work of God, Humility Is Cultivated in Us and Our Pride Is Crushed

With these great words "for it is God who works in you" (Phil. 2:13a), Paul ascribes the whole of our progress in the Christian life to the sovereign, gracious, divine activity of sanctification in us, and thus our humility is cultivated and our pride is crushed.

Calvin is emphatic in the way he explains this. Our obedience and actions are ascribed by Paul "wholly to God," Calvin says.[3] "Paul wants to ascribe everything to God and to take everything from us."[4] This is vital, because there can be no growth in godliness, no maturing as a Christian, no pursuit of holiness, no consecration to kingdom service that does not also and especially involve the killing of pride. Humility and its cultivation are not incidental but essential to Christian growth. The true weapon we have against pride is the sovereignty of God's grace. Thus it is only a right apprehension of God's grace at work in us for our sanctification that provides an adequate foundation for growth

3. Ibid., 254.
4. Ibid., 255.

in the Christian life. In other words, only when we realize and acknowledge that we are utterly dependent upon God and his grace, not only for our salvation but also for our maturation, are we in a position to really grow in the Christian life, because only then is our pride vanquished—left, as we are, with no basis for boasting in any of our spiritual attainments—since all are the result of God's work in us.

To say it again, yet another way, the acknowledgment of God's monergistic grace at work in our lives for sanctification crushes pride and cultivates humility. Only undiluted grace, perceived by the believer to be at work in his heart and life, kills pride; and pride-killing and humility-cultivating are essential aspects to Christian life and growth.

Why is the crushing of pride and the cultivation of humility essential to Christian growth? Well, for many reasons, but especially for these two.

First, pride is a root sin, and a part of every sin. Whenever we sin, we are preferring ourselves, our desires, our plans to God's, and that is always an arrogant and prideful thing to do. Thus every sin entails pride. So if we are going to mortify sin, and quicken graces, and mature in the faith, and grow as believers, and become more like Christ, then pride is going to have to be addressed, checked, and killed.

Only recognizing God's sovereign, gracious work in us for sanctification can prevent us from becoming prideful about our sanctification; this is a reality we struggle with. (1) If we are naturally inclined to self-discipline, we may be impatient with and censorious toward those who struggle with a lack of it. But such a spirit indicates that we are taking credit for what God has naturally gifted us with. He deserves the credit, not us. (2) Or if we have come to be self-disciplined through a long process of effort and supplication, we can look down on those who have failed to achieve our attainment. When we do this, we betray a prideful attitude that takes credit for what ought to be attributed to God as the product of supernaturally endowed growth in grace. Either way, pridefulness about our own level of spiritual maturity and personal character is sin! As such, it impedes real growth in holiness and must be killed. But the only way is attributing all good in us to God. "It is God who works in us," Paul says.

There is a second reason why the crushing of pride and the cultivation of humility is essential to Christian growth, and that is simply that humility is of the essence of Christlikeness. If we want to be like Christ, and that is the goal of sanctification, then we must be humble. But if we have not cultivated humility, or are prideful about other qualities that we have cultivated, then we have failed to attain to the crowning jewel of the Christian life, which is true gospel humility.

The only way to do this is to acknowledge that every shred of good in us, every scrap of humility in us, is due to God, to his Spirit, to his grace at work in us. So when Paul says that "it is God who works in you," he is cultivating humility and crushing pride.

By Calling on Us to Labor and Strive, with Due Reverence and Godly Fear, for Growth in Holiness and Obedience and Service, Our Indolence Is Rebuked and Our Laziness Corrected

The second great thing that Paul is doing is challenging our spiritual indolence or laziness. When he says "work out your own salvation with fear and trembling," he is calling on us to labor and strive, in the reverent, humble fear of the Lord, for growth in holiness, obedience, and service. These words are a rebuke to passivity in sanctification.

Calvin stresses here that God's working in us motivates us to work. Since he is at work in us, we work. Calvin expressly says that the logic "God works in us, therefore we don't have to" is an unbiblical view of how God's sovereignty and our responsibility work together in sanctification.[5]

This is hugely important because some Christian teachers will assert that any call for believers to obey is to undermine grace. In fact, some people will say that if someone wants to talk about obedience, then he just doesn't understand grace. "Obedience? That's for legalists!"

But that kind of thinking ("we're saved by grace, not by doing, so our doing doesn't matter anymore") never entered into the mind of the apostle Paul. He is challenging these Philippian Christians, and you and me. He is saying that obedience is a vital, essential part of the Christian life—even, and especially, obedience and service that we have to work hard to do, that we have to strive to offer.

That is so important for us to understand because there are some people who break out in hives and get the heebie-jeebies when someone starts talking about "duty" and "must" and "ought" and "commands" in the Christian life. They just do not know what to do with that. Because what is their logic? Their logic is, "I've been accepted by God apart from my doing; therefore, my doing doesn't matter." And the apostle Paul says, "No, no, no. You don't understand. You have been accepted by God apart from your doing, and now, therefore, your doing matters." It is a very different logic that the apostle Paul is operating with, and so his first exhortation is "continue to obey" (2:12a), and his second is "work out your own salvation" (2:12b). The principle we learn from this is that obedience is a natural, vital, and essential part of the Christian life.

Isn't it interesting? God is doing what here? Equipping you. To do what? "To will and to work for his good pleasure" what is well-pleasing in his sight (see Heb. 13:21). Did you notice that? God is at work in you, equipping you to do what? His good pleasure—what is well-pleasing in his sight. If he is equipping

5. Ibid.

you to do that, what do you have to do? What is well-pleasing in his sight, but it is God at work in you, enabling you to do it! Over and over in the New Testament we see this principle that God is at work in us for our godliness; and therefore, precisely because he is at work in us, we are to work to grow in grace. That truth is all over the New Testament; and therefore, the sovereignty of God in our salvation and sanctification is not permission to be lazy, but it is a reason to hope.

The sovereignty of God makes us hopeful that change is possible; it does not make us passive, as if no change were necessary. Growth in godliness is the work of God in us by his grace, by his Spirit. But precisely because it is the work of God in us by his grace, it requires our effort. And our effort will never be wasted, because he has given a promise to us and a reason to hope. I love the way that Calvin puts it: "God acts in us in such a manner, that he does not allow us to be inactive."[6]

A Huge Encouragement

Now, there is a huge encouragement here, friends, and I do not want you to miss it. Philippians 2:12–13 is an encouragement, not just an exhortation. It is not only Paul saying to us that we need to live life in light of the humble, obedient service of Christ displayed in his humiliation and exaltation. It is not only the apostle Paul exhorting us to work out our sanctification with fear and trembling. It is the apostle Paul giving us an encouragement that we can and we will make progress in driving sin from our lives.

Here is the encouragement. Paul is not teaching that "God accepts you, and therefore no change is necessary in your life." Rather, Paul is teaching that "God accepts you, and therefore change is now possible in your life." He is not saying (as many do today) that "God accepts you, and therefore it doesn't matter

6. Ibid., 257.

how you live." He is saying instead that "God accepts you, and therefore real gospel change, gospel freedom, and gospel holiness are now possible."

I want to tell you that this is the most encouraging possible news, because every real Christian wrestles with this reality: "Lord, I know that you have accepted me not because of who I am, not because of what I've done, not because of what you saw that I would do. I know that you've accepted me not because of me but because of Jesus. I know that you've forgiven me. I know you've justified me. I know you've adopted me. But, Lord, there are sins in me that have a hold on me that make me wonder whether I really love you and trust in you."

And you know, there are a lot of well-meaning teachers that come along, and they are trying to encourage you—I'm not impugning their motives at all—they are trying to encourage you, and they say, "You know, Christian, you don't need to worry about that, because God accepts you and so there's no change necessary in your life." There are two problems with that! The two problems are as follows.

First, it's not biblical! Paul, over and over and over again, says two things: (1) God freely, mercifully, graciously accepts you, and (2) change is an essential part of what he is doing in you in his great work of salvation. Change is not optional in God's plan, so one reason that the well-meaning but misguided counsel that "God has shown you grace and therefore it does not matter whether you change or not" does not work is because it is not biblical. Think back to the passages in Ephesians 2, Romans 6, 2 Thessalonians 1, and Galatians 5. Repeatedly, the apostle Paul stresses that change does matter, obedience does matter, godliness does matter, growth does matter. God is in the business of transforming how we live, and so what we do does matter. It does not contribute to our justification; it does not contribute to our acceptance with God; it does not contribute to our adoption. But it is a part of what God the Holy Spirit is doing in us to make us be more like Christ. It is a part, in short, of our sanctification.

Second, it's unsatisfying. But there is a second reason why this teaching does not work, and it is that if a Christian really thinks about it, the message "stop worrying about your ongoing sin, change isn't necessary" is not going to satisfy the deep, deep questions of the heart that continue with even the apostle Paul in Romans 7: "Lord, how can it be that you have saved me with such a great salvation and that I continue to do what I do not want to do, and I continue to not do what I so want to do? Lord, help me." Paul's message to you here in Philippians 2 is so much more helpful and encouraging than the message that "God has shown you grace, and therefore it doesn't matter how you live." It is so much more helpful; it is so much more encouraging; it is so much more practical than "you are accepted by God; you are about as good as you are ever going to be; therefore don't worry about it." And that leads us to our third and final point.

By Pointing Us to the Indefatigable Work of God's Holy Spirit in Us, Both to Give Us the Desire and Ability to Do That Which Is Well-Pleasing in God's Sight, Our Discouragement Is Diminished and Our Despair Comforted with a Sure and Certain Hope

When Paul says that "it is God who works in you, both to will and to work for his good pleasure," he is pointing you to the relentless, inexhaustible, indefatigable work of the Holy Spirit in us to give us the desire and the strength to do what God has called us to do and to be what God has made us to be. This gives us an inextinguishable hope when we are tempted to despair in the fight of faith and in the struggles of sanctification.

This is what encourages me so much. Two things. (1) You might have expected Paul to say, "Continue to obey, to work out your salvation in reverent humility, lest you face God's judgment as a hypocrite." But that is not what he says. He says, "You work because God himself is at work in you already, so that you will want to do the work he created you to do, and so that you will do it for his good pleasure in you." That is incredible.

But do you know what else is encouraging to me about this? (2) He says this in the present tense, not the past tense. He doesn't say, "I want you to work out your sanctification in reverent humility because God has already changed you." Now, of course, that is true. God has changed us. When we become believers, the Holy Spirit causes us to be born anew. He regenerates us; he gives us a new heart and a new spirit. He causes us to love Christ in a way that we have never loved him before and to hate sin in ways that we have never hated it before. But that is not Paul's point here. He does not say, "keep on obeying, keep on pursuing Christian maturity in humble service to others because you have already been changed." Instead he says, "God is at work in you now to change you." Let me tell you, my friends, that truth keeps me from despair, because one of the great realities that I live with every waking moment is that I know that I am not what I ought to be. The apostle Paul is simply saying to us here, "Child of God, he's not finished with you yet. He is at work with you, in you, for you, for his pleasure and glory." I cannot imagine a more comforting and encouraging thing to know in the pursuit of godliness in the Christian life than that my God is not done yet. It keeps me from going over the edge. It keeps me from the brink of despair.

The fact of the matter is that the thing that tires the believer most, that saps his strength the most as life wears on is his own sin. It is not so much the trials of life but the trials that the believer brings upon himself by sin. It is hurting those he loves the most by his own sin. It is grieving his Lord by his sin. This is the greatest burden.

And here is Paul saying that "the Lord isn't finished with you yet." "I am sure of this, that he who began a good work in you will bring it to completion at the day of Jesus Christ" (Phil. 1:6). "Even your struggles with your thorn in the flesh are going to prove that my grace is sufficient, and that your sanctification is all of grace, and thus redound to my glory, and lead you to praise me, and in the final analysis aid your own comfort."

If I may paraphrase Newton, "we may not be what we want to be or what we should be nor what we one day will be, but by the grace of God, we are what we are, and we are not what we once were." God is at work. He is still working. He will not quit working until the work is done.

Let us not forget that the power that is at work in us is the same power that raised Christ Jesus from the dead. Paul says that the power at work to grow us in grace is the same power that raised Jesus from the dead and seated him at the right hand of the Father in heaven (see Eph. 1:19–22).

In this great passage, Paul *cultivates humility* (and *crushes pride*) *in us*, *challenges our indolence*, and *comforts our discouragements* in our sanctification. How does this happen? Calvin says it happens by the Spirit teaching us that "it is God who calls us and offers us salvation; it is our part to embrace by faith what he gives, and by obedience to respond to his calling. But we have neither from ourselves. Hence we act only when he has prepared us for acting." Therefore, let us humble ourselves, and shake off our indolence, and take courage, and grow in hope. There is good news for us, even for our sanctification.

Delivered July 7, 2009, at St. Pierre Cathedral, Geneva, Switzerland.

11

God's Sovereign Election—Ephesians 1:3–14

Geoffrey Thomas

> For he chose us in him before the creation of the world to be holy and blameless in his sight. (Eph. 1:4)[1]

I want to take my life in my hands and preach you a second sermon in this commemoration on this text. I am well aware that to preach once on the subject of election is too much for those who do not believe it, but I am going to speak again on this theme for a number of reasons. Some of you have questions about election that I want to try to answer in this sermon. I also need to address the theme because Paul himself returns to it in the next verse where he says, "in love he predestined us" (v. 5), and then once again in verse 11 he repeats both the terms: "In him we were also chosen, having been predestined according to the plan of him who works out everything in conformity with the purpose of his will."

1. All quotations of Scripture in this chapter are from the NIV, unless otherwise indicated.

He won't let go of this theme, and if it were that important to an apostle (and John Calvin, whom we wish to honor this week), then it must be important enough for us to understand it.

Again, I want to speak on it because it is a wonderfully encouraging truth, easy to preach on, and full of comfort to God's people. Also, it has been some years since I spoke on election. It is crucial that every preacher has an all-round ministry. Every Sunday morning, I preach about the Lord Jesus Christ. My priority is that you see him in the beauty of his person, and understand the glory of his work, so that you love and serve him all your lives. That is far more important to me than your having a perfect grasp of the Bible's teaching on election, but we also know this: the Holy Spirit has taken such pains to breathe out the Scriptures to their very jots and tittles. We don't want to grieve the Spirit, and so we must seek to understand everything we've been given, if only in the name of the fellowship of the Spirit.

Election is the simplest of all doctrines to understand, because it just says that God is the one who took the initiative, and he chose us. There was once a lady who came to a minister and said to him, "I'm really confused about this business of election. Can you help me?" "I can surely try," he said, asking her, "Now, Mary, are you sure you are saved?" "Yes, Pastor," she said, "Thank God, by his grace I know that I am." "Did you save yourself, or did the Lord save you?" "Pastor, you know it was all of the Lord." "Did he do it on purpose, or was it an accident?" Mary paused. "I reckon he did it on purpose." "That's the doctrine of election," her pastor told her. Let us begin with the basic truth of the words of our text.

God Chose Us in Christ before the Foundation of the World

Everyone can understand those simple words. Before we had any existence, before there was a creation, before there were any dimensions of space—height, depth, length, and breadth. We are being taken back to the time when there was unimaginable nothingness—nothing whatsoever. We are told that then there was, as there had always been, the triune God—Father, Son, and Holy Spirit. Before all things else had their beginning, there was the unbegun true and living God. Our text tells us that then, in that deep quiet and profundity, this God was moved with love for his chosen ones. Their names were written on his heart; they were dear to his soul. Jesus tells us that it was then that God gave us to Christ. The Father attached us to the Son before he made the light, plugging us right into him. He, the Son of God, lovingly received us from his Father, then and there, before the beginning of beginnings—before the very angels had been made. From that time onward, the elect never had any existence apart from Christ, and they never will a million years from now. Once in Christ, in Christ forever: thus the eternal covenant stands. How awesome! True, but the decree of God to elect sinners is not inscrutable. It has a face in Jesus Christ. Indeed, we could say that ultimately there's no such thing as "the decree"; there is only loving Father and redeeming Son, decreeing. There is no more comforting truth than this being preached to any congregation anywhere in the world today. Before the stars existed, and before God said, "Let there be light," he had chosen me and many of you and millions like us.

It was not that when God saw our beauty he chose us, because we can lose our beauty; our faces can be ravaged by illness or by fire or acid. And if he had chosen us because of our beauty, then might he not discard us because of our ugliness? It was not because we were brilliant that he chose us, because we can fall a victim to Alzheimer's disease, and the man who could repair a TV set last year is no longer even able to switch one on. If he had chosen us because we were clever, might he not reject us when we grow senile? Or if he had chosen us because we were righteous, what would happen to us when a temptation became too strong—if we were to catch sight of a woman washing herself, and we sent for her, and slept with her, and got her pregnant, and then had her husband killed? Would a God who allegedly had chosen us because he judged us to be law-abiding people discard us when we behaved like devils? But Paul says that it was not at all that in time God began to evaluate us and then chose us, but before we were born, before we had done right or wrong, before anything existed except himself. Then it was that he chose us and countless multitudes like us. He did it that we should become holy and blameless, not because we were holy and blameless.

Does this concept fit in with Paul's own self-understanding of how he became a Christian? It certainly fits into Luke's treatment of the conversion of Paul, in each of the three places he recounts Paul giving his testimony in the book of Acts. The apostle never tells us that he was seeking and praying and agonizing so that eventually God saved him, but rather that he was breathing out threats and hatred against the church. Then God intervened in his life—as he was walking along a road to kill and imprison Christians, not when he was kneeling by his bed. God arose and came and saved him. Here was a man totally conditioned against Jesus, and if you try to explain Paul's conversion in terms of psychology, sociology, heredity, environment, or any basis other than the divine work of God, you will have a real problem on your hands. How does Paul describe his own conversion? Let's look at this testimony in Galatians 1:15–16: "But when God, who set me apart from birth and called me by his grace, was pleased to reveal his Son in me so that I might preach him among the Gentiles, I did not consult any man." In the previous verses you hear Paul talking about himself, and it is all ego: "I persecuted the church of God and [I] tried to destroy it" (v. 13). "I was advancing in Judaism beyond many Jews of my own age and [I] was extremely zealous" (v. 14). Then he comes to the account of his conversion and it is all God, what the Lord did—"set me apart . . . called me by his grace . . . was pleased to reveal his Son in me." What a difference!

All his own decisions and energy resulted in death and destruction, while all God's decisions result in life and usefulness.

There are times when people stand here before us, and they give their testimony before they are baptized and join the church and come to the Lord's table. Their testimonies are usually fascinating sermons in themselves, but my point is that everyone thinking of confessing Christ and being baptized should read this testimony of Paul. Notice what he doesn't say: "When I decided to give God a chance." No! Or, "When I opened my heart and let Jesus come in." No! That is the way many people speak today. They don't go back before the creation of the world, but they start with themselves and what they did. But Paul says that God, working according to an eternal plan, set him apart from his birth, before he took his first breath and uttered his first cry; then God had a plan for him. That's how Paul saw his conversion, not "I had the courage to make the all-important decision to accept Christ." Where does anyone anywhere in the Bible talk like that? You will search in vain looking for it. Those men were full of the Spirit, and so they knew that before the foundation of the world God had loved them and purposed that they were going to be his people.

Imagine that we had an actual baptismal service, and a candidate got up and said, "I suppose that it all comes down to this: I'm a little better than other people. I have more discernment and insight than most people. I was willing to give God a chance to save me, and it was because of my willingness that God was able to save me." I could imagine seeing your faces drop, and my own heart would sink. What was I going to do? Could I baptize a man who boasted in himself like that? No way. This man evidently had never seen the grace and power of God. He was glorying in autosoterism, in self-salvation. I was told of a very different Christian who came from China. He was in an informal meeting, and was asked to give his testimony. "How did you come to know the Lord?" He spoke modestly of how God had sought him, and then the Lord had opened his heart to receive the truth, and how the Holy Spirit had given him a new birth and made him a new creation. When he had ended, the chairman smiled and said, "That was wonderful, but you left out what you did." The man from China said, "I don't know what you mean. There was nothing I did." The chairman said, "God did his part, and then you must have done something. What was your part?" The Chinese brother's face finally was wreathed in a smile: "Oh, yes, my part! I ran and ran as far from God as I could. I tried to get away from him, but his part was to run faster, tackle me, and totally overcome me by his mercy and love."

Has God ever taught that truth to you? Your part in salvation had been backing away from God, continuing to find excuses why you didn't want to be converted, looking for a hiding place where you could escape from the Word of God. What could you bring with you to God? Only your sin and need. "Nothing in my hand I bring." What did God bring to you? His forgiveness and salvation in Jesus Christ. Do you see why I'm returning to this theme of God choosing us today? It teaches us that God (all by himself) saves (not just attempts to save) sinners (the most undeserving and helpless of people). "Election" means "God saves sinners."

You will protest and say, "But I was the one who believed in Jesus Christ. I repented of my sin. I confessed him as my Savior." Of course you did, but it was God's grace that enabled you to do so, wasn't it? Predestination does not take away our liberty. Please understand that. God hasn't merely foreordained what we shall choose. He has foreordained that we shall choose freely. We will know, afterwards, that we could have chosen differently. When unconverted Keith Underhill (who has been a missionary in Kenya for thirty years) came to this university forty years ago, it was God who arranged that he should be sharing a room with a Christian from South Wales called Brian Williams. The university authorities didn't arrange that ("We'll put him with a Christian so that he can get saved!"). It was God who constrained Keith to accept freely Brian's invitation to go along to the Christian Union meetings with him. The God who has given the Bible also brought gospel preachers whom he had called and gifted to speak the message of the Bible to Keith (and the other students in the Inter-Varsity). So the scene was this: God revealed his Son to Keith and the other men and women, by the preached Word; but then, by the inward witness of the Holy Spirit that accompanied their preaching, he revealed his Son in Keith in all God's loving particularity. Thus Keith inwardly knew the beauty of Christ, and so God enabled Keith freely to trust in Jesus Christ. It was God who overcame all Keith's resistance and changed his will so that he came freely to bow before Christ as his Savior. Keith was drawn against his will and made a new creation, and then he freely bowed and acknowledged God as his Savior and Lord. We humans could never control an operation in which individuals made free choices while materials behaved randomly. But God can. He controls without compelling. We live in a world where everything is foreordained by God, but we also live in a world where saints and sinners make free choices, and where individual subatomic particles behave with complete randomness.

Sometimes we are amazed at the erratic behavior of our teenage children. It can seem completely random, but then some action will show what powers control their actions. Once there were two women sharing a pot of tea. One watched her son walk out of the door with his shoes shined and his hair neatly combed. His mother said to her friend, "That's the most frustrating thing in the world." Her friend said, "I don't know what you're so uptight about. I wish my son would shine his shoes and comb his hair. He dresses like a slob." The mother replied, "Oh, that's not what's frustrating. What bugs me is that a pair of blue eyes and a blonde head did in ten minutes what I couldn't do in eighteen years." You understand the point of that illustration? She had nagged her son for years to clean up his life, but all her expostulations had failed. Then he fell in love, and he wanted to look dapper. It was the expulsive power of a new affection that drove out his dirty habits! I am explaining to you God's sovereign election and his effectual grace by which God creates a new inward motive that makes us desire Christ and please him. Christ's salvation becomes the thing we long for most of all in life. The fellowship of Christ is something we can't do without. Somebody radically altered the attitude of that mother's son, and so he willingly changed his lifestyle. The mother knew that a blonde head and a pair of blue eyes had achieved more than all her exhortations. So it is with God's grace. When God is pleased to reveal the beauty of Jesus Christ in us, to our minds, our emotions, and our hearts, then all of our resistance to salvation is taken out of us. We gladly repent and believe. We can't resist him, and we trust him with all our hearts because we sincerely want him. The God who chose us before the foundation of the world drew us to himself in time.

Listen to the testimony of Charles Haddon Spurgeon:

> One weeknight, when I was sitting in the house of God, I wasn't thinking much about the preacher's sermon, for I didn't believe it. The thought struck me, "How did you come to be a Christian?" I sought the Lord. "But how did you come to seek the Lord?" The truth flashed across my mind in a moment—I shouldn't have sought him unless there had been some previous influence in my mind to make me seek him. "I prayed," thought I, but then I asked myself, "How came I to pray?" I was induced to pray by reading the Scriptures. How came I to read the Scriptures? I did read them, but what led me to do so? Then, in a moment, I saw that God was at the bottom of it all, and that he was the Author of my faith, and so the whole doctrine of grace opened up to me, and from that doctrine I have not departed to this day, and I desire to make my constant confession, "I ascribe my change wholly to God."[2]

2. Charles H. Spurgeon, *Autobiography, 'The Early Years,' 1834–1859* (Edinburgh: Banner of Truth, 1973), 1:165.

A preacher recently was heard to say, "God will never mess with your free will." Well, I'm sure glad that God "messed with" my free will. Though raised in a Christian home, I was beginning to turn away from the things of God when the Spirit of God began to work in me and make me willing to bow before Christ. In Galatians 1:15, Paul attributes his whole change of life from Christ-hater to Christ-preacher to the intervention in mercy in his life of almighty God: "But . . . God . . . set me apart from birth and called me by his grace, [and] was pleased to reveal his Son in me."

God's Choosing People Is Not Horribly Unfair

Two things. First, this little point: there isn't the least connection between what God says here and the idea that only a tiny proportion of men will be saved. This seems to arise every time the Bible's words "election" and "choose" arise. People seem to think that these "hot" words mean some terrible contraction of the number of people who are going to be saved, as if election meant that at last God would have only a handful of people in heaven. Now, there is no reason to believe from Scripture that only a tiny group of folk are going to be saved. The great promise of the covenant of grace with Abraham is that his seed is going to be numerous, like the sands on the seashore and the stars in heaven. The vision in Revelation 7 is of a multitude that no man can number around the throne of God and the Lamb. No way is the devil going to carry the bulk of the human race down with him to hell. So we are to understand from the Bible that God has been utterly prodigal in the number of people he has chosen, his vast arms extended wide, wide, wide—as far as the east is from the west—as he takes to his bosom uncountable masses of people, far beyond human calculation. Our vision should be that where sin abounds, grace did much more abound. However, whatever their number, let's make sure we are counted amongst them. Nice, lovable people aren't going to hell simply because they have the misfortune not to belong to the elect. Men are condemned to dishonor and wrath only for their sins.

The second thing is this: people protest in an outraged tone, "Suppose a father condemned some of his children to misery before they were born, while he gave his other children supreme happiness, all out of his own arbitrary will. Would that be right and just? Wouldn't it be brutal and detestable?" Of course it would be; it would be execrable to the highest degree, so that we may never charge the God of love with behavior like that. What we are dealing with is as far from that as light is from darkness. Fallen men and women are not in the position of being innocent children, and God is not a tyrannical monster. How does the righteous God, before whom the angels hide their eyes, crying, "Holy, Holy, Holy," see the world? "All that is in the world, the lust of the flesh, and the lust of the eyes, and the pride of life, is not of the Father, but is of the world" (1 John 2:16 KJV). Those of the world are not of the Father; they are not his offspring, John says. When God looks into the thoughts of man, what does the Lord see? "The LORD saw how great man's wickedness on the earth had become, and that every inclination of the thoughts of his heart was only evil all the time" (Gen. 6:5). When God describes the state of man, how does he sum him up? As dead in trespasses and sins (Eph. 2:1). His heart is deceitful above all things and desperately wicked. Man is sick and covered in bruises and putrefying sores from head to toe in the sight of God. That is the situation—not children of a father but rebels and criminals who have defied God with a high hand, because they hate him. We will not have this Lord ruling over us. Thus the wrath of God is revealed from heaven against them all.

Even non-Christians do not consider a limited display of mercy to be unjust. Let me use this illustration. Think of a high-security prison. Islamic terrorists who have blown to bits boys and girls are kept there. IRA killers, the murderers of innocent men and women shopping on a Saturday afternoon, are there behind its bars. Drug barons and rapists who in their different heinous ways have destroyed the lives of many are kept incarcerated there. Con men are there—those who have plundered the pensions of thousands so that retired people have discovered themselves to be virtually penniless. Pedophiles are there. Thieves who have half-killed old ladies and taken all their best possessions are there. Drunken joyriders who have mowed down schoolchildren and shown no remorse are there. Two hundred such desperate criminals are there, and these prisoners are told one day that the parole board is meeting. Every prisoner applies for parole. The parole board examines all the cases and they decide to give parole to ten men. Is that unfair? Shouldn't they have released all two hundred? Is there anything cruel or unrighteous in leaving 190 criminals behind bars to serve out their sentences? Have their sentences and punishments honored the justice of the courts? Yes. Were the judgments that were passed upon them fair? Yes. Did their punishments fit their crimes? Yes. They were enemies of the citizens of the state as lawbreakers without a conscience, and they were justly found guilty. You can see immediately my application. The Bible tells us that all the world lies guilty before God. There is none righteous, no, not one. God in his extraordinary love saves vast numbers of criminal rebels at the cost of the crucifixion of his own dear Son. Is he unjust that he has not saved every one? No. He would be unjust only if he failed to deal with a single person absolutely fairly, and that he has not done. God has taken every fact into consideration as he has dealt with the world.

Let me use another illustration of particular love not being unjust love. The media periodically announce that there are hundreds of children needing fostering. A husband and wife hear of this; they talk together about offering to help, and they apply and receive two children to be fostered. All their family and neighbors admire them for taking into their home these needy children.

They didn't have to foster any! Will we dare to criticize them for showing such love to only two? No. We admire them. However, let almighty God, the Lord who has been so terribly offended, bring many sinners to glory (when he could bypass all sinners, since he owes no sinner anything but justice), and God somehow becomes unfair or mean for not choosing to save every single person without exception. In the case of the couple who take to their hearts two children, we magnify their gracious act. In the case of God and wicked sinners, some of them affect a pose of moral outrage—they are "offended" at the divine Sovereign's discrimination. They would "reject" such a God, they say, and they will vilify his character for claiming to be their sovereign judge. He will certainly put them in hell, he will be just in doing so, and every one of their vile mouths will be stopped. Now let us press on and ask why in the world God did choose to save sinners.

God Chose These Multitudes Because He Loved Them

Paul makes this glorious statement: "He chose us in him before the creation of the world to be holy and blameless in his sight. In love he predestined us" (vv. 4–5). Because he loved them, he chose them and predestined them to all the blessings of salvation. The logic of the whole foundation of God's election is God's love. Paul goes back behind God's election to God's love. Then should we ask the further question why did God love them? To that question, no answer exists. We can get back behind his election to his love, but I can't get behind the love to anything. The love is the bedrock. The love is ultimate reality. The love is the foundation. The love is the great source of all of God's redemption. It is like the throne of God. It is the controlling center of heaven and earth whence God works all things after the counsel of his own will. Someone may ask, for example, "But what lies behind the throne of God?" Nothing. That is the heart of the divine omnipotence. You can't go behind that to something more powerful. Nothing more powerful than the sovereignty of God exists. All the rivers of life flow out of the throne of God and of the Lamb. They all come from that sovereignty.

So it is with the divine love. That is the alpha and the omega. That is God himself. Who created God? No one. God is unoriginated and uncreated. He is from eternity to eternity. There never was a time when there was no God. There never was a time when he was not omnipotent. There never was a time when he was not love. I cannot get beyond the love of God to something more rational, more involved, more understandable. The love is the headwaters. God's love is the source. The love of God is the ultimate reality of God. God is love, and beyond that we cannot go. This vast creation was made by God, and this God is infinite love. This God has loved his own people, and if we ask when he began to love them, Paul tells us before he created the world he loved them. In the beginning he loved them. He has loved them with an everlasting love. I cannot conceive of God as not existing. I cannot imagine God not being eternal. I cannot think of God as not being Father, and Son, and Holy Spirit. I cannot speak of God not in love with his people. That is part of the reality of God. Of course, it is voluntary, and gracious, and so it is an act of God; but it is still an eternal love, the only way God has been, always in love with his people, always having a bride to present to his Son, always completely passionate for their salvation. It is in that fact that our election is rooted. He chose us in Christ before the foundation of the world because he loved us.

God chose individuals with identities, not a gray, faceless group. It was personal love: "Jacob is the name of the man I have loved," God says, "and I loved the prophet named Jeremiah even before he was formed in the womb." Now, that is surely one of the most marvelous aspects of the whole of our relationship with God—the minuteness of his concern, his intensive care of us. It is our names that are engraven in the palms of Jehovah's hands. We are approaching a time when new computers will be able to react more intimately and personally with us. Their letters will have little giveaways to show that they know more about us and even how we feel, because they themselves have been made to "feel." Will that fact make us feel loved? The old person living alone, and feeling so insignificant and anonymous in a vast and bewildering universe—how will she feel when a machine starts writing more personally to her? More lonely than ever, I'm sure. We are all tiny creatures, clinging desperately to a little planet on the very outskirts of the universe. That is all we are. Our lives are quickly over and gone. Is there no alternative to machines? Then we see this individual love of a personal God for ourselves, and we say with the psalmists, "I am poor and needy, but the Lord thinks on me. He cares for me today. He is touched by this feeling of how infirm I am. He is my own shepherd, and I will lack nothing I need." That is where we Christians find our peace, our dignity, our personhood, the worth of our own identity. That is where we cease to be nonentities. We are proud of a God who knows and loves his own chosen people. We are contemplated by the deep affection of God, so that we can no longer say, "Nobody cares . . . I don't matter . . . I'm nothing . . ." because God cares. He has cared so much, he has given me his own Son.

Paul cries with wonder, "He loved me and gave himself for me." It is even possible for me to stand before Calvary in all humility and wonder and say, "And I am the meaning of that! You gave up your only Son to that, because you loved me? Amazing pity! Grace unknown! And love beyond degree!" The Lord of glory inhabited the womb of Mary and, in the fullness of time, he was born in the stable of Bethlehem. He lived long years in an insignificant village, off the beaten track, called Nazareth, and he suffered Golgotha, and breathed his last, and his body was laid in a tomb—and all out of love for me! Our hymns abound with such wonder at his personal love for us. "Who was the guilty? Who brought this upon Thee? Alas, my treason, Jesus, hath undone Thee, 'Twas I, Lord Jesus, I it was denied Thee: I crucified Thee." "In my place condemned He stood; Sealed my pardon with His blood." "Living, He loved me, dying, He saved me, Buried, He carried my sins far away." Scores of hymns acknowledge I am what I am all because of the Lord's dying love for me.

Harry Kilbride wrote this:

> God's choice is not a cold, arbitrary decision. Rather, it is as if a great king ruled his kingdom with perfect justice. All those who were in prison were being justly punished for crimes willfully committed. Some faced the death penalty. However, this loving king determined to display his grace in pardoning the guilty. So he made his way to death row and he offered a full and free pardon to any man who would confess his crimes and repent of them. Alas and sadly, none would. So hard of heart were they that they all despised their goodhearted monarch and his laws and spat in his face. Incredibly, he wouldn't be defeated. He singled out the very worst offender and visited him, again and again. He poured upon him words and gifts of love, pleading with him to accept the gracious offer of forgiveness. Eventually, the hard heart was melted by such sincere love and personal sacrifice. Weeping with sorrow, the criminal fell at the feet of his king, confessed his crimes, and declared how utterly undeserving he was of such grace. He begged the king to allow him to live a new life of devoted royal service. In joy, the king signed the papers of pardon and brought him home to the palace actually adopting him into the royal family. From then on, this erstwhile murderer from the gutter would be a prince.
>
> My friend: God's love for us was much greater than that of this king. What if this king could only pardon this villain if the king's own beloved son, his prince and heir, would die in his place? Why, no one would believe such a story. They would say it was too farfetched. Yet that is the Gospel story. For God so loved the world that he gave his only Son. For

God demonstrates his own love for us in this: while we were still sinners, Christ died for us. God's love for you and for me cost him the Cross. If guilty sinners are punished, shall God be charged with injustice? If the justly condemned despise his love and his offer of forgiveness, shall God be blamed? But if God, determined in love, to yet redeem a people and if in love he includes you in that number, is your heart not overwhelmed with the amazing love and grace of God?

"Why was I made to hear Thy voice,
And enter while there's room,
When thousands make a wretched choice,
And rather starve than come?
'Twas the same love that spread the feast
That sweetly drew us in;
Else we had still refused to taste,
And perished in our sin." (Isaac Watts).[3]

"Chosen by Grace" is not a story of God's choosing names at random out of a hat. It is a love story, the most wonderful love story the world has ever heard.

The Teaching of Election Is Going to Affect You Very Positively

First, it is going to humble you. There is the great command to us to humble ourselves under the mighty hand of God. There is the warning that God resists the proud, but gives grace to the humble. There is the example of Christ who humbled himself. Three different indications of the importance of the grace of humility are there. So we need all the help we can to become more humble, if God is going to entrust us with new and needed blessings. The Bible's teaching on election is one of the means to achieve that. It emphasizes that we are

3. Harry Kilbride, *Chosen by Grace* (privately printed), 10.

what we are by the grace of God. If we have faith, and our eyes have been opened, and we can see the glories of Christ, and if we have light and hope, then we owe it all to no attainment of our own whatsoever. We owe it all entirely to the grace of God. Remember those wonderful words of Paul: how did he become a Christian? "It pleased God," he says. "It pleased God." It was God who chose him before the foundation of the world. It was God who separated him from his mother's womb. It was God who revealed his Son in him. The initiative was all of God. The accomplishment was divine. The keeping power was the Lord's alone. Paul was saved by the will of God and kept by the power of God. The Christian says, "I am what I am by the grace of God." Boasting is excluded. What do you have that you have not received from God? Nothing. God has given us everything. All things bright and beautiful, every good and perfect gift, temporal and eternal, material and spiritual, all comes from God. He gave us his Son, and with him he has freely given us all things. We are debtors to God for everything. What a humbling truth! Imagine that it were any different. Imagine that God's hands were, in fact, really tied, and that ultimately the decision to enter glory had actually been ours. Imagine it! Do you understand what I am imagining—that the critical choice of heaven had been, in fact, our choice? That would be the end of humility. What a desperate virus to take with us into eternity! We would soon be saying to the angels in some lordly way, "Yes, I'm rather glad that I gave Jesus a chance." No, it is all of grace that sinners will be in heaven. Our boasting is left outside the pearly gates.

Origins are crucial. It is essential to start off the Christian life with the realization that I am a child of sovereign grace. We did not enter into a partnership with God at conversion. We were slaves of sin, and have been redeemed by what Jesus Christ did. We have neither the ability nor the right to boast about the power of our wills or our right to make our own choices. A Christian can have only one boss, and the sooner we learn that it is God himself, the better off we'll be. God's purpose is that we learn that from conversion. We see that in the redemption of Paul, where amongst the first words he heard when he regained his sight were, "The God of our fathers hath chosen thee" (Acts 22:14 KJV).

Second, God's choosing us is a profoundly encouraging teaching. God knew all about me. He had seen the file. He understood my personality, my hang-ups, my duplicity, my carnality, my personal problems, my laziness, my hypocrisy, my depression, my self-pity, and my cold heart. He knew all my sins—the sins that my wife and children don't know about God knew about before the foundation of the world. The sins my congregation isn't aware of God has always been aware of. He knew the whole life in its every detail, and yet he still determined to have me as his own and to change me. He chose David, though he knew what depths David would plumb. He chose Peter, though he had heard the curses at the fireside. He chose Paul, though he saw his lust for blood and delight at seeing Stephen being stoned to death. He still chose those men, and he chose millions like them—not one of them worthy or perfect. He chose me, knowing my whole life—all the disappointments and the falls. He still determined he would never be separated from me. I would share his eternity. What an encouragement to keep going, knowing my certain destination. I am to be glorified together with Christ, so let me get my priorities right this day. First, let me be always seeking God's kingdom and righteousness. Then let me be abounding in the work of the Lord.

Third, God's choosing such a vast company of people is a tremendous support to evangelism. If we didn't believe in election, we wouldn't witness. Men are dead in sins and at enmity against God. How hopeless the situation could seem. Satan would say to us, "It's hopeless. You can't persuade anyone in this dark town to become Christians. Give it up!" The greatest evangelist the world has ever seen, the apostle Paul, once felt just like that, and God came and supported him by reminding him of the truth of election. He said to him on that occasion, "Paul, you are safe wherever I call you to go, until your life's work is over. I want you to go into this city of Corinth, and don't stop preaching there because I have some people I have chosen in Corinth. They will certainly respond to your preaching and praying and personal witness because I am going to be with you, and I will open their hearts, and they will pay heed to you" (see Acts 18:9). Some people were bound to be saved because God had made up his mind. That thought so dominated Paul's attitude to evangelism that he was willing to suffer anything and everything for that purpose: "Therefore I endure everything for the sake of the elect, that they too may obtain the salvation that is in Christ Jesus, with eternal glory" (2 Tim. 2:10).

John Gibson Paton was a missionary to what was called in his day the New Hebrides islands in the south Pacific. He suffered very much there. He buried his wife and child on those islands, digging their graves with his own hands. He labored for twenty-five years with no evangelistic success. Were there not many times when he felt discouragement? Didn't the devil often tell him to move on with his ministry? "Get a life, John!" What kept this missionary preaching in such a situation? Paton stood one day over the graves of his wife and their wee bairn, and this is how he prayed: "Father, you have chosen a people out of every tribe and tongue to be saved. Some of those chosen ones are on this island, and I won't leave until they are safely in the fold." That is what the biblical teaching of election did for evangelists like Jonathan Edwards and George Whitefield, and what it did for pastors like Spurgeon, and missionaries like William Carey and Adinoram Judson. That is what has kept Keith Underhill all these years laboring in Kenya.

It is fascinating to see what follows the conclusion of Romans chapter 9, which is packed with God's awesome distinguishing mercy. Paul begins the next chapter with these words: "Brethren, my heart's desire and prayer to God for Israel is, that they might be saved" (Rom. 10:1 KJV). The doctrine of election didn't make him a fatalist; it rather encourages him to pray. He tells us that he longed to see those same persons he has described in chapter 9 converted and becoming real Christians. He sincerely prays for them, and walks to the synagogues in every town he visits to witness to them that they might trust in Jesus as the Christ. If he believed in mere man it would be a fruitless task, for nobody is seeking after the Christ Paul offered to them. If Paul depended on human logic, it would say, "Why bother to talk to people? If they are predestined to be saved they will be saved anyway." But Paul knew that the way God's decrees work is through the means God has appointed, and that is by bearing witness and praying and living a holy, loving, courageous life.

So the fact that God elects sinners makes a Christian a praying Christian. Listen to these counsels of J. I. Packer:

> You pray for the conversion of others. In what terms, now do you intercede for them? Do you limit yourself to asking that God will bring them to a point where they can save themselves, independently of him? I don't think you do. I think that what you do is to pray in categorical terms that God will, quite simply and decisively, save them: that he will open the eyes of their understanding, soften their hard hearts, renew their natures, and move their wills to receive the Savior. You ask God to work in them everything necessary for their salvation. You would not dream of making it a point in your prayer that you are not asking God actually to bring them to faith, because you recognize that this is something he cannot do. Nothing of the sort! When you pray for unconverted people, you do so on the assumption that it is in God's power to bring them to faith. You entreat him to do that very thing, and your confidence in asking rests upon the certainty that he is able to do what you ask. And so indeed he is: that conviction, which animates your intercessions, is God's own truth, written on your heart by the Holy Spirit. In prayer, then (and the Christian is at his sanest and wisest when he prays), you know that it is God who saves men; you know that what makes men turn to God is God's own gracious work

of drawing them to himself; and the content of your prayers is determined by this knowledge. Thus, by your practice of intercession, no less than by giving thanks for your conversion, you acknowledge and confess the sovereignty of God's grace. And so do all Christian people everywhere.[4]

Fourth, it is going to make you a more courageous and faithful witness. Surely John Reisinger is right when he says:

> Nothing kills self-sufficiency like the truth of election. Nothing humbles a proud religionist like sovereign grace. How do you respond to a sinner who says, "Leave me alone; when I get ready to believe, I will believe"? I clobber him over the head with election. I tell him that he can't get ready. I press on him the truth that God does not have to send another witness to him but can leave him alone and let him go to hell for sure. Romans 9 is not a secret for God's sheep alone. It is the message for every proud Pharaoh in this world. It is the hammer of God that destroys the damning myth of the power and rights of one's "free will." Sovereign election, rightly preached, will lead men to seek grace.[5]

How You Can Know if You Are Elect

I believe that there is just one criterion, and it is this: do I have Christ? If I have Christ, then I know I am elect because in Christ I have election. Our text tells us that before the creation of the world God chose all the elect in Christ. I am simply asking if we can't put our confidence in that, whether we have Jesus Christ in the grasp of our own faith. Do we have him as his invitations

4. J. I. Packer, *Evangelism and the Sovereignty of God* (London: InterVarsity Press, 1961), 15.

5. John G. Reisinger, *Chosen in Eternity* (Frederick, MD: New Covenant Media, 2000), 29. The whole booklet is valuable and has been a real help in the preparation of both these sermons on election.

and promises are made to us? "The person who comes to me—there's no way I'll throw him out." Have you come to him? That is the great sign that a man is God's elect—if a man wants Christ, and needs Christ and longs for Christ. He may not have strong faith, or mountain-moving faith, but he has a faith that longs and yearns and needs. Do we have an emotional dependence on Jesus Christ? Is there in the depth of our hearts some elemental yearning and longing—an urgency to have the covering of the blood of Christ for our sins, the robe of Christ's righteousness to hide our defilement? If to lose him is desolation, and if the proof of his nonexistence would drive us crackers, then that person is God's elect person. Do we have a longing that Christ should dwell in our hearts? That is a sign of our election. Let me close with an illustration of John G. Reisinger's (from whom a number of the earlier illustrations were also gratefully taken):

> Imagine you are a four-legged sheep caught in a thicket from which you cannot free yourself. You are cold, hungry, thirsty, and your throat is sore from bleating. The more you struggle to get free the more the briars dig into your flesh and make the blood flow. Finally, in utter despair you resign yourself to your pitiful situation, quit struggling, and prepare to die. If, in that most hopeless situation, you heard the familiar voice of the shepherd, what would you do? You would cry, "Baaaa! Baaaaa!" as loudly as you could.
>
> Well, let me tell you that if you are a two-legged sheep in the same condition, you will react in exactly the same way. If you are caught in a thicket of sin and cannot get loose, and the harder you try to get free the more you fail because the bonds of sin get stronger, and you are hungry, tired, and thirsty, then I have good news. There is a gracious Shepherd calling your name. Cry out to him! Cry, "Baaaa! Baaaaa!" as loudly as you can. Tell him how sick you are of sin and its awful consequences. Tell him how totally helpless you are and how badly you need his grace and power. He will be at your side in a moment. He

will free you from the thicket of sin, bind up your wounds, give you bread and water, and put you on his shoulders and carry you safely back to the fold.

The only person who will not cry out "Baa! Baa!" is the person who either doesn't believe he is caught in the thicket of sin but imagines he is totally free, or the person who loves the sin despite the misery it brings.

If you are a chosen sheep, you know what it is to be set free from the thicket. You have tasted the bread of heaven and have drunk the water of life. You will praise forever he who loved you with an everlasting love and washed you in his own precious blood.[6]

Delivered July 8, 2009, at St. Pierre Cathedral, Geneva, Switzerland.

6. Ibid See also the conclusion where a number of articles from the journal that Reisinger edits, *Sound of Grace*, have been gathered.

12

Cherishing the Church—Matthew 16:18b

Joel R. Beeke

How important is the church in the life of the individual Christian? This question has been answered in various ways. At one end of the spectrum is the clericalism and absolutism of Roman Catholicism, in which the visible and institutional church, administered by a hierarchy of priests, bishops, and pope, claims and wields total power over the believer in matters pertaining to this life and the next. At the other end is the intense subjectivism and individualism of modern American evangelicalism, which holds that Christianity consists only in personal faith and which suspiciously regards the church as "organized religion." Many agree with the notion that the church is a voluntary society.[1] "You don't have to attend church to be a Christian," they say. As

1. Michael Horton, *We Believe: Recovering the Essentials of the Apostles' Creed* (Nashville: Word, 1998), 193.

a result, the church commands scant regard for her ordinances and office-bearers, and even less loyalty from her adherents. As an institution, the church must compete for support with the whole welter of Christian crusades, mission agencies, schools, publications, broadcasts, charities, and fund drives that crowd the landscape of evangelical America. The net result is that the church has lost all authority, and has been reduced to a revolving door where people are leaving as fast as they are coming in.

Both extremes are rooted in unbiblical views of the church. Both are unacceptable to the mind of the Reformers like John Calvin. While breaking with the clericalism, authoritarianism, and absolutism of Rome, Calvin nonetheless maintained a high view of the church: "If we do not prefer the church to all other objects of our interest we are unworthy of being counted among her members," he wrote. Calvin agreed with Cyprian and Augustine, who said, "He cannot have God for his Father who refuses to have the church for his mother." To this Calvin added, "For there is no other way to enter into life unless this mother conceive us in her womb, give us birth, nourish us at her breast, and lastly, unless she keep us under her care and guidance until, putting off mortal flesh, we become like the angels."[2] Therefore, the church is essential for spiritual nourishment and maturation.

Calvin warns us to avoid a church that is an absolute authority, an infallible teacher, and a center of habitual grace. But he also urges us to avoid a church that is a center for rallies, entertainment, rehabilitation, or politics—a church that becomes a music hall, a social institution, or an evangelistic circus. Instead, Calvin calls us back to Scripture to consider what Christ has said about his church.

In the past, Reformed believers have profoundly cherished the church. Today, that sense of appreciation is waning in general.

2. John Calvin, *Institutes of the Christian Religion*, ed. John T. McNeill, trans. Ford Lewis Battles (Philadelphia: Westminster Press, 1960), 4.1.1, 4.1.4.

Many Protestants have depreciated the place the church occupies as Christ's institution.[3] This lowered view of the church is fostered by a lack of understanding about what the church truly is as Christ's institution. It disregards Jesus' words to Peter: "Upon this rock I will build my church" (Matt. 16:18).[4] Calvin would say that we cannot really understand what the church is and why we should appreciate her until we truly understand the meaning of those words. To that end, I want to address three things: first, the *status* of the church as belonging to Christ ("my church"); second, the *substance* of the church as founded on Christ ("upon this rock"); third, the *success* of the church as the workmanship of Christ ("I will build")—all of which should increasingly move us to cherish the church.[5]

The Church's Status: Belonging to Christ

In Matthew 16:18, Jesus speaks about the church as the epicenter of his vision. There is a programmatic ring about the words he uses. He doesn't just say, "Peter, by the way, I am planning to build the church." Rather, he tells Peter with absolute certainty that he will build his church, despite the gates of hell that will try to prevail against it. It is as if he says to Peter and to us, "Since you have recognized my true identity as the Son of God, I want you to understand what lies at the heart of my ministry. The reason I have come into the world as the Christ is so that by my Spirit-anointed ministry I might bring into being a church that belongs to myself." So right from the beginning of this Christian community, Jesus makes clear that he has come not simply to save

3. John Murray, "The Church—Its Identity, Functions, and Resources," in *Collected Writings of John Murray* (Edinburgh: Banner of Truth, 1976), 1:238.

4. All quotations of Scripture in this chapter are from the KJV.

5. Parts of this paper have been adapted from my "Glorious Things of Thee Are Spoken," in *Onward, Christian Soldiers: Protestants Affirm the Church* (Morgan, PA: Soli Deo Gloria, 1999), 23–67.

isolated sheep, but rather to bind his chosen sheep together in an amazing community that he is pleased to call his own church.

Jesus used the Greek word *ekklesia* to describe his church.[6] The only other place in the Gospels where *ekklesia* is used is Matthew 18:17. But the term is used throughout the Septuagint (the Greek translation of the Old Testament) and the New Testament to translate the Hebrew word *qahal*, which describes the congregation or assembly of God's chosen and privileged people, Israel. As God's *ekklesia*, Israel is called to know, love, and serve him.

John Murray wrote, "When Jesus speaks of 'my church,' he is thinking of those gathered and knit together after the pattern provided by the Old Testament as the people for his possession, as the community which he is to constitute, and which stands in a relation to him comparable to the congregation of the Lord in the Old Testament."[7] Several aspects of God's relationship with the *ekklesia* are still true of the church today. Both Israel and the church are called by sovereign grace out of Egypt (Hos. 11:1–5) and the world. Both are called by God into a covenantal relationship with him to accomplish a vital kingdom task. Both are called to worship God in community. And both are called to future inheritance in the heavenly Canaan.[8]

When Jesus said "my church" in Matthew 16, he was claiming God's people as his own. The *ekklesia* is thus his assembly, his people, bound to him with ties far deeper than those of family or friendship. The *ekklesia* is defined in Matthew 16:18 by her saving relationship to Jesus the Messiah, who has done for her what the

6. Lothar Coenen, "Church," in *The New Theological Dictionary of New Testament Theology*, ed. Colin Brown (Grand Rapids: Zondervan, 1975), 1:291–307; D. Douglas Bannerman, *The Scripture Doctrine of the Church* (Grand Rapids: Eerdmans, 1955), 571–76; Thomas Lindsay, *The Church and the Ministry in the Early Centuries* (London: Hodder and Stoughton, 1907), 4–5, 10–11.

7. John Murray, "The Nature and Unity of the Church," in *Collected Writings of John Murray*, 2:323.

8. David Watson, *I Believe in the Church* (London: Hodder and Stoughton, 1978), 67–74.

sacrificial system in the old economy merely foreshadowed in its attempt to atone for sin. The *ekklesia* is a people bonded to Christ in love, mercy, forgiveness, and dependence.[9]

Christ's assembly started with a small group of ordinary people. When he looked at his disciples, he spoke concerning his whole church: "You are mine; you belong to me." The word *my* in the original is moved from its normal grammatical position to show that emphasis. Jesus did not use that possessive pronoun lightly. Significantly, he talked about "my Father," "my friends," and "my church," but never about "my money" or "my property."

Now, we value what belongs to famous people. If I were to ask you how much you would give me for an antique pen, you might offer me $20 to $50. But if I were to say, "This is the pen that John Calvin used to write the *Institutes of the Christian Religion*," you would probably offer me considerably more. The value of the object would increase substantially because of the person who owned it.

The church belongs to Jesus Christ. The church is his by *gift*, for all that the Father gives him shall come to him (John 6:37; cf. John 17). The church is his by *promise*, for the Father promised her to his Son (Ps. 2:8). And the church is his by *purchase*, for Christ has bought her with his own precious blood (1 Peter 1:19).

To make the church his, Christ will engage in a threefold task. First, he will build his church through his crucifixion. He will die for his people to cleanse them from their sin and make them fit for the presence of God. Second, he will build his church by his exaltation. He will rise from the dead in triumphant glory on the third day to send his Holy Spirit to draw men and women, boys and girls to himself and into his kingdom. Third, he will build his church by the proclamation of the gospel. And so he says to Peter in Matthew 16:19, "I will

9. Cyril Charles Richardson, *The Church through the Centuries* (London: Religious Book Club, 1938), 19–23.

give unto thee the keys of the kingdom of heaven"—keys that the Heidelberg Catechism rightly and famously refers to as the preaching of the gospel (Q. 83)—"and whatsoever thou shalt bind on earth shall be bound in heaven: and whatsoever thou shalt loose on earth shall be loosed in heaven."

All three of these tasks coalesce on Pentecost when the Spirit says, as it were, to Peter, "Bring out now the keys that Jesus put into your pocket, proclaim the crucified and exalted Christ, and thereby open the kingdom of heaven to those who will repent and believe." And suddenly, the very man who only weeks ago had denied that he ever knew the Lord Jesus Christ is filled with the Holy Spirit and preaches the gospel, and the Christian church, from being a small company of 120 men and women in Acts 1, becomes a church of 3,120 by the end of Acts 2, as Jesus fulfills his glorious promise, "I will build my church."[10]

Because the church is the center of the vision of Christ, the Savior was willing to give his all for her. In Ephesians 5:25, Paul says that Christ "loved the church, and gave himself for it." In Acts 20:28, Paul speaks of "the church of God" that God "hath purchased with his own blood"—that is, with the atoning blood of his Son.

Golgotha, where Christ died for his church, was not a pretty place. It was not a sentimental spot for tourists but a place of blood and death and punishment. Yet this bloody punishment of sin is precisely what we deserve, for the wages of sin are death and hell (Rom. 6:23; Rev. 21:8), where the smoke of torment justly ascends day and night forever (Rev. 14:10–11). Only when we see how ugly sin is and how justly we deserve such punishment do we perceive the wonder of what transpired at Golgotha.

Reformed evangelicals are often criticized for being preoccupied with sin. Yet the most appalling utterances about sin are

10. Sinclair B. Ferguson, "The Church That Christ Builds," lecture delivered at Puritan Reformed Theological Seminary, May 14, 2009.

found in Scripture, not in our confessions of faith or in the words of Calvin or Bunyan. What is human society really like? The prophet Isaiah said Israel as a society was like a man covered in boils and ulcers from the crown of his head to the soles of his feet (Isa. 1:6). Jesus said that "out of the heart proceed evil thoughts, murders, adulteries, fornications, thefts, false witness, blasphemies" (Matt. 15:19). Paul likened human society to a community of snakes with poison under their lips (Rom. 3:13). The book of Revelation compares the condition of man to a bottomless pit opened by a great, divine hand, with the smoke of depravity and the everlasting burnings of hell pouring forth and obscuring the light of the sun (Rev. 9:1–3).

Lest you think such biblical illustrations go too far in describing the depravity of man, consider what Western civilization has done. What kind of depravity was exhibited when Africans were enslaved and whipped into submission? What about those who subjected Jews to gas chambers, incinerators, and torture? What about those who vacuum unborn children out of wombs, cut them up, incinerate them, then boast of "the right to choose"? We stand before God in a corporate silence of guilt.

Society's history is no different from our own as individuals. The record of each of us testifies against us. Our thoughts, fantasies, emotions, resentments, bitterness, and self-pity condemn us. Our words, which are so often harsh, cruel, and cold, repeatedly condemn us. And our actions are little better: what we do even to our dearest friends and those who most depend on us condemns us.

So immense is our depravity before God that there is only one way we can be reconciled to him. That way is through God's Son, who came into this world to take on our flesh and dwell among us. The eternal Son of God—born in a stable to dwell among men! The immortal Son—clothing himself with rags of mortality! God, who made man after his image, himself made in man's image! And if that wasn't enough, he also offered that life as a ransom for us. "I must die," he said from the beginning. "The bridegroom will be wrenched away from you and you will fast in that day. But I must go to Jerusalem for your welfare, to be a ransom for your sin. I did not come to be ministered to but to minister" (cf. Matt. 20:28; Phil. 2:6–8).

The only way God can forgive our sin is through Christ. Jesus endured the wrath of a sin-hating God against us, tasting death for us, entering the lake of fire for us, going into the bottomless pit as our substitute. "He descended into hell" and "gave up the ghost." That was what Golgotha was all about. When you sing about the wondrous cross on which your Savior died, you should not think of something pleasant and beautiful and refreshing, but rather of everything that is ugly and atrocious and revolting. Golgotha was a place of skulls and bones and bleeding flesh.

Three crude crosses, dingy and bloodstained, support three naked bodies in that awful place. Every insult possible is shouted against one of those prisoners—the one in the center, whose name is Jesus. Soldiers, spectators, priests, and elders hurl their hate against Jesus. The only one who dares to speak in his defense is a dying thief. The tenderhearted women who followed him are silent; the disciples who loved him are too terrified to rise in his defense. His brothers and his friends have forsaken him. Worst of all, so has God. The face of the Father that Jesus always turned to in love and adoration is now turned away. He has become an outcast from his Father's house.

This is what God thinks about sin and depravity. Sin is terrifying in the presence of Sinai's thunder and lightning, but sin is most bitter, as Thomas Watson said, in the "red glass" of Christ's suffering. There Christ hangs in the naked flame of God's holiness, bearing our sin, wounded for our transgressions. The unclean place, the passions of the mob, the sufferings of the soul, the darkened sun, the coldness of God, and his holy revulsion against sin—such are the wages of sin!

This is the dowry that Jesus Christ paid to his Father for his bride, the church. As William Gurnall wrote, "The church is taken out of dying Jesus' side, as Eve [was born] out of sleeping Adam's" side. We must remember that incalculable dowry of suffering and blood when we are tempted to slight the church, take her for granted, or neglect our duties toward her. If the Lord Jesus Christ cherished the church so much that he died for her, is it too much for him to ask his followers to cherish the church and live for her?

Cherishing the church as the purchased bride of Christ doesn't negate all criticism of the church. But healthy criticism, which is based on Scripture, is measured out with sorrow and pain. Unhealthy criticism is sour and destructive and is wholly subjective. Men who love their wives can take a great deal of criticism against themselves, but they do not take kindly to unkind comments directed against their spouses. Similarly, Jesus Christ does not approve of us when we thoughtlessly criticize his bride (cf. Eph. 5:22–33).

What do we think of the church? Do we cherish her as Jesus did and weep for her weaknesses as Jeremiah did? Does the church stand in the center of our vision as well?

For most Christians today, I suppose the family represents the center of our vision. We promote and defend our personal family, which is a great thing to do, but not at the expense of the church family. Have you ever considered that as precious as our family is, our personal, immediate family is only an interim arrangement? Our church family life, however, is for all eternity, as Calvin emphasized. Therefore, my great responsibility as a father is to share Jesus Christ's vision and, by the Spirit's grace, to fold my family into the greater and more lasting family of the people of God—a family united by common faith. Here in our text Jesus is promoting this vision for us, so that we might understand that the living church consists of our brothers and sisters, not merely of the flesh, but of the Spirit. When a congregation gets hold of this, it becomes such a gloriously new and different community that people begin to ask, "What is it that God is doing among these people? They seem so addicted to the apostle's teaching, and to fellowship and priestly ministry among one another." The answer, of course, is that they have caught sight of the vision of the Lord Jesus Christ, and that the church is not an added extra to their personal salvation or their personal family life. The church of Christ is that new community he is creating, into which our faith in Jesus Christ and our personal family lives are folded, in order that we might be enriched by the community of the people of God. What a great vision the Lord Jesus Christ has of building his very own church![11]

The Church's Substance: Founded on Christ

Jesus said, "Upon this rock I will build my church." Wars have been fought over the meaning of those words; people have shed blood and spilled ink over them; and church leaders and synods have argued endlessly over them. Those very words are also inscribed in letters of gold on the great dome of St. Peter's in Rome. In fact, Roman Catholicism says that the rock is literally Peter, who served as Christ's vicar on earth. Peter in turn is claimed as founder of the church of Rome. His role as "vicar of Christ" was passed to succeeding bishops, Rome claims.

Most Protestants acknowledge that these words refer partly to Peter, whose name derives from the word for "stone."[12] But the

11. Ibid.

12. This acknowledgment is not a capitulation to Rome's view. Even if the rock were referring wholly to Peter, the Roman Catholic would still have to prove several things that are not supported by the text. John A. Broadus said that these include that Peter alone was to be the founder of Christianity, that he was vice-regent of God and the sovereign of all Christians, that his supposed authority was transmissible as well as actually transmitted to the leading official of the church at Rome, and that Peter lived and died at Rome (*Commentary on the Gospel of Matthew* [1886; repr. Valley Forge, PA: Judson Press, n.d.], 356–57).

rock refers more to the content of what Peter is confessing than it does to his person. As Lenski points out, "Thou art the Christ, the Son of the living God" (Matt. 16:16), refers to "the divine revelation from which that confession sprang and to which Jesus refers so significantly in verse 17, 'Blessed are thou, Simon Barjona: for flesh and blood hath not revealed it unto thee, but my Father which is in heaven.'"[13] Peter here is spokesman for the rest of the disciples, whose confession of this divine revelation matches his. That is evident from Jesus' question, "Whom say ye that I am?" (Matt. 16:15). And that explains why in Matthew 18:18 the rest of the disciples receive the same keys of the kingdom that were previously given to Peter (Matt. 16:19). If the rock were Peter, Christ would probably have said, "You are Peter (*petra*, rock), and upon this Peter (*petra*, rock), I will build my church." Instead, Christ used a diversity of form and gender in Greek words (*petros* and *petra*) that is "too abrupt and marked to be . . . fortuitous," wrote Joseph Addison Alexander.[14] The rock was not the natural, unstable reasoning of Peter, but the mighty truth the Father had revealed to Peter—namely, the messiahship and divine sonship of Jesus. Though Peter himself cannot be entirely separated from his confession of the divine revelation, the focus in this context is on the divine revelation that lay behind his confession of Christ's true identity.

When Christ therefore declares, "Upon this rock I will build my church," he refers to what Peter has confessed: his own identity and office as the Son of God and Israel's promised Messiah.[15] The church shows the foundation on which she is built by her confession. She rests on the reality of the objective revelation that Peter confessed. That is the church's true foundation; the true church

13. R. C. H. Lenski, *Matthew* (Minneapolis: Augsburg, 1964), 626.

14. Joseph Addison Alexander, *The Gospel according to Matthew* (London: James Nisbet, 1861), 439.

15. R. B. Kuiper, *The Glorious Body of Christ* (London: Banner of Truth, 1966), 67–68.

is built on it. "The truth that Jesus Christ is the promised Messiah, very God and very man in one person, the anointed Savior of the world, is the main groundstone whereupon the faith of all believers is founded, as upon a rock," David Dickson said.[16]

Thus the rock on which the church is built is Jesus Christ, the Son of the living God. This does justice to the classical distinction Jesus maintained between *petros* (stone) and *petra* (rock), which may indicate, according to Alexander, that "while Peter was a stone, i.e., a fragment of the rock, his Master was the rock itself."[17] According to the Bible, three revealed truths flow out of this.

First, Christ alone, as he is revealed in the Scriptures, is the chief cornerstone of the church's structure. That's why 1 Corinthians 3:11 says, "Other foundation can no man lay than that is laid, which is Jesus Christ."

Second, the apostles build their doctrine on Christ as the chief cornerstone. That's why Ephesians 2:20 refers to believers' being "built upon the foundation of the apostles and prophets, Jesus Christ himself being the chief corner stone."

Third, believers themselves are living stones, built on the foundation of the apostles, who in turn are built on the chief cornerstone. That's why 1 Peter 2:4–5 says that believers come to Christ "as unto a living stone, disallowed indeed of men, but chosen of God, and precious, [so] ye also, as lively stones, are built up a spiritual house, an holy priesthood, to offer up spiritual sacrifices, acceptable to God by Jesus Christ." Each particular believer, like a stone in God's ever-growing temple, has a unique place in the purpose of God.

Thus these revealed truths were never intended to be for Peter alone or only for the stream of his supposed papal successors. All the disciples of his age and of ours share in this divine revelation. As Lenski notes: "Luther is right: 'All Christians are Peters on account of

16. David Dickson, *Matthew* (Edinburgh: Banner of Truth, 1981), 224.
17. Alexander, *Matthew*, 439.

the confession which Peter here makes, which is the rock on which Peter and all Peters are built'—understanding Luther to refer to the truth held and confessed by Peter and these Peters."[18]

Whatever else we may say about these words, we can certainly say that the church is founded on Jesus Christ and that the chief article of the Christian faith is trust in Christ. That's the basic mark of belonging to what the Reformers, following Augustine and John Wycliffe, called the invisible church. Calvin said that the invisible church consists of the elect, whose names are in the Lamb's book of life (Rev. 21:27) and who will become known by saving faith and its fruits (Matt. 7:20).[19] Thus a person can be a member of the visible church (the church as we see it) of professing believers, yet not be a part of the invisible church (the church as God sees it) of genuine believers who have a true, saving relationship with Christ.[20] The invisible church is the true church, said Heinrich Bullinger, a great Swiss Reformer.[21]

18. Lenski, *Matthew*, 626.

19. Johannis Wyclif, *Tractatus de Ecclesia*, ed. Johann Loserth (London: Treubner, 1886), 2; Calvin, *Institutes*, 4.1.7; David N. Wiley, "The Church as the Elect in the Theology of Calvin," in *John Calvin and the Church: A Prism of Reform*, ed. Timothy George (Louisville: Westminster/ John Knox Press, 1990), 96–117. Cf. Geddes MacGregor, *Corpus Christi: The Nature of the Church according to the Reformed Tradition* (Philadelphia: Westminster Press, 1958); George H. Tavard, *Holy Writ or Holy Church: The Crisis of the Protestant Reformation* (New York: Harper & Brothers, 1959); Kilian McDonnell, *John Calvin, the Church, and the Eucharist* (Princeton: Princeton University Press, 1967); Paul D. L. Avis, *The Church in the Theology of the Reformers* (London: Marshall Morgan & Scott, 1981); Harro P. Höpfl, *The Christian Polity of John Calvin* (Cambridge: Cambridge University Press, 1982).

20. James Bannerman, *The Church of Christ: A Treatise on the Nature, Powers, Ordinances, Discipline, and Government of the Christian Church* (Edinburgh: Banner of Truth, 1974), 1:29–40. Many in the Reformed community in recent decades have voiced concern about the formula and doctrine of the invisible church, including John Murray (*Collected Writings*, 1:231–36), though Murray later muted that criticism (ibid., 4:262). Cf. Kuiper, *Glorious Body of Christ*, 26–30; Peter Toon, *God's Church for Today* (Westchester, IL: Crossway, 1980), 26–28; Jelle Faber, "The Doctrine of the Church in Reformed Confessions," in *Essays in Reformed Doctrine* (Neerlandia, Alberta: Inheritance, 1990), 112–15; Stuart R. Jones, "The Invisible Church of the Westminster Confession of Faith," *WTJ* 59 (1997): 71–85.

21. Thomas Harding, ed., *The Decades of Henry Bullinger*, trans. H. I. (Cambridge: Cambridge University Press, 1852), 5:7–9.

That distinction guards us against equating membership in the visible church with salvation. Just belonging to a church doesn't make someone a true believer any more than owning an organ makes one a true musician. The saving work of the Holy Spirit welds Christians together. Whatever their differences, all true Christians are saved by Spirit-worked faith and trust in Christ alone (*solus Christus*). A church so constituted builds on Christ as on a rock.

Jesus Christ is the mediator, minister, and surety of his church. But the substance with which he builds his church is sinners. Jesus changes sinners by his power, makes them confessors of his name, and works commitment in their lives. When this is forgotten, the church weakens and begins to die. It is scandalous when churches list dozens, sometimes hundreds of families on their role of membership who seldom attend worship services and show that they have no personal faith in Christ, no living relationship with him. Many churches today are strong in membership but weak in discipleship. Such churches may seem strong numerically, but they are built on sand and will soon break down under stress. "The church is most evangelistic when she is least concerned about impressing the world or with adding to her numbers," Iain Murray says.[22] An inactive church member is a contradiction in terms.

Implied in the rock of Peter's confession in Jesus Christ are the historic attributes of the church, best summarized by the Nicene Creed's confession of "one holy, catholic, and apostolic church."[23] Roman Catholics and Protestants have always taught that those attributes are inseparable from the essence of the church. But while Roman Catholics

22. Cited in John Blanchard, *The Complete Gathered Gold* (Darlington, UK: Evangelical Press, 2006), 86.

23. G. C. Berkouwer, *The Church*, trans. James E. Davison (Grand Rapids: Eerdmans, 1976) is entirely devoted to the unity, catholicity, apostolicity, and holiness of the church as she expounds her true ministry. Cf. standard works of systematic theology and works on the Belgic Confession of Faith (Articles 27–29), the Heidelberg Catechism (Q. 54), the Westminster Confession (Chapter 25), and the Larger Catechism (Q. 61–64); Joel R. Beeke and Sinclair B. Ferguson, *Reformed Confessions Harmonized* (Grand Rapids: Baker, 1999), 188–93.

emphasize the visible, institutional form of those attributes, Protestants focus on their Spirit-worked and experiential character. As Charles Hodge said, "If the church is the body of those who are united to Christ by the indwelling of the Holy Spirit, then the indwelling of the Spirit must make the church holy, visible, perpetual, one, catholic."[24] Each attribute begins with and finds fulfillment in Jesus Christ.

When Protestants say they believe in "one holy, catholic, apostolic church," they confess that Christ, not the church or any man, is the rock on which every attribute of the church is built. Christ is the rock of the church's unity, sanctity, catholicity, and apostolicity. He builds his church by means of office-bearers and apostolic doctrine. Christ leads the church in all truth through the Holy Spirit. Ministers, said Calvin, must be "duly ordained, as ambassadors of God"; filled with the Spirit, his ministers speak words of comfort and lead the church in a holy course.[25]

We do not believe *in* a church, however, for that would mean we place our trust in it. We believe only in Christ. We believe only that there is a church that is holy, catholic, and apostolic. As Calvin put it, the church is of divine appointment but is not divine; it is one, not many; true, yet imperfect; and free, being in bondage to no man.[26]

It takes faith to confess these attributes of the church, because we often fail to see so many of them. When we gaze on the church's external appearance, her garments appear soiled and torn. We see disunity rather than unity, unholiness rather than holiness, denominationalism rather than catholicity, and apostasy rather than apostolicity. We see a church that tragically withholds the gospel from people and then wonders why

24. Charles Hodge, *Discussions in Church Polity* (New York: Charles Scribner's Sons, 1878), 8.

25. For an excellent treatment of Calvin's view of ministers and preaching, see Benjamin Charles Milner Jr., *Calvin's Doctrine of the Church* (Leiden: E. J. Brill, 1970), 102–4.

26. R. B. Kuiper, "Calvin's Conception of the Church," *Torch and Trumpet* 10 (Feb. 1959): 13–17.

she has lost her audience. Cold preaching, lukewarm members, love of power, lack of discipline, worldliness, entertainment, and politics usurp the gospel.

When we see the church's decline from within and society's threats from without, we are tempted to say that the church cannot survive. Nevertheless, we are not tempted to abandon her, for she, said Calvin, is our "mother." Though she appears to age and fail, we still cherish the church. By faith, we still trust that "the Son of God from the beginning to the end of the world, gathers, defends, and preserves to himself by his Spirit and Word, out of the whole human race, a Church chosen to everlasting life, agreeing in true faith; and that I am and for ever shall remain, a living member thereof" (Heidelberg Catechism, Q. 54). Because the church is Christ's bride, she cannot fail. By faith, we believe she will complete Christ's purpose for her. Jesus guarantees that success when he says, "I will build my church."

The Church's Success: The Workmanship of Christ

Some believers belong to small, weak fellowships. They struggle from year to year while attendance dwindles. No new people are attracted to the church; there are few conversions; and people seem to have lost a true sense of the presence of God. People get discouraged. They become embarrassed, apologetic—even cynical about the church. They gradually start distancing themselves from the congregation as well as its ministries.

That slow but sure separation from the church in response to discouragement is part of Satan's strategy. It's the same kind of thing that prompted the disciples of Christ to forsake their master as he was led away to be crucified. To fight Satan's efforts to separate us from the church, we must be reminded of the magnificent promise of the almighty Son of God: "I will build my church."

The Battle against Darkness

Christ did not say, "I will try to build my church," or "I wish I could build my church." He said, "I *will* build my church. I created the heavens and the earth; I have called the world from nothing by my power. I, the Almighty, will build my church."

That is what Christ has determined to accomplish. It's his vow, backed by his authority in heaven and on earth. "Let me tell you what I will do," Christ says to Peter. "I will build my church. And even the gates of hell will not prevail against it."

The gates of hell (or hades) lead to more than death. They lead to all the powers of darkness and evil. Jesus sees hades, as it were, as an organized city with gates. A city gate in the ancient world was the place where judgment and wisdom were dispensed by the elders and rulers of the city. So what Jesus refers to here is what Paul describes in Ephesians 6:10–20 as the powers of darkness organized to destroy the people and kingdom of God. Jesus thus says that though the church is built in the midst of the conflict promised in Genesis 3:15 and pursued through the ages, it will not founder before the gates of the enemy. Christ's church may lose many skirmishes, but it will win the great battle. Christ is stronger than Satan; therefore, his church will defeat Satan's army. The seed of the woman will prevail over the seed of the serpent.

That statement must have seemed preposterous to a handful of nobodies who followed Jesus. Yet Jesus looked at the fishermen, the tax collector, and the other disciples and promised, "Upon this rock I will build my church; and the gates of hell shall not prevail against it."

What seemed so preposterous has happened and is still happening. Throughout history, even when the church seemed overwhelmed by the powers of darkness, she has survived and grown. "God in the midst of her doth dwell," John Flavel admonished people who were quick to mourn a faltering church. "Be not too quick to bury the church before she be dead."[27]

The church may stagger, but she will surely continue her march through history to ultimate triumph. That is because Jesus Christ guarantees her success. He will never dismiss her as irrelevant as others do. Individual churches may close their doors, denominations may wither, but the church of Christ will grow and prosper. As the Belgic Confession (Art. 27) says, "This holy church is preserved or supported by God against the rage of the whole world, even though she sometimes (for a while) appears very small and in the eyes of men, to be reduced to nothing: as during the perilous reign of Ahab when nevertheless the Lord reserved unto him seven thousand men who had not bowed their knees to Baal."

If we truly grasped God's perspective of the church, many of the problems we struggle with in the local church would seem so small. Consider this, for example. While Israel saw only the rubbish of Jerusalem, God saw rebuilt walls (Isa. 49:16). When we see a church torn by dissension, God sees a glorious church built up, as the living stones of New Jerusalem (1 Peter 2:5). She is elected by the Father (Eph. 1:3–6), redeemed by the Son (Eph. 1:7), and adopted by the Spirit (Rom. 8:15). She is glorious because of her role in the plan of God (Eph. 3:10–11), her holiness (Eph. 2:10), her access to God (Heb. 4:16), and her distinguished inheritance (Eph. 1:14, 18). As John Newton wrote:

> Glorious things of thee are spoken, Zion, city of our God,
> He whose word cannot be broken formed thee for his own
> abode:
> On the Rock of Ages founded, what can shake thy sure repose?
> With salvation's walls surrounded, thou may'st smile at all
> thy foes.

27. John Flavel, *The Works of John Flavel* (London: Banner of Truth, 1968), 5:19, 449.

A Work under Construction

True Christians are members of the only successful institution on earth. "No group, no movement, no institution of any kind in the world can even approach to the glory, the splendour, the honour, the beauty, the magnificence, the wonder, the dignity, the excellence, the resplendency of the church of God," writes Daniel Wray.[28] We should serve the church, and Christ through the church, with all our hearts, always remembering that our labor is not in vain in the Lord (1 Cor. 15:58).

Christ's building is not without organization. Calvin devoted almost all of Book IV, nearly one-third of his *Institutes*, to the subject of the church, and a good part of that was devoted to how Christ wants his church to be structured and organized by means of office-bearing. Calvin stresses that wherever Paul went in Acts 14, he established elders over the church. This, said Calvin, is essential for our well-being as the people of God. We are not to be lone rangers or rugged individualists. Being sinners, we need one another, we need the body of the church, and we need the structure that Christ gives to his body.

Calvin's old Genevan liturgy had the minister pray regularly before sermons, "Lord, we are miserable sinners." Since we don't get beyond that in this life, and we remain far too slothful and fickle and weak, Calvin said, we need the authority of preaching, the rule of elders, the compassion of deacons, and the communion of saints to assist, teach, and nurture us.[29]

28. Daniel Wray, *The Importance of the Local Church* (Edinburgh: Banner of Truth, 1981), 4–7. Cf. Kuiper, *Glorious Body of Christ*; Wilhelmus à Brakel, *The Christian's Reasonable Service*, ed. Joel R. Beeke, trans. Bartel Elshout (Grand Rapids: Reformation Heritage Books, 2005), 2:58–60.

29. For Calvin on the teaching office, see Robert Henderson, *The Teaching Office in the Reformed Tradition* (Philadelphia: Westminster Press, 1962); on the ministry, see John H. Leith, "Calvin's Doctrine of the Proclamation of the Word and Its Significance for Today," in George, *John Calvin and the Church*, 206–29; on the eldership, see Elsie Anne McKee, *Elders and the Plural Ministry: The Role of Exegetical History in Illuminating John Calvin's Theology* (Geneva: Librarie Droz, 1988); on the deaconry, see Elsie Anne McKee, *John Calvin on the Diaconate and Liturgical Almsgiving* (Geneva: Librarie Droz, 1984).

From one perspective, we who are New Testament believers are the adult children of God. We are the inheritors of the new covenant. We have the fulfillment of the revelation of God in Jesus Christ and the blessing of the poured-out Spirit of Christ. We are a privileged people far beyond anyone in the old covenant. Yet, from another perspective, we are still growing children who have a long way to go. We need encouragement, admonition, and direction. And Christ provides us with this in the structure of his church.

No wonder, then, that Calvin, like many of the ancient fathers, loved the title of the church "the mother of the faithful." The church is to be a good mother—loving, supporting, disciplining—so that believers might grow in the grace and knowledge of Christ.

The church, then, is a fleet of fishing boats, not a yachting club—a hospital for sinners, not a museum for saints. We dedicate our lives as office-bearers and as members to a work in progress—to what Christ has promised and paid for with his own blood, to what is worthwhile and will be successful in the end, though there will always be dross amid the gold. The church's work, therefore, is never in vain. It is the product of God's sovereign grace in Christ, not the product of the mind and efforts of men.

Christ's promise that he will build the church is always being fulfilled. But on this side of the day of judgment, the church is under construction. And like any building site, this place of construction isn't necessarily tidy or impressive. It includes piles of bricks and boards, ugly trenches, waste, rubble, and scattered tools.

If we look at that mess, we can easily become discouraged. We see in the church so many unfinished people who are full of imperfections and weakness. If we think we're going to find something better than that, we only set ourselves up for disappointment. Instead of criticizing people who fall short of our expectations, we ought to put on our boots, overalls, and helmets, and get busy on the worksite.

We should also prepare ourselves for a lot of hard work that may not seem to get much accomplished. Regardless, *ora et labora* ("pray and work!") must become our work song. "The church of Christ needs servants of all kinds, and instruments of every sort; penknives as well as swords, axes as well as hammers, Marthas as well as Marys, Peters as well as Johns," wrote J. C. Ryle.[30] Though we'll struggle with many challenges and experience much discomfort along the way, we ought to press on, always remembering what the church is going to be someday—a bride adorned for her husband, without spot or wrinkle. "The church shall survive the world, and be in bliss when that is in ruins," wrote Matthew Henry. "When men are projecting the church's ruin, God is preparing for its salvation."[31]

Finally, before we complain about the messiness of the church's building site, we should think about the growing process of every believer. Isn't every one of us under construction? Some of us aren't very impressive yet; we have a long way to go. Our faith, which may be true faith, is not very strong. But little strings are needed as much as big strings in God's concert of grace. "Christians in concert are an abridgment of heaven, shining like a firmament of bright stars," George Swinnock wrote.[32]

The work of the church may be small in our eyes, but it is Christ's work and it will abide forever. As builder and maker, God will not rest until his city is complete. The church chosen from eternity past will glorify the triune God forever. Christ will lose none of those given to him by the Father, chosen to everlasting life (John 17:12). The church is the only institution in the world that never loses its members, even by death.

One day Christ's work will also be finished in us, and our bridegroom will present us to his Father in glory, sanctified and perfected by his work in us. When we pass from the militant to the triumphant church, all sorrow will be forgotten, all sighing will

30. Cited in Blanchard, *Complete Gathered Gold*, 83.

31. Ibid., 93.

32. Ibid., 91.

flee, and we will forever praise the Lamb who sits on the throne. As John Murray concluded, "It is both the privilege and obligation of believers to appreciate more and more the complementation of Christ and his church."[33]

This complementation is the center of Calvin's ecclesiology. That's why his doctrine of the church is so consistent with Christ's doctrine of the church. Calvin would say to us: Let us embrace a love for the church, for she is the bride of Christ. Let us embrace a love for faithful pulpit ministry, for such preaching is Christ's speaking to us. Let us embrace a love for sanctification, for holiness fostered in the church greatly honors Christ. And let us embrace these truths under the realization that they are all gifts of Christ to us.

What about you? Do you love the church because you love her surety, king, and mediator, and because she is his bride? Let us confess together: I believe there is a holy, catholic, apostolic, and eternal church, built and maintained by Jesus Christ on the solid rock of Peter's confession, "Thou art the Christ, the Son of the living God" (Matt. 16:16). I believe in the perseverance of the saints and of the church because I believe in the perseverance of the Christ of God. I believe that "the church is nothing but Christ displayed," as William Gurnall quipped,[34] and that he will not forsake the work of his own hands.

"Christ is the King of his church, and the church is the greatest queen in the world," said Richard Sibbes.[35] Let us therefore keep courage and cherish the church for Christ's sake, for she is heir to his cross and his glory. As the Puritan Stephen Marshall concludes:

> The glory that He looks for to eternity must arise out of this one work of building Zion; this one work shall be the only monument of His glory to eternity; this goodly world, this

33. John Murray, *Collected Writings*, 1:244.

34. William Gurnwall, *The Christian in Compleat Armour* (London: J. Fuller, 1747), 2:314.

35. Cited in Blanchard, *Complete Gathered Gold*, 88.

heaven and earth, that you see and enjoy the use of, is set up only as a ship, as a workshop, to stand only for a week, for six or seven thousand years; and when His work is done He will throw this piece of clay down again [as] . . . a gourd which springs up in a night and withers in a day; but this piece [His living church] He sets up for a higher end, to be the eternal mansion of His holiness and honor; this is His metropolis, His temple, His house.[36]

Delivered July 8, 2009, at St. Pierre Cathedral, Geneva, Switzerland.

36. Cited in I. D. E. Thomas, *The Golden Treasury of Puritan Quotations* (Chicago: Moody Press, 1975), 58.

13

John Calvin and Psalm 110: The Psalm for Yesterday and Today—Psalm 110

Martin Holdt

I have never heard a sermon on this psalm. Compared to all that has been written and said about Psalm 23, Psalm 110 is surely a very neglected part of the sacred Scriptures. Jesus quoted from it in Matthew 22:41–45. The apostles did as well in Acts 2:34–35. The letter to the Hebrews does so in Hebrews 1:13; 5:6; 10:12–13. The whole of Hebrews chapter 7 is a commentary on verse 4.

The psalm is messianic. It must have been of paramount importance to the apostles and the early Christians, and so should it be to us. John Calvin says about this psalm, "The Psalm is thus, beyond all controversy, a very clear prediction of the divinity, priesthood, victories, and triumph of the Messiah. We have so many Scriptural helps to its exposition that we can be at no loss as to its meaning."[1]

1. John Calvin, *Calvin's Commentaries* (Grand Rapids: Baker, 1981), 6:4.296.

It teaches the greatness of David's great Son. Verse 1 teaches that he is coequal to the Father. He is distinct as a person in the Godhead, and yet one with God in lordship. What the Father has, he has. He is holy as God is. He is omnipotent as God is. He is sovereign as God is. He is merciful as God is. There is nothing about God that is not true of him. He is God, and he is seated on his throne! Romans 1:2–4 adds, "which he promised beforehand through his prophets in the holy Scriptures, concerning his Son, who was descended from David according to the flesh and was declared to be the Son of God in power according to the Spirit of holiness by his resurrection from the dead, Jesus Christ our Lord" as the fulfillment of Psalm 110:1. The sacrifice has been accepted. It pleased the Lord to bruise him. Now the Father invites the Son to take his place on the throne. Plumer says, "Sitting denotes permanence of position. Sitting denotes majesty and authority."[2] In his ascension, Jesus was exalted to this position.

This is not a symbolic throne, as is, for example, the throne of Queen Elizabeth II. Christ is not merely a figurehead. This is not a nonexecutive position. It is an executive throne! From this proceeds the dictates of his will! By gradual process of subjugation, he is conquering human hearts. One of his devout enemies was Saul of Tarsus, who in one moment was breathing out threatenings and slaughter against the body of Christ, but the next moment was conquered by the Son of God. Another one was you, and see what he has done! His enemies put up fierce resistance. However, he shatters the spear and the sword. It is God who does all this. The subjugation of his enemies is not confined to his elect, who start out hostile and end up as his willing slaves. It includes all others.

Christ rules all his enemies. The incorrigible are crushed. The rest are saved. There was Herod, who in all his pomp was struck down by the Lord in judgment of his arrogance. Acts 12:21–23 says, "On an appointed day Herod put on his royal robes, took

2. William S. Plumer, *Commentary on the Psalms* (Edinburgh: Banner of Truth, 1975), 973.

his seat upon the throne, and delivered an oration to them. And the people were shouting, 'The voice of a god, and not of a man!' Immediately an angel of the Lord struck him down, because he did not give God the glory, and he was eaten by worms and breathed his last." There have been others. No monarch has ever succeeded in getting the better of the Son of God. Psalm 2:4–6 states, "He who sits in the heavens laughs; the Lord holds them in derision. Then he will speak to them in his wrath, and terrify them in his fury, saying, 'As for me, I have set my King on Zion, my holy hill.'" Calvin comments: "Let us learn that, however numerous those enemies may be who conspire against the Son of God, and attempt the subversion of his kingdom, all will be unavailing, for they shall never prevail against God's immutable purpose, but, on the contrary, they shall, by the greatness of his power, be laid prostrate at Christ's feet."

The story is well known of Julian the Roman, who once pointed his dagger to heaven to find the Son of God whom he used to call the Galilean. But when he was wounded in battle and saw that it was all over, he took some of his clotted blood and threw it into the air, saying, "You have conquered, oh you Galilean." For those whose status changes from enemies to friends, it is called irresistible grace. To others, it is certain defeat and a forced admission that he is, after all, Lord! Philippians 2:10–11 declares, "So that at the name of Jesus every knee should bow, in heaven and on earth and under the earth, and every tongue confess that Jesus Christ is Lord, to the glory of God the Father." Calvin writes, "However much the world may rage against Christ, it will never be able to hurl him from the right hand of the Father. Moreover, as he does not reign on his own account, but for our salvation, we may rest assured that we will be protected and preserved from all ills under the guardianship of this invincible King."[3]

3. Calvin, *Commentaries*, 6:4.301.

Second, the place from which he will rule is proclaimed. In the execution of his gracious plans, he will extend his mighty scepter from Zion. Calvin comments: "If God had not told us in this place respecting the extension of Christ's kingdom, we would not this day have been classed among his people."[4] Since Zion is the place of his rule, are we not to see the church, the body of Christ, the city of our God as the place in which and through which he does his will on earth as it is in heaven? First Corinthians 1:2 is a most brilliant definition of the church. Here is our *ecclesia*. This is God's Zion—a people called out of darkness into light by God himself, a local, visible church, either in Corinth or wherever it is and functions. It consists of "those sanctified in Christ Jesus," that is, set apart in him and for him. They alone are not the only people he rules, for a spiritual body of believers in a local church are only a part of "all those who in every place call upon the name of our Lord Jesus Christ, both their Lord and ours" (1 Cor. 1:2). There he rules.

Third, his glorious following is shown in verse 3. Like the disciples, his people then and now are a motley bunch. Remarkably sensitive, easily provoked, so very vulnerable, and still struggling with sin! For all that, motivated by the grace of God, led by the Spirit of God, and moved by the love of Christ, this is what the people of God are. This is what verse 3 is teaching. Calvin comments on this magnificent verse: "In relation to the number of his subjects, and their prompt and cheerful obedience to his commands . . . they shall be a willing people, spontaneously and cheerfully consecrating themselves to his service."[5] This is what he had seen in the Reformation. People, many of them, transformed by the grace of God, gathering eagerly to hear the Word of God and enthusiastic about the will of God.

In the second part of verse 3, there is a reference to the "dew of your youth." The freshness of the dew of early morning com-

4. Ibid., 301.
5. Ibid., 301–2

pared to the weariness that precedes retirement at night is a fitting analogy of the condition of true believers from the moment of conversion until they die, unless they lapse into lukewarmness. Note the irony of Acts 8:1b–5: "And there arose on that day a great persecution against the church in Jerusalem, and they were all scattered throughout the regions of Judea and Samaria, except the apostles. Devout men buried Stephen and made great lamentation over him. But Saul was ravaging the church, and entering house after house, he dragged off men and women and committed them to prison. Now those who were scattered went about preaching the word. Philip went down to the city of Samaria and proclaimed to them the Christ." Note the deep commitment of Paul's friends in Christ from Romans 16:3, 4a, 6, 12. They did it for nothing! The love of Christ constrained them. You know God's people by their willingness to serve him who died for them.

Why did this psalm mean so much to Jesus, the apostles, and the early church? Why is it so important to God if quoted as often as it is in the New Testament? One of its verses was the sword of the Spirit that formed part of the sermon that led to thousands of conversions on the day of Pentecost! Psalm 110 seemed to have rolled off the tongues of early believers, and it seemed to have gripped their thinking. Take the letter to the Hebrews, and think of chapters 1, 5, and 7. Persecuted Jews were being told, "We have a high priest and we have a temple and we have sacrifices; what do you have? All that you have is a stranger from Galilee who was ignominiously crucified!" Among the key words in the letter to the Hebrews are the words "we have." Hebrews 8:1; "Now the point in what we are saying is this: we have such a high priest, one who is seated at the right hand of the throne of the Majesty in heaven."

Well, then, what do we have in our Messiah? First, we have a priest who is a king (v. 4). The New Testament writers had no difficulty identifying Jesus as the fulfillment of this verse. Luke 24:44: "Then he said to them, 'These are my words that I spoke to you while I was still with you, that everything written about me in the Law of Moses and the Prophets and the Psalms must be fulfilled.'" He was the result of God's promise made under oath (v. 4a)! Did God need the oath? No! He cannot but be true. Numbers 23:19 says, "God is not man, that he should lie, or a son of man, that he should change his mind. Has he said, and will he not do it? Or has he spoken, and will he not fulfill it?" We do need an oath! We tend to doubt even him! Shame on us!

The incarnation should settle all our doubts; against all odds, Jesus came. Born of a virgin, threatened by Herod, hated and killed by the Jews—God knew that would happen. Yet he never changed his mind (v. 4a). His purposes are fixed and glorious! What are they? They are centered in his Son (v. 4b). Throughout the Old Testament, no priest dared assume the role of a king. Godly Samuel did not. No king was to be a priest. Saul was judged for trying to do the work of a priest. So was Uzziah. The two offices were kept separate and very strictly so. If you needed the help of a priest, you went in one direction. If you needed the help of a king, you went in another. Had Jesus come to be another Levitical priest, an Aaron, he could not have been a king! He came by God's appointment as a priest and a king (v. 4b). Hebrews 7:1–3, 24b–28 repeats what Psalm 110:4 is saying to us. Again from the pen of Calvin:

> The priesthood of Christ is invested with great importance, seeing that it is ratified by the oath of God. And, in fact, it is the very turning point upon which our salvation depends; because, but for our reliance on Christ our Mediator, we would be all debarred from entering into God's presence. In prayer, too, nothing is more needful for us than sure confidence in God, and therefore he not only invites us to come to him, but also by an oath hath appointed an advocate for the purpose of obtaining acceptance for us in his sight. . . . When he promises a new priest, it is certain that he would

> be one who would be superior to all others, and would also abolish the then existing order.[6]

All your needs are met by him. By his bloody sacrifice, you have a priest who sacrificed his own body as a ransom for sin. By his ascension, you have a king (v. 1a) who commands everything to favor your salvation and sanctification. Ephesians 1:11 says, "In him we have obtained an inheritance, having been predestined according to the purpose of him who works all things according to the counsel of his will." Matthew begins with a reference to his priesthood. Matthew 1:21 says, "She will bear a son, and you shall call his name Jesus, for he will save his people from their sins." Matthew 28:18 ends with a reference to his kingship: "And Jesus came and said to them, 'All authority in heaven and on earth has been given to me.'" He has all power over kings (for our day and age, that means presidents), all power over events, and all power over nations. All power over everything! To have all your sins forgiven is wonderful. But to know that he governs the universe to make Romans 8:28 true is equally glorious. What it must have meant to hurting Christians in the first couple of centuries A.D. What it should mean to us in our century in this topsy-turvy world! He governs the world as his will is done on earth as it is in heaven. The Lord God omnipotent reigns.

He is a conqueror who will overcome all opposition. Do you sometimes feel as Lot did? 2 Peter 2:7–8 says, "And if he rescued righteous Lot, greatly distressed by the sensual conduct of the wicked (for as that righteous man lived among them day after day, he was tormenting his righteous soul over their lawless deeds that he saw and heard)." Are you not deeply disappointed in your country's leaders, respected and revered as they may be? Are they examples of morality? How many rulers in our time are not quite the role models we want our children or grandchildren to fol-

6. Ibid., 306

low? Many of them cover up for their dishonesty. Others legislate in favor of sin—sin that nailed our Savior to the tree! Yes, and they legislate to make the homosexual comfortable in his sin, to kill babies in the womb, to favor the indolent and lazy, and to discriminate against the industrious. Why, then, do we pray for them? We do so that they may be converted. Our only real hope in an earthly government is the conversion of those who rule. We are encouraged to pray for them. 1 Timothy 2:1–6 teaches: "First of all, then, I urge that supplications, prayers, intercessions, and thanksgivings be made for all people, for kings and all who are in high positions, that we may lead a peaceful and quiet life, godly and dignified in every way. This is good, and it is pleasing in the sight of God our Savior, who desires all people to be saved and to come to the knowledge of the truth. For there is one God, and there is one mediator between God and men, the man Christ Jesus, who gave himself as a ransom for all, which is the testimony given at the proper time." But what if they stubbornly refuse? Verses 5 and 6 indicate what the Lord will do with kings, presidents, and prime ministers who protect false religion or promote pluralism at the expense of pure and undefiled religion. Here are Calvin's brilliant words: "In these words David celebrates the dreadful nature of that power which Christ possesses for the dispersion and destruction of his enemies; and by this means he affirms, that though encompassed by bands of deadly foes, yet their malignant attempts would not prevent God from upholding the King whom he has set up."[7] Imagine that day! Revelation 6:14–17 says: "The sky vanished like a scroll that is being rolled up, and every mountain and island was removed from its place. Then the kings of the earth and the great ones and the generals and the rich and the powerful, and everyone, slave and free, hid themselves in the caves and among the rocks of the mountains, calling to the mountains and rocks, 'Fall on us and hide us from the face of him who is

7. Ibid., 308

seated on the throne, and from the wrath of the Lamb, for the great day of their wrath has come, and who can stand?'"

Isaiah 66:22–24 also foretells that day: "For as the new heavens and the new earth that I make shall remain before me, says the LORD, so shall your offspring and your name remain. From new moon to new moon, and from Sabbath to Sabbath, all flesh shall come to worship before me, declares the LORD. And they shall go out and look on the dead bodies of the men who have rebelled against me. For their worm shall not die, their fire shall not be quenched, and they shall be an abhorrence to all flesh."

Is this terrible vindictiveness? Is this intolerance? No, it is the verdict of the king, against whom kings and nations have taken their stand. It is against kings and nations who have not taken his warning seriously—his warning given in Psalm 2:10–12: "Now therefore, O kings, be wise; be warned, O rulers of the earth. Serve the Lord with fear, and rejoice with trembling. Kiss the Son, lest he be angry, and you perish in the way, for his wrath is quickly kindled. Blessed are all who take refuge in him." Already now he warns in love. A few years ago, our state theater in Pretoria was closed. We believe it was an act of God. There were those who knew how often blasphemous stage shows made the hearts of the godly ache with grief. What was put on did not go unnoticed by him who sees and knows all things! The final blow will yet be struck (v. 5–6). Present evil structures cannot hold. They already have within them the seeds of their own destruction. God is not mocked; whatever a man sows that shall he reap. Evil will not last, whether it is protected now in parliament or in a brothel. The final blow will yet be struck.

The psalm concludes with verse 7. This is the picture of a conqueror returning from the conquest of his enemies, and having exhausted himself in the process, he refreshes himself by a stream of cool clean water. It is a picture of satisfaction with a mission accomplished, and yet with a full and final goal still to come. Two things are yet to happen. Every single enemy of the gospel, from presidents down, will be brought down. Every vestige of sin will be dealt with, and all evil, including Satan, will be crushed forever. Then all the elect will be brought safely and perfectly home. Jesus' prayer, "Father, I desire that they also, whom you have given me, may be with me where I am, to see my glory that you have given me because you loved me before the foundation of the world" (John 17:24), will be finally answered. And he, our Melchizedek, will love it (v. 7b). All his designs for each one of his chosen people will be perfected. All the rough edges of every believer will be gone for good; we shall be like him.

Calvin comments on this verse: "As a shepherd is gentle towards his flock, but fierce and formidable towards wolves and thieves; in like manner; Christ is kind and gentle towards those who commit themselves to his care, while they who willfully and obstinately reject his yoke, shall feel with what awful and terrible power he is armed."[8]

Derek Kidner has this to say: "The Psalm, by its very form, recalls us to a situation still in movement. We are left with the picture of the warrior following up his victory, like Gideon and his 300 at Jordan, faint yet pursuing, pausing only to renew his strength and press on to complete the rout. Such is the leader, we are to infer, who beckons us to follow."[9]

Then let us follow him to victory! It won't be long! The full and final victory is in sight! All that Jesus died for as priest and to accomplish as king will soon be fully realized. Let us take courage and continue to fight the good fight of faith. Since we have such a king and such a priest, we have all that we need for life and living, as we look forward to an eternity with him who is seated at the right hand of his Father, the king upon his throne.

Delivered July 8, 2009, at St. Pierre Cathedral, Geneva, Switzerland.

8. Ibid.,

9. Derek Kidner, *A Commentary on Books III, IV, and V of the Psalms* (London: Inter-Varsity Press, 1975), 396.

14

More Than Conquerors—Romans 8:35–39

Edward Donnelly

Chronic indigestion, bleeding from the lungs, kidney stones, abscessing hemorrhoids, blinding headaches, and gout—John Calvin was never physically strong, and he rarely knew what it was to be free from pain. His son died shortly after birth, and this bereavement was followed after only nine years of marriage by the death of the wife whom he had grown to love. He spent much of his life in circumstances that he would have done almost anything to avoid. He was hated, opposed, and slandered. Enemies in Geneva set their dogs on him in the streets. Yet this frail, shy man changed the face of Europe. By any standard, he is one of the influential figures of world history, and the 500th anniversary of his birth is being remembered by millions.

How was he able to accomplish so much? How can we explain his prodigious achievements in the midst of so many trials? What can we learn for ourselves from his productive, pain-racked life? The apostle Paul deals with the paradox of suffering and fruitfulness in the closing verses of Romans 8. He has brought the first part of his magnificent doctrinal exposition to a close at verse 30. Man's lack of righteousness has been displayed in all its guilty helplessness. God's gracious provision of righteousness in Jesus Christ has been luminously set forth, together with the profound implications of the gospel for Christian experience. Now, before moving on to Israel's refusal of God's righteousness, he pauses and writes (v. 31): "What then shall we say to these things?" "Now that we have grasped the truth, what effect should it have on us; how are we to use it in the struggles of daily life?" The heart of his answer is found in verse 37—fifteen simple words, almost all of one syllable, but pulsating with power: "No, in all these things we are more than conquerors through him who loved us." The Lord brings these words before us so that we can make them our own confession, and experience the reality of which they speak. Here is the victory of the believer.

The Sphere of Victory

"In all these things"—what things? In verse 35 Paul gathers together most of the troubles we can imagine: "tribulation, distress, persecution, famine, nakedness, danger, sword." Here we have life at its blackest, circumstances at their most difficult—what he refers to in verse 18 as "the sufferings of this present time." Nothing painful seems to be excluded. Such is the sphere of our victory.

"*In* all these things." He chooses his preposition carefully. Not "after all these things." While it is true that an eternity of happiness is coming for the Christian, that is not what Paul is saying here. Not "apart from all these things," for he is not making the point that life isn't always grim and that we are often happy and prosperous. Nor is he advocating a stoic "in spite of all these things," where we grit our teeth and make the best we can of the bad times. It is "in all these things"—in the middle of them, while we are experiencing them, by means of them, that "we are more than conquerors." "These things" form the arena in which our victory is being won.

This is encouraging, for it reminds us that biblical Christianity is invigoratingly honest—the polar opposite of sentimental escapism. The apostle looks at life in this world as it really is. He confronts head-on what Hamlet calls "the heart-ache and the thousand natural shocks that flesh is heir to," and he defies them. The believer's victory can be won, he declares, in every possible situation. It is not dependent on ideal circumstances, for who would then qualify? Wherever we may be at this moment, no matter how difficult our position, wherever we may find ourselves in the future, no matter how painful or testing, we can and will overcome. "In all these things" encompasses everything. Nothing is outside its scope. The promise will never be invalidated.

But these words are also challenging. A better translation of the verb might be "we are *in the process* of more-than-conquering." Paul isn't referring to a time after the victory—the triumphal procession, the official reception, the medals and cheering. As Alexander Maclaren writes, "It is not that we shall be conquerors in some far-off heaven, when the noise of battle has ceased. It is here and now, in the hand-to-hand death grapple that we do overcome."[1] The picture is of a bloody battlefield, a place of carnage and screaming. Those involved are filthy, frightened soldiers, staggering with exhaustion, aching in every limb. The sphere of victory is a place of intense struggle and pain. "Conquering" refers to war, which is never antiseptic, relaxed, or risk-free. It implies enemies, fierce fighting, and wounds. This battle is not to be won by dropping smart bombs from thirty thousand feet. Victory comes only in the hand-to-hand combat of the trenches.

Is that a fair description of your Christian life at present? Are you a warrior? Have you been wounded recently? What are you

1. Alexander Maclaren, *Expositions of Holy Scripture*: Romans (Grand Rapids: Baker, 1978), 205.

attempting for Jesus that is dangerous? When were you last terrified at what he was asking you to do? Is it not the case that many of the Lord's servants are far too comfortable? We have tended to internalize and privatize Christian warfare. We reduce it to our personal struggles against temptation and indwelling sin. These are vital, and plucking out an eye or amputating a hand does hurt, but the battle we are called to is also more extensive and public.

Paul's list of troubles—"tribulation—persecution—danger—sword"—focuses particularly on those that came upon him not because he was a human being but because he was a Christian. They were the outcome of his zeal for Christ—the occupational hazards of a soldier. He suffered because he was faithful to the gospel. And Calvin suffered not simply because he was born with a weak constitution at a time when medicine was rudimentary, but because he was called to be a warrior for Christ. He left behind the cloistered life of scholarship, so attractive to his reserved, studious temperament, and marched into the hateful clamor of controversy. He stood, contended, and bled in the front rank of the battle line, where the fighting was fiercest. He didn't think that he was exceptional in this, for it seemed to him to be the duty of every believer. His comment on "sheep to be slaughtered" is that "the condition of the Church in all ages is here portrayed . . . A state of continual warfare in bearing the cross is enjoined upon us by divine appointment."[2] "In all these things." He knew very well what the "in" meant.

It is all too possible to build tombs for the prophets while being careful at the same time to insulate ourselves from most of what they suffered. To read and admire Calvin, to become an expert on his theology, to attend or speak at conferences in his honor, does not necessarily mean that we have inherited his passion.

One of his favorite terms for the believer was "hero," and there are too few heroes in our churches today. We are capti-

2. John Calvin, *Calvin's Commentaries*, vol. 5 (Grand Rapids: Baker, 1998), 170.

vated and nourished by the God-centered grandeur of Reformation theology, and we are eager to see it taught to others. We seek to live by God's grace, in the path of his commandments, and for his praise. Our people are solid and stable, and they pass on the faith to their children and their children's children. For all this, we should be profoundly thankful. But there is an inertia, a timidity, a lack of enterprise, and a love of ease among us. We are fonder of repeating William Carey's exhortation about expecting and attempting great things than of obeying it. Persecution? Danger? Can we honestly say that we are "in . . . these things"?

Our text is a summons to heroes, a wake-up call from the soul-numbing enjoyment of personal peace and affluence. We need to put ourselves "*in* all these things" by proclaiming, evangelizing, ministering, caring, loving, forgiving, and suffering with a self-sacrificing passion that will make beautiful the faith that we profess. We need to pursue reformation in our churches, whatever the cost. We need to move out of our comfort zones into the dark places of a needy world. We need to assault the citadels of Satan in our culture. We are called to sweat and bleed, to weep and tremble. There is no victory available for those who do not fight. But if we want to overcome, opportunities are all around us.

In God's mercy, a new generation of young people is turning to biblical Christianity. They are hungry for transcendence, for the solidity of historic confessionalism, and they are coming in the thousands to be taught. But they will not be satisfied with theory or with business-as-usual Christianity. They are in earnest, on fire, and they won't be tame or tidy or easy to manage. What draws them is the strange thrill of lives given over to God—devoted completely to glorifying and enjoying him forever. And if we are to commend the truths for which Calvin stood, we must also, in all integrity, become more involved in the warfare in which he ceaselessly engaged.

The Superlative of Victory

In face of enemies so powerful and pressures so daunting, what can we hope for? Should our goal be mere survival, coping somehow with what comes against us? Are we to expect nothing more than winning through by the skin of our teeth? "We are more than conquerors," says Paul. The rare word he uses means total, overwhelming victory. We will utterly overcome the troubles that come upon us. They will prove unable to defeat or even significantly damage us. We conquer them.

More than that, we turn them to advantage. A conqueror defeats his enemy. A more-than-conqueror turns his enemy into an ally and enlists him in his own cause. Paul the apostle is the perfect example of this. He had once been Saul of Tarsus, but the risen Jesus had met him on the Damascus road. He could simply have struck Saul down, taking away his life, which would have been victory. But the Lord had a greater triumph in mind. The persecutor of Christians was to become a preacher of the gospel and the supreme interpreter of the person and work of his Savior. The next thirty years of service and suffering were to prove that, in Paul's life, Jesus Christ had been "more than conqueror."

It is exactly the same with our troubles as Christians. Not only do they fail to harm us—they help us. Instead of defeating us, we find ourselves strengthened by them. What seems to be a curse is transmuted into blessing.

This can be hard to accept while we are in the depths of pain. We aren't ready at that moment to hear how valuable suffering can be. "Whoever sings songs to a heavy heart is like one who takes off a garment on a cold day" (Prov. 25:20), and it sounds horribly glib to suggest to someone in agony that troubles are blessings in disguise.

But that is not what the apostle is saying. "These things" in themselves are not blessings. They are intruders in the world, due to sin, and God hates them. Death is not in the nature of created things, but is instead "the last enemy" (1 Cor. 15:26). "Jesus wept" at the tomb of his friend Lazarus, "deeply moved" by a mixture of sorrow and outrage (John 11:35, 38). Paul himself knew far too much about trouble to treat it lightly or to think that it could be anesthetized with pious phrases. When he wrote of "tribulation, distress, persecution, famine, nakedness, danger," he had already experienced all of these in his missionary endeavors. Only the "sword" was still to come when, on the day of his death, a Roman soldier would bring a blade down on his neck.

But God was taking all these things, painful though they were, and overruling them for good. As he himself tells us, Paul learned lessons through them that he could have assimilated in no other way: "We rejoice in our sufferings, knowing that suffering produces endurance, and endurance produces character, and character produces hope, and hope does not put us to shame" (Rom. 5:3–5). What had been intended by Satan to damage him was being used for his benefit.

John Calvin's testimony would have been identical. He became the man he was and achieved what he did not in spite of the suffering that he experienced but *because* of it. His trials shaped him, and his theology was forged in the furnace of affliction. The controversies with which he had to wrestle compelled him to clarify his understanding of Scripture. Betrayals and disappointments cast him back on God. Persecution purified the church, and in some cases awakened sympathy for the gospel, as again and again the devil overreached himself. It is no coincidence that Calvinism at its best is a fighting faith, producing men and women with steel in their spines, for this is the matrix out of which it sprang. It was the "all these things" that made the "more than conquerors."

And it is still the same, for we have found it so in our own experience. Troubles have come, some of them trying us to the limit, but what has happened? Our faith has been strengthened, our priorities corrected, our vision sharpened, our character refined, our hunger for heaven intensified. Like the psalmist, we have been able to testify: "I know, O LORD, that . . . in faithfulness you have afflicted me" (Ps. 119:75).

Here is the antidote to unbelief. This is the promise that can persuade us to throw off caution and renounce the easy path. For everyone who fights, there is certain, overwhelming victory! We should not fear "all these things," but welcome them, for it is as we venture boldly into them that the gospel triumphs. In this life, the victories are paradoxical and often look like defeat. Like the heroes of Hebrews 11, we will be derided as losers by the world. But faith assures us that our triumphs, though not yet complete, are already real and will be fully revealed in God's time.

It is a thrilling perspective! No disaster can touch us apart from the sovereign will of our loving Father. Not a single person can be lost for whom the Savior died. Nothing in all creation can hinder the building of Christ's church or the irresistible advance of his kingdom. God "works all things according to the counsel of his will" (Eph. 1:11), and before his mighty, redeeming purpose, Satan's worst is powerless. "In all these things we are more than conquerors."

The Source of Victory

Does it sound arrogant? If the text ended at this point, it would be. But Paul adds the transcendent factor that turns weakness into strength and defeat into victory: "through him who loved us." Apart from Jesus Christ, all our talk of conquering would be empty boasting or pathetic whistling in the dark. With him, we are certain to overcome.

He enables us to overcome by *his presence*—"through him." "I am with you always" is his permanent promise to all his people, but to those who are suffering he is particularly close. A mother loves all her children equally, but when one of them is ill, there is a particular outflow of affection to that little one. It doesn't mean that the others are any less dear to her—just that when extra love is needed, it is instinctively given. So it is with Christ. While he loves us all, always and to the end, he has a special concern for those in trouble. The context here is the constancy of his love in circumstances in which it might be questioned, as Paul answers his own rhetorical question: "Who shall separate us from the love of Christ?" by affirming that not anything in all creation "will be able to separate us from the love of God in Christ Jesus our Lord" (vv. 35, 39).

Our Lord has "all authority in heaven and on earth" (Matt. 28:18), and it would be a simple matter for him to remove our troubles or to overcome our enemies with a word, no matter how impossible that might seem to us. But he chooses not to, for "all these things" are part of his sovereign plan. Does he not then care for us in the trials that he allows to come upon us? In our struggling, is his heart not moved with compassion toward us more tenderly than we can imagine? Is he not unceasingly and effectively channeling his infinite power to help and sustain us when we need him most? Throughout history, God's people have found Christ to be especially near in times of darkness. They sense his presence; they feel his upholding hand; they know themselves to be empowered, far beyond anything they could have expected. They are "more than conquerors through him."

But there is more here than the assurance of Christ's presence. The source of victory is ultimately in *his passion*—"through him who loved us." He always has loved his people and always will, from before the creation of the world, during all time and throughout the endless ages of eternity, but the tense of the Greek verb points to one supreme moment in the past when Christ's love was extended in a uniquely significant way. That moment was Calvary, for "greater love has no one than this, that someone lays down his life for his friends" (John 15:13). When Paul speaks elsewhere of "the Son of God, who loved me and gave himself for me" (Gal. 2:20), the love of which he is thinking is that seen in the body on the cross outside Jerusalem. Here is the source of victory—"him who loved us."

Victory because, on the cross, Christ paid the full penalty for our sins, robbed death of its sting, and broke the power of the grave forever. By the sacrifice of himself and his subsequent resurrection, he secured everlasting life for every one of his own. More than that, in this act of love the Lord faced the full force of evil and not only overcame it but used it to serve his good purpose. In that moment of deepest despair, with the Son of God hanging accursed and dead, it seemed as if hell had won. But in all these things God was more than conqueror. For every act of cruelty, every blow of Satan was helping to atone for sin and being overruled for the salvation of Christ's people. It was not a tragedy but a triumph, not a defeat but a victory.

Souvenirs, as the word itself means, are reminders of something important. The holiday souvenir serves as an aid to memory by representing something characteristic of a place we have visited—a model of the Eiffel Tower from Paris or the Parthenon from Athens. And Jesus Christ has left his church a souvenir. It isn't a reminder of his incarnation or of his heavenly glory. He has given us, rather, bread and wine—symbols of his broken, bleeding body, a reminder of his cross. "When you remember me," he said, "remember me like this." For here is where our salvation was accomplished and where victory was won. "Conquerors through him who loved us."

Christ's path to victory is to be ours also. The key verse in Calvin's understanding of the Christian life is Matthew 16:24: "If anyone would come after me, let him deny himself and take up his cross and follow me." "Whomever the Lord has adopted and deemed worthy of his fellowship," he writes, "ought to prepare themselves for a hard, toilsome and unquiet life, crammed with very many and various kinds of evil."[3] This should not daunt

3. *Institutes*, 3.8.1.

us, for since Calvary we can look at suffering without fear and confront all that Satan can do without being shaken in our faith. Why? Because Jesus Christ has been there before us. He loved us with a bloodstained love, and we are privileged to follow in his steps. Our victories aren't marked by swagger and bombast. We aren't smooth or impressive; we don't give the impression that we are riding high above the troubles of less enlightened men and women. We are often tired and troubled; we make mistakes and fall down a lot; we struggle and are sometimes sad. But Christ is with us; he is seen in us; he bears witness through us—and we do overcome! This is how his work is done in the world. He is the source of our victory, and for it he receives all the praise.

It may seem an unnecessary question at a Calvin celebration and he wouldn't have liked the title, but I need to ask: are we really Calvinists? For it is more than standing in a historic tradition or embracing, however wholeheartedly, a marvelously coherent and comprehensive theology. It is a life, a commitment, a willingness to say, "I know that I am not my own master. I offer my heart to the Lord in sacrifice." For Calvinistic role-models we could hardly do better than look to the five young men who were burned for Christ in Lyons on May 16, 1553. Calvin had urged them to be faithful: "Be ready to give your life at any time . . . May the Son of God be glorified by your shame . . . This is sufficient cause to despise the whole world with its pride, till we be gathered into that everlasting Kingdom where we shall fully enjoy those blessings which we now only possess in hope."[4] His students proved true as steel. Dressed in gray shirts and tied together, they were taken in a cart to the place of execution. And as they passed through the streets, they began to sing. It was the ninth psalm. Listen to them:

4. Quoted in Emanuel Stickelberger, *John Calvin* (Cambridge: James Clarke & Co., 1977), 116–17.

Wholehearted thanksgiving to you I will bring;
    in praise of your marvelous works I will sing.
For joy I will shout and exultingly cry in praise of your name,
    Lord my God, O Most High.
The Lord is a stronghold, a refuge, a tower,
    for all the oppressed in their dark, troubled hour.
Those knowing your name, Lord, trust you for your grace;
    you have not forsaken those seeking your face.

This has been a memorable week. We have given thanks for John Calvin and honored God's grace in him. But it isn't real life. Our commitment to the truth he taught is not to be proved in days of recreation, luxurious hotels, historic places of worship, stimulating lectures, or delightful fellowship. These are aids, stimuli—no more. The value of our time together will be demonstrated in the days to come—in our homes, churches, communities, nations—in our laboring and contending and enduring and rejoicing—and in our keeping on.

When the five young men had been fastened to the stakes, they were bound together with a heavy chain and the fire was lit. They stood fast and for a little while, until they entered glory, they could be heard calling to each other, "Courage, brother, courage!" We who have gathered here will never be together again on this earth. But until we do meet once more, let us cry to each other as we separate and take up our crosses, "Courage, brother, courage!" "In all these things we are more than conquerors through him who loved us."

Delivered July 9, 2009, at St. Pierre Cathedral, Geneva, Switzerland.

15

One of a Thousand—Job 36:1–4

Hywel R. Jones

And Elihu continued, and said:

Bear with me a little, and I will show you, for I have yet something to say on God's behalf.

I will get my knowledge from afar and ascribe righteousness to my Maker.

For truly my words are not false; one who is perfect in knowledge is with you. (Job 36:1–4)

Much has been written on the book of Job in the last hundred years or so, and Elihu, the speaker of our text, has been treated dismissively in almost all of it. Although Old Testament scholars no longer deny him a place in the original narrative, they do not assign him a significant role in the history it records. And the same is true of devotional studies of the book, even in those that were written from the perspective of a high view of the Bible! All too often the best that is said about him is that he provides something by way of relief for Job (and the readers of the book) after the hubbub of the speeches and before the fearful interrogation by the Lord. So widespread is this view—and you may well have read it, heard it, or even hold it or some version of it—that it may come as a real surprise to learn that prior to the eighteenth century, Elihu was seen very differently. Not only was he regarded as having a most significant role in Job's recovery, he was also closely associated with the intervention of the Lord that brought it about.

John Calvin did not write a commentary on the book of Job, but he preached his way through it. In the opening sermon he made a comment that provides a key to understanding its most difficult section that, if it had been adopted, would have vastly improved (not to say corrected) many commentaries that have been written on the book. He said that Job had a good case, but he handled it badly, whereas the friends had a bad case that they handled well. By anticipation, we may say that Elihu not only had a good case, but also argued it well.

Calvin described him as a "faithful teacher," compared him to the prophets of Israel, even though he was not an Israelite, and declared that he brought "the pure word of God" and spoke by "the Holy Ghost."[1] Theodore Beza, Calvin's successor, did much the same. In the seventeenth century, the English Puritan Joseph Caryl followed that line of thought in his sermons on the book, and preaching on the opening verses of chapter 32, he made the remark that "after the disputants, come the mediators." By "disputants" he, of course, meant Job and his friends. But who are the mediators? Note the plural noun, for it is significant. It shows that Caryl was not thinking just of the Lord but also of Elihu, and by the use of the one word "mediator," he was associating them in terms of adjudicating and reconciling activity. Elihu's ministry paved the way for the coming

1. All quotations from Calvin in this chapter are from his *Sermos on Job* (Edinburgh: Banner of Truth, 1993).

of the Lord (see Mal. 4:5; James 5: 7–11), and that is why he fades from the scene when the Lord appears and is not censured by him. He can therefore be compared with John the Baptist, the forerunner of "the messenger of the covenant" (Mal. 3:1). To use his own words, Elihu was a rarity—"one of the thousand" (33:23)—a man of God with a message from him.

With that in mind, let us turn to our text. It is the beginning of Elihu's final speech. He has already spoken three times, addressing Job in the main (33:1), but also making an appeal to the friends (34:1). In these words, he claims that he is a messenger for God, that his message is true, and that his burden is to magnify the righteousness of God. We will consider these matters, using material from his speeches to do so; and in the course of doing so, we will be confronted with aspects of the preaching ministry that are so needed in today's church and world—perhaps you have already realized that connection.

A Messenger of God

The closing words of our text, "*One who is perfect in knowledge is with you,*" are often quoted as supplying the final piece of supporting evidence for the derogatory view of Elihu that has been referred to. On the basis of them, he is pilloried as a "Know-All," and that in addition to his being called an "Angry Young Man" and a "Pompous Windbag," on account of his introduction to his first speech (32:1–14). Given such doubtful characteristics, how can Elihu be regarded as a messenger of God?

One way of answering these charges is to say that such faults—and faults they certainly are (see 1 Tim. 3:1–7; 2 Tim. 22–26; Titus 1:7–8 where the apostle Paul declares them to be unworthy of a gospel minister)—would not by themselves prohibit Elihu from being considered as a messenger of God, even if they were true. Think of the prophet Jonah, and also remember that "there is not a righteous man on earth who does good and never sins" (Eccl.

7:20). But each of the three charges seems to be so well grounded in the text that some cautionary remarks should at least be made about them, and even some corrections advanced.

Angry Young Man

There can be no doubt but that the author of the book of Job intends to draw attention to Elihu's anger. He mentions it four times in the first five verses of chapter 32, which open this section of the book. But it should *also* be noted that the author points out that Elihu's anger is roused by what Job and the friends have said.

His anger is therefore not irrational. It is not the fitful passion of people who flare up unaccountably and cool down as inexplicably. It has a cause, and that lies in what people have said—and not what they have said about him. It is not the result of personal pique. Its explanation lies in what all four participants in the debate have said about God and how they have variously represented him. Elihu is impartial. His anger is roused against Job for one reason and the friends for a different one.

First, Job has been concerned to justify himself more than God—that is, he has been intent on putting himself in the clear rather than God. In fact, he has blamed God while exculpating himself. Second, Job has been found guilty by the friends, without a fair trial. In God's name, they have declared him to be in the wrong, without adequate proof. Job had "justified himself more than God," and the friends, speaking in God's name, had "found no answer but condemned Job." Elihu's anger is therefore not mindless but moral.

The word "anger" is not an inaccurate translation of the Hebrew, but "indignant" would make things clearer. Elihu's anger is related to what is right—or rather to the lack of it. Interestingly, the expression "his anger burned" is also used by the Lord at the end of the book (see 42:7), again with regard to Job and the friends and on exactly the same grounds as Elihu had specified. Elihu's anger is therefore like that of the Lord—not as pure, of course, because God's anger is sinless, but it is of the same kind. It is morally based, discriminating, and just. Does that not sound much more like God's jealous concern for his own honor, which, when it is reflected in human experience, amounts to godly zeal and not blind rage?

Pompous Windbag

It is true that Elihu does refer to himself many times in his first speech, and what is more, he is not diffident about doing so. But this should not be understood without giving full weight to other details in the text, for he has been present all through the debate, listening to what has been said, expecting that the friends would deal with Job's case thoroughly, but no one has. And now that they are all silent, he cannot be so because he sees that the matter cannot be left where it is! God's honor has been sullied by each and every one of them, and that moves him. He is no more impulsive than irrational, but being young and deferential, he has to stand alone and speak unsupported. In such circumstances what could be more understandable than that he says "I"—and that he does so a lot! (This chapter should not be read from the pulpit in a tone that accentuates a negative view of Elihu.)

Mr. Know-All

Even in the sixteenth century, there was some difference of opinion as to who Elihu had in mind when he used the words "one who is perfect in knowledge is with you." Calvin refers to some who thought that Elihu could have been referring to God, while himself preferring to read the text in a straightforward manner (as he so often does). Calvin therefore understood Elihu to have been speaking about himself, but he immediately added the rider that by this expression Elihu did not mean "to vaunt himself in his own person but to [the] end that the doctrine which he bringeth (according as it is of God) might be received and every man humble himself under it." "Perfect in knowledge" is therefore a statement about *what* Elihu had to say rather than about himself as a speaker. Although the net difference between these two sixteenth-century readings is not that great, they do give an alternative to the modern view that is intent on seeing Elihu's words as almost amounting to a claim to omniscience. However, it should not be forgotten that Elihu does speak later of God as being "perfect in knowledge" (see 37:16), and so the view that he is referring to God by these words (which I prefer) does not amount to special pleading.

Thus we regard Elihu as being zealous, not pompous, "full of words" for God, not full of self-importance (32:18). He had a profound awareness that God was his maker and judge (32:22; 36:3), but also an equally profound desire to see Job restored to fellowship with God. He says, "I desire to justify you" (33:32). As surely as Haggai was "the Lord's messenger in the Lord's message" to the people of his day (Hag. 1:13 KJV), so was Elihu to Job. And like Abel, "he being dead yet speaks" to Christians today, whether they are suffering themselves or speaking to such in God's name.

A Message from God

Any messenger worthy of the name knows that he has been entrusted with something to say. That is especially so for every preacher of God's Word, and Elihu is a classic example of such conviction and assurance. He knew that he had been speaking words for God and also that he had still more to say for him (36:2). His message consisted of words that were "not false," that is, words that would neither misinform nor mislead (v. 4). His message was characterized by "knowledge," and it concerned "righteousness"

(v. 3). These are central elements of the gospel of Christ (Rom. 1:16–17). We will consider each of these.

I Will Get My Knowledge from Afar

Elihu is speaking metaphorically here. In his day, knowledge, and especially wisdom, was regarded as being so far removed from the generality of human beings (see 11:7–12; 28:1–28) that it was those who had lived longer than others or farthest away from any region who were likely to have it (see 8:8–10; 11:7–12; 15:7–10; 21:29). By claiming "knowledge from afar," Elihu is declaring that God, his maker, has disclosed his message to him. It consists of convicting Job of his sin and confronting him with the restoring righteousness of God.

Job has sinned against God by his outspoken criticism of him. Elihu has heard Job's outbursts, and concluded that he has "justified himself rather than God" (32:2). Instead of acknowledging the supremacy and authority of God and the limited nature of his own understanding, Job has turned everything on its head. It is indeed true that man cannot absolve himself without condemning God. To prove this charge, Elihu quotes Job's own words back to him (see 33:9–11; 34:5–7) with the prefatory remark, "Surely you have spoken in my ears, and I have heard the sound of your words" (33:8). Elihu is not at odds with the friends over the offensiveness of Job's scornful speech (see 34:34–37; 35:16) or their recognition of the justice and power of God (see chapter 34). Indeed, he claims that Job has been speaking like the wicked who rebel against God and so deserve his judgment (see 34:1–15).

God's message to human beings does not ignore their sin, and so his messengers are not to make light of it. Sin is always against God. It is never just against other human beings. To address it *as such* is one of the hallmarks of the true messenger of God. The way to peace with God is never by way of ignoring or minimizing sin. "Whoever conceals his transgressions will not prosper, but he who confesses and forsakes them will obtain mercy" (Prov. 28:13). That truth is proclaimed by the friends, as well as by Elihu (see 5:17–27; 11:13–20; 33:24–28). Repentance is the way to restoration, and that truth was borne out in what happened to both Job and the friends (42:1–9).

But such an agreement does not mean that Elihu only repeats what the friends say. That has often been said, in spite of Elihu's own words: "[Job] has not directed his words against me, and I will not answer him with your speeches" (32:14; see also 35:4). Elihu knows that he has something to say that is both different from and additional to their "speeches," just as the gospel of Christ counters and exceeds all the wisdom of the world (see 1 Cor. 1:18–2:16). As the bearer of God's revealed word, Elihu can teach "wisdom" (33:33), and so he lays claim to a knowledge that is "*perfect*." What does that mean?

The adjective that is translated "perfect" can also mean "complete," that is, something that is in contrast to what is partial. In this setting what is limited is, of course, the knowledge of the friends and of Job himself. Job's piety is described by this adjective in the opening verse of the book, along with the adjective "upright." This couplet could be rendered as "rounded and straight," which means that Job's piety was without glaring deficiencies and deviations. It was coherent and consistent. Applied to Elihu's message, it means that what he had to say dealt with the situation fully and that he knew it. It met the need of that hour, just as the good news of Jesus Christ and him crucified is always the wisdom and power of God to ignorant and enslaved sinners (see 1 Cor. 1:18–2:5).

Job's friends have all been majoring on the cause of Job's sufferings, which they declare to be sin on his part. This is true even of Eliphaz, who, though he gives some sensitivity to Job's anguish and speaks of divine "chastisement" and "discipline," does so only in the context of suffering being a sign of divine displeasure on account of human sin. Eliphaz says, "As I have seen, those who plow iniquity and sow trouble reap the same. By the breath of

God they perish, and by the blast of his anger they are consumed" (4:8–9). This is the unvarying diagnosis of the friends—Job is suffering grievously *because* he has committed some terrible sin (8:2–6; 11:5–6).

By contrast, Elihu never says such a thing. He is silent on the *cause* of Job's sufferings. His concern is that Job has been sinning grievously *because* he is suffering—and not the other way around. This is part of the reason why they all, and Job, too, remained silent in spite of the fact that Elihu paused from time to time and invited comment. He is focusing on facts they all know, rather than advancing a theory that they can debate. Their silence is therefore significant, given the fact that previously each of them had been so keen to speak. New ground was being cut altogether.

How many Christians have from time to time been told that they are suffering because they have sinned, and that they are continuing to suffer because they either will not repent or do not have any or enough faith when they do? Such was the satanic lie the friends presented. It was calculated to provoke Job, who knew that he had not sinned prior to the day when his afflictions began, to "curse God to his face" for having become so unjust. It is true that all suffering is *ultimately* traceable to sin, but that it is only *some* sufferings that are the *direct* result of sins committed—and God has a good purpose in them all. Such a distortion was common thinking in our Lord's day. Remember that his disciples asked him, "Rabbi, who sinned, this man or his parents, that he was born blind?" and that Jesus answered, "It was not that this man sinned, or his parents, but that the works of God might be displayed in him" (John 9:1–3).

Elihu's message is therefore in line with our Lord's correction. He does have something to say as to why Job was afflicted, but this is not the "why" of cause; it is the "why" of purpose. True, it does not amount to an account or even a hint of what had transpired in the heavenly court, for that had not been revealed to him—just as it would not be to either Job or the friends. Inscrutability is part of divine sovereignty. Secret things belong to the Lord (Deut. 29:29), and he is to be trusted and served by his believing people however dark his ways may be to them.

God is all-powerful and all-wise, but he is also *good*, and that is the something "new" that Elihu has to say to Job and the friends. The Most High does not do whatever he does just to show he has the authority and the power to do it. Nor does he merely do it for his own glory. He does it for his people's good. As Elihu senses the approach of the Lord in wind and rain, thunder and lightning, and snow and ice, he can say that God acts in "a perfect storm," not only for "correction" but also for the "land" (it is his and he made it) *and also for "love"* (37:13). Hardships, disasters, and suffering do not have to be a severe judgment. They may be a severe mercy, for "behind a frowning providence he hides a smiling face." Suffering is not always punitive; sometimes it is not even purgative. It may just be preventive, as Elihu says, to "hide pride from man" (33:17 KJV); and when it fails to achieve that end, due to sinful human frailty, it can then be productive of restoration by the goodness and mercy of God.

I Will Ascribe Righteousness to My Maker

Elihu has been hearing a debate about whether God is being righteous in relation to Job's sufferings. Job has been denying it, claiming that he has "not denied the words of the Holy One" (6:10). The friends have been maintaining it, declaring that God does not "pervert justice [and] the Almighty [does not] pervert the right" (8:3), and so Job is being justly punished for his sin. Still Job asserts that his "vindication [righteousness] is at stake" (6:29), although he acknowledges that, speaking generally, no one can "be in the right before God" (9:2).

Job is convinced that his is a special case, which of course it is at that time. He therefore believes that God alone has an answer to it, if only it could be presented to him. But could Job plead his case successfully before him, even if he were to be given the opportunity? He doubts it because God "is wise in heart and mighty in strength" (9:4). In a really dark moment, Job claims that God is immoral or amoral because he "destroys both the blameless and the wicked" and "mocks at the calamity of the innocent" (9:22–23). Then in a better moment he longs for an "arbiter between us [that is, God and himself], who might lay his hand on us both" (9:33). If only God were to make himself bearable to Job, then there would be hope of a settlement of the dispute over who is righteous (13:20–22). All this makes clear that Job's relationship with God has been disrupted.

Elihu had heard all this. He knew that he was the answer to Job's request and the arbiter in Job's dispute with God (33:23). He could say that he was "according to [Job's] wish in God's stead" (33:6 Geneva Bible) so that righteousness might be restored between them. He says to Job, "I desire to justify you. . . . I will teach you wisdom" (33:32–33), and he sets about this by "ascrib[ing] righteousness to [his] maker" (36:3). Like the apostle Paul, Elihu is convinced that the just God is also a justifier (Rom. 3:26).

We have already noted that Elihu connects hardships in the realm of nature and human affairs not only with divine power and judgment but also with God's love (37:13). God is good, even though he speaks by way of afflictions, even an illness that is mortal. His thoughts and ways are his own. They are higher than those of man, but his purpose is good! It is to "turn man aside from his deed and conceal pride from a man; [to keep] back his soul from the pit [and] his life from perishing by the sword" on account of it (33:17–18). In his opening speech (33:12–33), he shows that Job is "not right[eous]" in saying that God is silent. God is not dumb; it is Job who is deaf. God is not heartless; Job is unjust.

And so Elihu goes on in one of the most beautiful Old Testament messages about God's restoration of righteousness to man, which is the good news of the gospel. In what he says, he refers to both man and God by the same third-person singular pronoun and makes rapid changes between them, as is often the case in Hebrew poetry, especially the psalms. He says:

> If there be for him [i.e., the afflicted) an angel, a mediator, one of the thousand, to declare to man what is *right* for him,
>
> and he [i.e., God] is merciful to him, and says, "Deliver him from going down into the pit; I have found a ransom; let his flesh become fresh with youth; let him return to the days of his youthful vigor";
>
> then he [i.e., the afflicted] prays to God, and he [God] accepts him; he sees his [God's] face with a shout of joy, and he [God] restores to man *his righteousness.*
>
> He [i.e., the afflicted] sings before men and says: "I sinned and perverted what was *right,* and it was not repaid to me.
>
> [But he (i.e., God)] has redeemed my soul from going down into the pit, and my life shall look upon the light."
>
> Behold, God does all these things, twice, three times, with a man, to bring back his soul from the pit, that he may be lighted with the light of life. (Job 33:23–30)

Here is the stock in trade of the preacher of "the glorious gospel of the blessed God" (1 Tim. 1:11 KJV).

Human beings lack righteousness and are heading for destruction, but God is merciful and provides a mediator and a ransom in Jesus Christ. The humbled sinner confesses his sin to God, and God delivers him from the punishment he deserves and restores him to a new life that he lives with gladness in the light of God's countenance. This is the message of reconciliation that God gives to his ambassadors (2 Cor. 5:17–21), which he himself delights to hear preached and is pleased to use. It is also what every human being needs to hear. Elihu is (to quote Calvin once more):

> A messenger of God's grace . . . an odd man among a thousand, and so rare a benefit, as we ought to esteem highly. Howbeit this is not said to make us esteem the persons, but to make us receive the benefit which is ministered unto us by them with the greater reverence, that is to say to make us receive the grace of God, for as much as it pleaseth him to draw us to him, and to justify us of his fatherly love, showing us that although we be wretched and miserable, and that there be nothing in us but death and damnation, yet he will not leave us there, but deliver us by the mean[s] of our Lord Jesus Christ.

Such men are what the church needs in every generation and the world even more. They are concerned with theology centered on the gospel and not a theodicy based on philosophy. Their goal is not to make the ways of God acceptable to human beings but to direct sinful human beings to Jesus Christ, who, though just, took the place of the unjust so that they might be made acceptable to God.

Delivered July 9, 2009, at St. Pierre Cathedral, Geneva, Switzerland.

16

Bowing before the Majesty of God—Romans 11:33–36

Derek W. H. Thomas

The publication in 1559 of the final edition of John Calvin's *The Institutes of the Christian Religion* is fascinating from several points of view, not least in tracing the changes that took place from the first pocket-sized edition in 1536 to its final form, which contained eighty chapters in four "books." What had begun as a commentary on the Apostles' Creed grew somewhat disproportionately in response to a variety of contentious issues that arose during the Reformer's ministry in Geneva. But perhaps most importantly, it was Paul's letter to the Romans that shaped the definitive change from the first edition of the *Institutes* in 1536 to the second edition in 1539. During Calvin's exile from Geneva in the city of Strasbourg, the young Reformer, barely thirty years old, wrote his first commentary on this epistle. It has been suggested that the contours of theology as defined by the *Institutes* owe more to Calvin's study of Romans than to any other single cause.

Not the least important in this suggestion of the influence of Romans on the shape of the *Institutes* is the location of the Reformer's discussion of the doctrine of predestination (including election and reprobation). It is a well-known fact that Calvin moved the location of this doctrine from the beginning of the 1536 and 1539 editions of the *Institutes* (where one might argue it logically belongs) to a point, in the final edition, subsequent to the discussion of the application of redemption by the Holy Spirit in the life of the believer. This, it should be noticed, is precisely its location in Romans (as opposed, say, to Ephesians, where it occurs in the opening sentences of the letter). The effect of this change was to suggest that predestination is a doctrine best understood by believers after they come to know the redemptive work of Jesus Christ applied by the Holy Spirit. Election belongs to those truths that the Holy Spirit enforces in the hearts of the faithful, rather than something to be discussed and debated in the prolegomena and apologetic arguments of the Christian faith.

In particular, Calvin found no embarrassment by the transition from the exalted phrases of the closing of the eighth chapter of Romans and the tension of the opening verses of the ninth chapter. Many have questioned the connection. How can Paul end with the peroration "neither death nor life, nor angels nor rulers, nor things present nor things to come, nor powers, nor height nor depth, nor anything else in all creation, will be able to separate us from the love of God in Christ Jesus our Lord," only to then go on and ask whether God's purposes have been compromised because so many of his own fellow Jews have rejected the gospel? But for Calvin, the segue to a discussion on predestination is natural. In beginning the discussion on predestination in the *Institutes*, Calvin had asked the question: Why do some respond to the gospel and others do not? The answer lies in the sovereign discrimination of God, nowhere more sharply drawn than the quotation in Romans 9:13:

"Jacob have I loved, but Esau have I hated" (KJV). In the end, the reason lies in the sovereign disposition of God. While believers may rejoice over the preservation of the saints to final glory, they must also ask why it is that they have believed the gospel and others have not. The reason, Paul has argued in Romans 9–11, lies in God's sovereign and mysterious purposes. And it is this consideration that leads Paul, by way of his concluding statement in Romans 11:33–36, to sing a hymn of praise to God's sovereignty in which three assertions are made.

A Vision of God's Incomprehensibility

Paul begins this song of praise by saying: "Oh, the depth of the riches and wisdom and knowledge of God! How unsearchable are his judgments and how inscrutable his ways!" (Rom. 11:33). Calvin, who takes Paul to mean that there are riches of wisdom and riches of knowledge (two facets rather than three), comments on verse 33: "Here first the apostle bursts into an exclamation, which arose spontaneously from a devout consideration of God's dealings with the faithful."[1] Paul is exulting in the greatness of the mind and wisdom of God. There are riches, or depths, in these that are beyond his (and our) grasp. And God's mind and wisdom are applied in twin directions: "How unsearchable are his judgments and how inscrutable his ways! 'For who has known the mind of the Lord, or who has been his counselor?'"

By any standards, the apostle Paul had a great mind. He had been educated under the most prestigious rabbinic scholar of the times, Rabbi Gamaliel (Acts 22:3). Furthermore, he had seen things that no one else had seen, having been taken into the "third heaven" (2 Cor. 12:2). But in comparison to the knowledge God himself possesses, the apostle's knowledge appears tiny and insignificant. The same is even more true of those who now read the Scriptures and the writings of the apostle—the thirteen epistles

1. John Calvin, *Commentaries upon the Epistles of Paul the Apostle to the Romans*, 22 vols. (Grand Rapids: Baker, 1981), 19:444; CO 49:230.

that bear his authorship. The information contained in them ranges over the entire encyclopedia of Christianity, and as his companion Peter reminds us, there are some things in these writings that are difficult to understand (2 Peter 3:15). Nevertheless, were we to attempt to fathom the depths of these writings, our understanding would still pale in comparison with the knowledge God has.

Knowledge of God and knowledge of the things God has made and how we should relate to them was absolutely crucial to Calvin. The opening sentence of the *Institutes,* reflecting something Augustine wrote in his *Soliloquies,* is among the most memorable lines the Reformer ever wrote: "Nearly all the wisdom we possess, that is to say, true and sound wisdom, consists of two parts: the knowledge of God and of ourselves." But even when, through the application of the redemptive work of Christ on our behalf, we are born again and made heirs of God and joint heirs with Jesus Christ, our knowledge of God, though true and sound knowledge, remains finite and contained. Were we to spend the rest of eternity exploring the depths of God's self-disclosure to us, we could never attain to the knowledge and wisdom that God has in himself. To cite something Augustine wrote when exploring the doctrine of the Trinity, "I am not silent in thoughts, even when I am silent in words." We may see the depths if not the bottom!"[2]

Paul, in Romans 11:34, cites from the prophet Isaiah when he writes, "For who has known the mind of the Lord, or who has been his counselor?" (Isa. 40:13). The prophet goes on to ask, "To whom then will you liken God . . . ?" (Isa. 40:18). The answer the prophet suggests is that all such attempts to compare God with someone or something end up as an "idol." The prophet mocks the idea that something that is made of metal or carved from wood can ever come close to being like God. The idea is preposterous, but as Calvin tells us in the opening of the *Institutes,* man's mind is a *idolorum factorum*—a

2. "On the Trinity," in *Nicene and Post-Nicene Fathers,* 1st ser., ed. Philip Schaff, 14 vols. (Peabody, MA: Hendricksen Publishers, 2004), 3:228.

"perpetual factory of idols." The natural man knows no limit in the degree of ingenuity with which he manufactures in his own mind a "god" before which he bows down and gives the affection and obedience of his heart. Such is the arrogance of the impious heart.

By contrast, piety consists in bowing before the majesty of God. Piety consists in acknowledging that everything we know—about God, about ourselves, and about the world we live in—is known because God has revealed it to us. In particular, Calvin makes the following comment when it comes to the issue of predestination (something Paul has just been talking about in the preceding chapters in Romans):

> Whenever then we enter on a discourse respecting the eternal counsels of God, let a bridle be always set on our thoughts and tongue, so that after having spoken soberly and within the limits of God's word, our reasoning may at last end in admiration. Nor ought we to be ashamed, that if we are not wiser than he, who, having been taken into the third heaven, saw mysteries to man ineffable, and who yet could find in this instance no other end designed but that he should thus humble himself.[3]

God's knowledge is vast and beyond our ability to conceive. We may in 2009 imagine the amount of information contained in the vast libraries of the world, or in the PhD dissertations that have been written (on Calvin or Paul alone!), or on hard drives of supercomputers, but these are tiny and insignificant compared to what an infinite mind can know. God is omniscient. He knows all actual and potential events. He knows everything exhaustively.

We are to be humble in our deliberations about God's judgments and ways. We must avoid speculation and firmly adhere to that which God has been pleased to reveal to us. If we stray from these paths, we will end up (so Calvin comments, employing one of his favorite metaphors) in a "labyrinth" from which it will be impossible to escape. God's

3. Calvin, *Romans*, 444; CO 49:181.

omniscience and wisdom means that he not only knows everything, but also knows how to achieve all of his aims and goals. In the outworking of providence, God's will is done perfectly. All we can do—all we *must* do—by way of response is "to admire and adore" him. It is what we were created for and for what we have been redeemed.

In the end, we must confess that God is incomprehensible. This does not mean that God cannot be known at all. Rather, it insists that God cannot be known fully and exhaustively. Indeed, what we know of God, we know only a little. God cannot be known by us except as he reveals himself to us in "baby-talk." At every point, God must accommodate his knowledge to our finite capacities. This is true of what God does, as much as how God *is* in himself. How can we expect to comprehend what God is doing in our lives? The providences of God are a deep mystery. His ways are not our ways (Isa. 55:8). Sometimes, when we find ourselves in the midst of difficult circumstances, all we can say is what the apostle writes in Romans 8:28: "And we know that for those who love God all things work together for good, for those who are called according to his purpose."

God is incomprehensible, and therefore our response should be one of wonder and awe in his presence.

A Vision of the Sovereignty of God

The second citation from the Old Testament in the passage under consideration is taken from the book of Job: "Or who has given a gift to him that he might be repaid?" (Rom. 11:35, quoting Job 41:11). The context of the passage in Job is fascinating, seeing that it comes at the very conclusion of the book. Basically, it is saying that God is no man's debtor. God may do as he likes because everything he does bears the stamp of his perfect integrity. There is no unrighteousness in God. We need to take a moment and examine the context of this statement in the book of Job itself.

God had not spoken to Job until chapter 38. There had been no answers to Job's questions. His pain and suffering had received a consistent interpretation by his friends. Calvin, who preached 159 sermons on Job in the years 1554–55, would say that Job's friends had only one song and they sang it to death! The lyrics of this song suggested that there was only one cause for suffering—sin. Job had sinned, and God was punishing him. Suffering is retribution for transgression.

Then there had been the contribution of Elihu. Calvin is much more sympathetic to Elihu, so much so that some scholars have suggested that Calvin's understanding of the book of Job is to be gauged by what Elihu says, which for Calvin means that pain is educative and disciplinary. Be that as it may, it is the contribution that God himself makes in the closing chapters that is of the greatest importance. And in citing the words of Job 41:11, Paul is placing his finger on a crucial aspect of Job's problem, as he wrestled with his adversity—his sense of entitlement to an answer from the Lord himself to his many questions.

What God said, of course, when he finally broke the silence at the beginning of chapter 38, was altogether unexpected. Job had been asking for a fight—a fight about knowledge and understanding. And God had challenged him to one in which God would ask the questions and Job would do the answering (the opposite of what Job had been asking for). We get a sense that all is not going in Job's favor when the first question seems altogether unfair: "Where were you when I laid the foundation of the earth?" (Job 38:4). Job, of course, has no answer to this question nor to the sixty or more questions like it that follow. Nor is Job able to give a reason for the creation of Behemoth and Leviathan in chapters 40 and 41. Whatever their exact identification may be (and various suggestions have been made from prehistoric dinosaurs destroyed by the flood, to an elephant and a whale, or a hippopotamus and a crocodile, or even representations of demonic creatures, perhaps Satan himself), the point of their inclusion is to conclude that Job has no answer to give. All he can do is put his hand over his mouth (Job 40:4)—a verse that Paul cites in Romans, following his exposition of man's sinfulness—"that every mouth may be stopped" (Rom. 3:19). And pain and suffering is just like that—the reason for their existence in Job's life lies beyond his ability to discern. Job is not entitled to demand that God provide him with a reason. He must trust both that God knows the reason and that it is a good one. In the end, Job is "shut up to faith."

Paul's point in citing this verse here in Romans, of course, is as a concluding statement to what he has just written about the doctrine of predestination in which some are saved and others are not. Why some are chosen to salvation and others consigned to perdition is a mystery, and we are not provided in Scripture or elsewhere with a reason for what seems to us to be an arbitrary decision on God's part. Does this make God a tyrant? Writing in the *Institutes*, Calvin would say:

> For God's will is so much the highest rule of righteousness that whatever he wills, by the very fact that he wills it, must be considered righteous. When, therefore, one asks why God has so done, we must reply: because he has willed it. But if you proceed further to ask why he so willed, you are seeking something greater and higher than God's will, which cannot be found. Let men's rashness, then, restrain itself, and not seek what does not exist, lest perhaps it fail to find what does exist. This bridle, I say, will effectively restrain anyone who wants to ponder in reverence the secrets of his God."[4]

In commenting on this passage in his commentary, Calvin adds another significant thought: namely, that as soon as man is created, even before he has sinned (even then he can demand nothing of God as of right), he is by virtue of his createdness

4. *Institutes*, 3.23.2; CO 2:699–700.

indebted to his maker. Even apart from any consideration of his wretchedness, man is not entitled as of right to demand anything of God. Even in the perfection of Eden, Adam must learn to accept that there is one fruit over which is written, "Thou shalt not eat," and if he asks for a reason why this is so, the only one forthcoming is "because God says so."

We must learn to live trusting in the Lord's sovereign providence over our lives. "Ours is not to reason why." We must learn to put our faith in God's sovereignty and accept it for what it is—the power of God at work in performing "good" for his people.

A Vision of the Glory of God

Calvin's exposition of verse 36 is masterful. For Paul, saying by way of conclusion that "for from him and through him and to him are all things," is continuing the line of thought from the previous verse that we are wholly indebted to God for everything. Calvin writes, "It is very far from being the case that we can glory in any good thing of our own against God, since we have been created by him from nothing, and now exist through him."[5]

The only fitting response to the fact that we have been created by God and redeemed by God and are continually upheld by God is to live our lives to his glory. Not to do so, says the Reformer, is "insane." For Calvin, Paul's words here summarize the very gospel—that it is of God's mercy that we are not consumed. All that we have and are is from his gracious hand.

This is a message we need to preach to ourselves every day. Most of our problems arise when we consider ourselves more highly than we ought, imagining that we have contributed to some aspect of our current well-being. Our chief end, as the first answer to the Shorter Catechism declares, is to glorify God and enjoy him forever. Nothing is more important in life than pursuing God's glory.

5. Calvin, *Romans*, 448; CO 49:232.

It is of considerable significance that Calvin's motto was a hand in which was placed a flaming heart offered up to God in love and devotion, surrounded by the words *Cor meum tibi offere Domine prompte et sincere*—"my heart I offer to the Lord, promptly and sincerely."

For Paul, as he comes to a conclusion of what we might call the doctrinal section of Romans, having surveyed the entire plan and accomplishment of redemption he wants us to understand that no shred of it is attributable to us. The plan of salvation, in its accomplishment and application, teaches me not merely that I can never do anything to earn, increase, or extend God's favor, or avoid the justified fury of his wrath, or to wring from him benefits that otherwise I might not receive, but also that I need not attempt to do so. God has loved me from eternity. In his sovereign predestination, his covenant mercy has been extended in my direction from before the foundation of the world. In Christ, God has sovereignly revealed his commitment to transform me into the likeness of his own dear Son so that I might be presented before him faultless and blameless for all eternity. When such committed love is shown me, promising to get me home to glory, my response, fed by motivations of gratitude, must be to ensure that the Lord be given the praise for every aspect of it.

Thus Paul concludes, "To him be glory forever." Hardly anything illustrates this more vividly than the manner in which Calvin died. The Reformer had never experienced good health, and in the latter part of his life, his health took a dramatic turn for the worse with regular bouts of malaria-like fever, tuberculosis, ulcerated veins, kidney stones, and hemorrhoids. In early February 1564, he gave his last lectures and sermons. However, even from his bed he continued to dictate letters and his final commentary on Joshua. When his friends appealed to him to get more rest, he replied, "What! Would you have the Lord find me idle?"

On May 2, Calvin wrote to his friend William Farel, expressing that he fully expected every breath he now took to be his last. He wrote, "It is enough that I live and die for Christ, who is to all his followers a gain in life and in death." Just over three weeks later, he was dead, and the next day—a Sunday—he was buried in an unmarked grace at a secret location somewhere in Geneva. He had lived for God's glory and not his own, and he despised the thought that future generations would superstitiously revere his grave. He desired that all the glory be given to the Lord alone.

It is one thing to accept this view of God and his ways—a God who is sovereign and majestic—and to acknowledge the need to bow before his unsurpassable greatness and glory. It is another thing to rejoice in it and to see it as the very place in which we find our reason for existence. We are created to reflect God's glory. Sin is defined by the apostle as "falling short of God's glory" (Rom. 3:23). Grace restores us into a right relationship with God, so that once more we may reflect his glory back to him, giving ourselves away to him in a life of unreserved adoration and commitment.

We need to ask ourselves if we are totally committed to this principle. Do we secretly aspire to greatness, anxious that our name or reputation be exalted above others, eager that the acclaim we think we deserve be given its due attention? There are no limits to the ingenuity of the human heart to apportion greatness to itself. And when we do, we must recognize that we diminish the glory of God and diminish the accomplishments of our Savior on our behalf. Our lives must be lived according to the principle of *kenosis* as espoused by the apostle in Philippians 2:5–7: "Have this mind among yourselves, which is yours in Christ Jesus, who, though he was in the form of God, did not count equality with God a thing to be grasped, but made himself nothing, taking the form of a servant." It is the servant's life to which we have been called.

For Calvin, this was the only possible response to the gospel. Writing in the *Institutes*, Calvin said:

> We see that our whole salvation and all its parts are comprehended in Christ [Acts 4:12]. We should therefore take care not to derive the least portion of it from anywhere else. If we seek salvation, we are taught by the very name of Jesus that

> it is "of him" [1 Corinthians 1:30]. If we seek any other gifts of the Spirit, they will be found in his anointing. If we seek strength, it lies in his dominion; if purity, in his conception; if gentleness, it appears in his birth. For by his birth he was made like us in all respects [Hebrews 2:17] that he might learn to feel our pain [cf. Hebrews 5:2]. If we seek redemption, it lies in his passion; if acquittal, in his condemnation; if remission of the curse, in his cross [Galatians 3:13]; if satisfaction, in his sacrifice; if purification, in his blood; if reconciliation, in his descent into hell; if mortification of the flesh, in his tomb; if newness of life, in his resurrection; if immortality, in the same; if inheritance of the Heavenly Kingdom, in his entrance into heaven; if protection, if security, if abundant supply of all blessings, in his Kingdom; if untroubled expectation of judgment, in the power given to him to judge. In short, since rich store of every kind of good abounds in him, let us drink our fill from this fountain, and from no other. Some men, not content with him alone, are borne hither and thither from one hope to another; even if they concern themselves chiefly with him, they nevertheless stray from the right way in turning some part of their thinking in another direction. Yet such distrust cannot creep in where men have once for all truly known the abundance of his blessings.[6]

Once we fully respect what is being said here, there can be no other fitting response than to bow in wonder and adoration before our blessed God and ask him to use us in whatever pleases him for his eternal glory.

Is this how you view your life?

Delivered July 9, 2009, at St. Pierre Cathedral, Geneva, Switzerland.

6. *Institutes*, 2.16.19, CO 2:385–86.

Index of Scripture

Index of Subjects and Names

Contributors

Joel R. Beeke is President of the Puritan Reformed Theological Seminary in Grand Rapids, Michigan.

Iain D. Campbell is Pastor of Point Free Church in Stornoway, Isle of Lewis.

Bryan Chapell is President of Covenant Theological Seminary in St. Louis, Missouri.

Edward Donnelly is Minister of Trinity Reformed Presbyterian Church, Newtownabbey, and Principal of Reformed Theological College, Belfast, Northern Ireland.

J. Ligon Duncan is Senior Pastor of the First Presbyterian Church in Jackson, Mississippi.

Sinclair B. Ferguson is the Senior Pastor of the First Presbyterian Church in Columbia, South Carolina.

W. Robert Godfrey is President of Westminster Seminary California in Escondido, California.

David W. Hall is the Senior Pastor of Midway Presbyterian Church in Powder Springs, Georgia.

Martin Holdt is Pastor of Constantia Park Baptist Church in Pretoria, Republic of South Africa.

Hywel R. Jones is Professor of Practical Theology at Westminster Seminary California in Escondido, California.

Steven J. Lawson is Senior Pastor of Christ Fellowship Baptist Church in Mobile, Alabama.

Peter A. Lillback is President of Westminster Theological Seminary in Philadelphia, Pennsylvania.

Henry Luke Orombi is the Archbishop of Uganda.

Philip Graham Ryken was appointed President of Wheaton College in 2010.

Derek W. H. Thomas is Professor of Theology at Reformed Theological Seminary in Jackson, Mississippi.

Geoffrey Thomas is Pastor of the Alfred Place Baptist Church in Aberystwyth, Wales.